Contacts and Contrasts

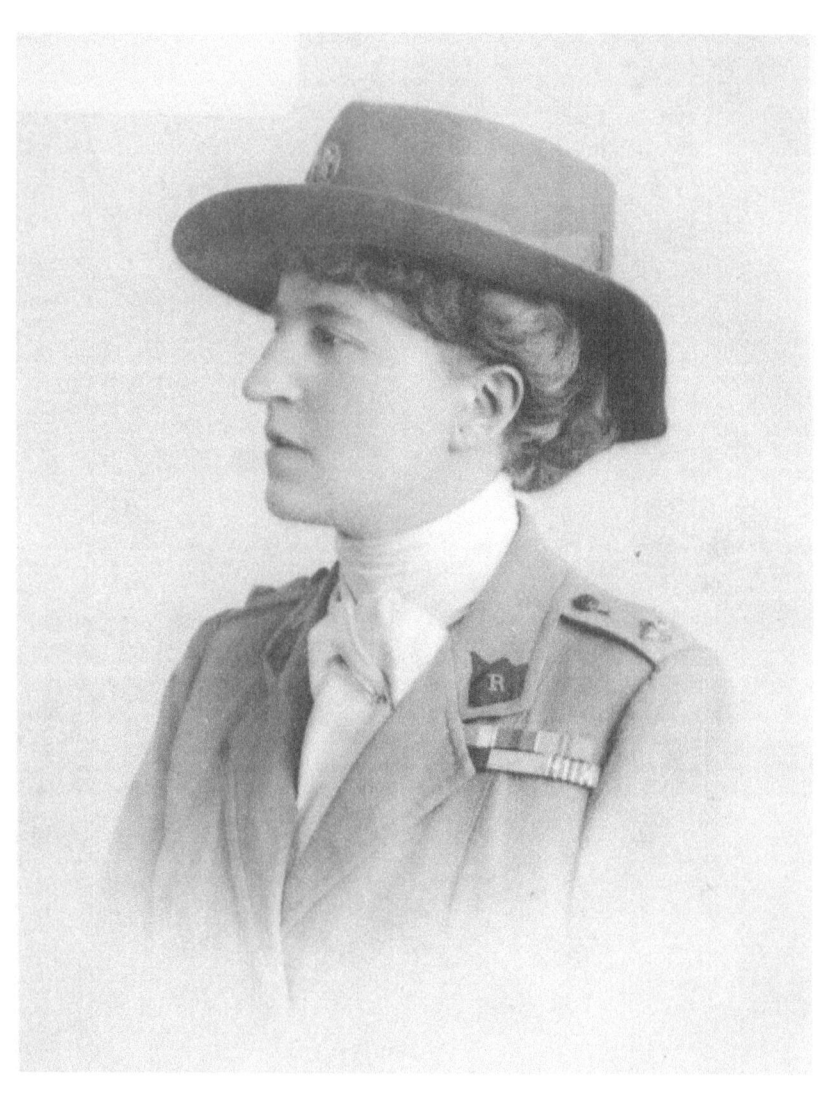

THE AUTHOR
[Photo Vandyk]

Contacts and Contrasts

Helena Gleichen

with a new introduction by
Caroline Stone

Mansion Field

Mansion Field
An imprint of Zeticula Ltd
The Roan,
Kilkerran,
KA19 8LS
Scotland

http://www.thegrimsaypress.co.uk

First published in 1940 by John Murray
This edition first published in 2013

Text © Estate of Helena Gleichen 2013
Introduction © Caroline Stone 2013

Every effort has been made to trace any possible copyright holders. The editor and publisher will be pleased to correct any oversights in future printings.

All rights reserved. No part of this publication may be reproduced, stored in a retrieval system, or transmitted in any form or by any means, electronic, mechanical, photocopying, recording or otherwise, without the prior permission of the publishers.

ISBN 978-1-905021-09-3

To
MY FAMILY

Contents

	Introduction to the New Edition	V
	List of Illustrations	XXI
	Introduction	XXIII
	Acknowledgements	XXIV

Early Years

1.	A Trip Abroad to Greece, Turkey, etc.	3
2.	Balls versus Studio	18
3.	Rome and Painting	25
4.	In France	40
5.	Pleasant Days	55
6.	Yachting with the Empress Eugénie	63
7.	Indigo and Mabbot's Farm	76
8.	About Horses	88
9.	Dogs	105

War

10.	Explanation	125
11.	Departure for Italy	132
12.	First Impressions	138
13.	Method of Working	145
14.	Adventure with Carabinieri	151
15.	Earthquakes, etc.	160
16.	Vipulzano	170
17.	The Real Thing	185
18.	The Attack on Gorizia	195
19.	Gorizia	211
20.	The Italian War as We saw it	223
21.	The Rosen Allee	243
22.	Return from Leave	256
23.	Gorizia	273
24.	A Holiday	286
25.	Bainsizza Plateau	299
26.	Scraps	310
	Appendix	339
	Index	341

Introduction to the New Edition

The Gleichen Family

Helena Gleichen was the daughter of Prince Victor of Hohenlohe-Langenburg (1833-1891), whose mother was the half-sister of Queen Victoria. He came to England, joined the Royal Navy and saw some twenty years of active service in the Mediterranean and the China Seas. In 1861, he married Laura Seymour, the daughter of one of his commanding officers. Since it was a morganatic marriage, she would not have been allowed to share his titles and so, when she was created Countess Gleichen, after one of the Hohenlohe estates, he adopted her style and was known as Count Gleichen. They had four children: Feodora, Edward, Victoria and Helena, whose full names and titles, German and English, are given under their entries in the Almanach de Gotha and the Peerage.

On retiring from the Navy in 1866, Count Gleichen took up sculpture and produced a number of monumental works, the best known of which are King Alfred in the main square at Wantage, the statue of Queen Victoria, and that of Thomas Holloway and his wife, at Royal Holloway College. He also produced numerous portrait busts, for example of some of his naval colleagues, of Queen Victoria, now in the Victoria and Albert Museum, and of Disraeli. Vanity Fair published a cartoon of him at work in the July 5th, 1884 issue. His most famous portrait is probably that of Mary Seacole, whom he knew from his time in the Crimea, and whom he tried to help throughout her difficult life; she made him an executor of her will.

Three at least of Count Gleichen's children had noteworthy careers and for this their father was in a good measure responsible. As Helena Gleichen remarks in this volume: 'In those days it was a terrible thing for one's daughters to insist on having professions, but my father encouraged us each to go ahead as if we had been boys.'

The eldest, Feodora (1861-1922), became a sculptor like her father, with whom at one stage she shared a studio. Her most notable works are the monument to Florence Nightingale for the Royal Infirmary at Derby, the Artemis Fountain in Hyde Park, the Memorial to the 37th English Division at Monchy-le-Preux, inaugurated in the presence of her brother, who had commanded the division in 1916, and the bust of the violinist Jan Kubelik. Among her other statues are a portrait of the Amir Feisal, one of Lord Kitchener, and a curious one of Satan. There were also smaller pieces in bronze and jade – a letter to Nina's sister, Mary Hunter, records the price of a jade carving as £13. She also drew and painted portraits, among many others, Axel Munthe and one of Florence Nightingale in bed during her later years. Feodora was given a number of decorations for her work, including the Légion d'honneur in the year of her death and she was made, posthumously, the first woman member of the Royal British Society of Sculptors.

Victoria (Valda) (1868-1951) was the musical one of the family and sang frequently in public, particularly before her marriage to Lt.-Col. Percy Wilfred Machell, killed in action in 1916, and the birth of their only son. This was always at charity concerts, not as a paid professional. It might have been expected that she would have known, and perhaps sung for, Ethel Smyth, but this does not appear to have been the case.

At the outbreak of World War I, Count Gleichen's only son, Edward (1863-1937), in common with the rest of the family, renounced his German titles. He joined the British army and had a distinguished career in the Grenadier Guards, which ranged from serving in the Guards Camel Regiment in the Sudan to Military Attaché in Washington. He saw active service throughout World War I, until in 1917 he was made Director of the Intelligence Bureau. Edward Gleichen received numerous decorations, among others for his part in the Boer War and his Mission to Ethiopia. He wrote several books about his military experiences, now largely forgotten, but lively and interesting sources for the events of the period. The Victoria and Albert has a volume of his sketches entitled *Count Gleichen's fellow officers at Alexandria*, combined with photographs of Egypt. He also wrote *London's Open Air Statuary*, to which both his father and his sister had contributed.

Helena Gleichen

The youngest of the family, Helena Gleichen (1873-1947) also trained as an artist, as she describes in the first chapters of this book, but her interest was always painting rather than sculpture. She had a passion for animals and they were her prime subjects, particularly horses and dogs, but she also recorded the war in a number of paintings, one or two examples of which are now in the Imperial War Museum. She also produced landscapes and sometimes illustrations, for example the frontispiece to Percy Landon's *The Opening of Tibet* (1904).

In the introductory chapters of *Contacts and Contrasts*, published in 1940, she gives an amusing picture of her life, swinging between her work as an artist and the upper class entertainments of the period – there is a wonderful picture of her as Joan of Arc in armour[1] at the Duchess of Devonshire's fancy dress ball given on 3rd July, 1897 to celebrate Queen Victoria's Diamond Jubilee. The contrast with her experiences on the Italian Front explains the title.

The Smyth Family

Nina Hollings, née Smyth, was such an important figure in Helena Gleichen's life and is mentioned so frequently in her book, that it seems relevant to say something about her and her background. Nina came from a military family – both her father and grandfather served in India, as indeed did her younger brother, Robert, with some distinction.

Nina's mother was brought up in France, but returned to England to keep house for her uncle in Norfolk after her own mother made what the family felt to be an injudicious second marriage. Nevertheless, it may well have been from this grandmother that Nina's generation inherited their musical and artistic inclinations. Mrs Smyth seems to have enjoyed her time in India, where the three oldest children were born.

In 1857, Nina's father, General Smyth, was in England on leave with his family when the Mutiny broke out and he returned to India, among other things to rescue his youngest daughter, Mary[2], who had been left behind. Letters recounting his experiences have survived. Afterwards, it was felt prudent for the family to settle in England.

Ten years later, having held various other posts, and having been seriously impoverished by the failure of the Agra Bank, General Smyth was given command of the Royal Artillery at Aldershot. He bought a house at Frimhurst, which Mrs Smyth seems to have found somewhat dull after the excitements of India, although she was much cheered by the arrival of the Empress Eugénie as a neighbour. The Empress was to prove a good friend, especially to Ethel, and it was perhaps at her house that Nina first met Helena Gleichen.

Nina Hollings

Nina was the fifth of the eight Smyth children, immediately after Ethel, who was, however, closer to her elder sister, Mary. Ethel tells a good deal about her siblings in her volumes of autobiography although, as she says, discretion prevented her from carrying their stories on beyond the nursery and the schoolroom. It is clear, however, that Nina greatly endeared herself to her father – and later to Helena Gleichen – by being a first rate horsewoman and completely fearless. A little of their later histories also emerges in Ethel's letters to her great niece[3].

Nina married Herbert Hollings, son of a Frimley family, living at Watchetts, who graduated from Oxford in 1878 and was called to the Bar in 1881. It was to a large extent the death of their eldest son, John (Jack) Herbert Hollings[4], of the 21st (Empress of India's) Lancers, on the 30th October, 1914 at Ypres, aged 26, only three months after the outbreak of war, that led Nina to take on an active role, going to the front with the Red Cross. In the few surviving photographs taken of her in the war zone, she is wearing a black armband in his memory. Nina, like Helena Gleichen was repeatedly decorated[5]. The *British Journal of Nursing* for December 16th, 1916 reports on one occasion:

> **MEDAL FOR VALOUR:** *A telegram from Rome states that the Military Bulletin announces that the Medal for Valour has been conferred on Countess Helena Gleichen and Miss Nina Hollings, both belonging to the British X-ray section at the Italian front. The Bulletin gives the following reason for conferring the decorations:- They gave their useful and valuable work for the Italian wounded on the Isonzo front, going willingly wherever called, even crossing zones under artillery fire, and being on several occasions a target for the enemy. They showed courage, intrepidity, and contempt of danger, always accomplishing their duty with equal self-sacrifice, lofty courage, and devotion.*

Nina was deeply concerned for her younger son, Richard, who survived the war but, while serving, contracted the tuberculosis that was to kill him a few years later. His son Michael, born in 1921, carried on the family military tradition and after serving with the Coldstream Guards – he was awarded the Military Cross in 1943 – was ordained a Catholic priest in 1950 and was much loved and respected by his parishioners in Notting Hill until his death in 1997.[6]

Later Years

After the war Nina and Helena remained close friends and lived together, partly at Hellens Manor, a magnificent house, largely Tudor, the recorded history of which goes back to the Norman Conquest[7]. They acquired it about 1931 and lived together, sharing their interests in animals – and ghosts. But their financial situation was always precarious and eventually it had to be given up.

In World War II, pictures were sent to Hellens from the Tate for safety. It seems to have been an unhappy experience on both sides. A letter from one of the staff preserved in the Tate Archives records:

> Lady Helena Gleichen asked me to go out and help with the hay making and, when I refused, loudly abused me in front of her three young maids.

When the paintings were removed in the spring of 1941, partly because of the impossibility of warming the house to the necessary 60°, Helena's response to the Director of the Tate was enthusiastic:

> Dear Mr Rothenstein - I was delighted to get your letter yesterday as our guests, although inanimate have spoilt the look of our hall - I will not deny....

She was active in organizing a Home Defense Corps[8] that was in effect a personal army. She lectured her staff, some 80 strong, on military tactics and allegedly demanded 80 rifles with ammunition from the local regiment, adding: "I could do with some machine guns, too, if you have any to spare."

World War I: The Italian Campaign

Because, until the very end, the British were only marginally involved, the Italian Campaign in World War

I is much less well known in the English-speaking world than the war on the Western Front, in spite of Hemingway's *A Farewell to Arms*. Italy, with the Austro-Hungarian Empire and Germany, made up the Triple Alliance, of which it had nominally been part since 1882. At the outbreak of war on July 28th, 1914, however, Italy refused to commit troops and by May 1915 had been persuaded to enter the war on the side of the Allies – the Triple Entente of Britain, France and Russia. The change of heart had much to do with territorial ambitions. Italy considered the Austro-Hungarians to be its historic enemies from the time of the Risorgimento and even earlier. In addition, the Italians were much less attracted by the inducement of the French colony of Tunisia, in the event of its being conquered, than by the Allies' offer of the restitution of Trieste and the Trentino, Istria and Dalmatia, which Italy felt to be rightfully its own and which were in the possession of Austria. Nevertheless, Italian politicians and intellectuals were very divided over the question of Italy's participation, although the Socialists, including Benito Mussolini, eventually came to be strongly in favour.

From the beginning, war on the Italian front centred on Gorizia and the Isonzo river – the area where Helena Gleichen and Nina Hollings were working – but the early offensives were disastrous, because of the rocky and hostile nature of the terrain and because the Italian army was poorly equipped and prepared. The brutal leadership of Luigi Cadorna, who allegedly introduced decimation – shooting every tenth man – in units that he felt had not performed adequately, played its part, although Helena Gleichen bears witness to the excellent discipline which obtained. The sense, common to almost all theatres of World War I, that untold blood was being shed for no purpose did nothing to raise morale. The first four Battles of the Isonzo resulted in the deaths of some 250,000 men and by the end of 1917, more than 600,000 were dead and innumerable wounded or missing, a large proportion of them in the Isonzo area. Fighting, as in the Dolomites, relied in part on trenches and tunnels. Deliberately provoked avalanches - the most famous being the "White Friday" avalanche of 13th December, 1916 which killed some 10,000 men - added a terrifying dimension.

Gorizia was taken from the Austrians in August 1916 as part of the 6th Battle of the Isonzo, described in this book. The attack was led by Luigi Capello, probably Italy's best general, who was later to be involved in a plot to assassinate Mussolini. The 12th Battle of the Isonzo – Caporetto[9] – took place in October-November, 1917, shortly after the two friends had left the area. It was marked by the use of poison gas on the part of the German units – Helena Gleichen describes its effect at an earlier stage in the fighting. Capello was too ill to command the troops and Cadorna's tactical ineptitude resulted in great loss of life and a disastrous defeat. Cadorna was sacked – he went on to be honoured by Mussolini in 1924 – and replaced by Armando Diaz, who completely rethought Italian military strategy and led the army to a decisive victory at the Battle of the Piave, fought at the summer solstice, 1918. The Austrian and German losses were estimated in excess of 100,000. After the Battle of the Piave, Armando Diaz, unlike his predecessor, did not wish to launch another offensive until his troops were rested and prepared. On the anniversary of Caporetto, 24th October, 1918, the Battle of Vittorio Veneto resulted in a resounding defeat for the Austro-Hungarian troops. By November 1st, half a million prisoners had been taken. On 29th October the Austro-Hungarians asked for an armistice, which was signed on 3rd November, becoming effective 24 hours later on 4th November; a week later World War I was over.

The Red Cross

On the 24th June, 1859, a key battle was fought in the Second Italian War of Independence – Solferino. That day, a Swiss businessman, Jean Henri Dunant, a man with a long history of social activism, happened to arrive at Solferino and found some 38,000 men dead or dying on the battlefield with, apparently, nothing being done to help them. Appalled, he organized the locals, especially the women, into a relief force and arranged for supplies and shelters that could be used as hospitals. On returning to Geneva, he wrote a book: *Un souvenir de Solferino*, which he published at his own expense and sent to a number of prominent political and military figures. His aim was a permanent organization that would provide humanitarian aid in war zones to all those who needed it and which would be considered as neutral and hence not liable to attack. On February 17th, 1863 the first meeting of what was to be known as the International Committee of the Red Cross took place.

A year later, again as a result of campaigning by Dunant and his group of supporters, the First Geneva Convention was signed. Its articles largely related to the protection of those in any way caring for the wounded and their automatic neutrality, to ensure that they would be able to operate in relative safety. Helena Gleichen mentions the repeated shelling of Red Cross installations by the Austrians, who were not signatories. Later the terms of the Convention were greatly expanded. In 1901, Dunant was co-recipient of the Nobel Peace Prize.

At the outset of World War I, the Red Cross combined with the St John's Ambulance Brigade, founded in the U.K. in 1877, to form the Joint War Committee. Besides providing medical and nursing support, they raised funds for mechanised ambulances for the first time and equipment such as the X-ray units described in this book. Volunteers included Ernest Hemingway, driving an ambulance for the American Red Cross, the historian G.M. Trevelyan, Commandant of the British Red Cross Ambulance unit in Italy and author of *Scenes from Italy's War* (1919), while Rudyard Kipling, at the invitation of the

British ambassador, Sir Rennell Rodd, went out to see and later report[10] on what was happening on the Italian Front, relatively little understood in England. Towards the end of the war, particularly in France, centres were set up by the Red Cross to record the names of the wounded and missing, and attempt to reunite them with their families. This was the origin of the International Tracing and Message Services, still very active today.

An account of the Red Cross activities on the Italian front, *Outposts of Mercy*, by E.V. Lucas, 1917, includes a brief chapter on the contribution made by Helena Gleichen and Nina Hollings, which has been reproduced as an appendix.

X-rays

Although other scientists had been working in the field, the discovery of X-rays is generally attributed to William Röntgen in November, 1895. A few weeks later, the first X-ray photograph was taken – of his wife's hand. On seeing it she is reported to have said: "I have seen my death." In February of the following year, John Hall-Edwards in Birmingham was the first to use X-rays to guide a surgical operation and, again in 1896, Russell Reynolds, a schoolboy at Winchester, built the first X-ray apparatus, now in the Science Museum in London.

Shortly after, in the States, Thomas Edison designed and produced the first commercially available machine for radiography, the prototype of the equipment used by Helena Gleichen and Nina Hollings. In 1901, when the U.S. President William McKinley was shot in an assassination attempt, efforts were made to make use of one of Thomas Edison's machines, but the President died of gangrene before the suggestion could be implemented. It did however serve to make the public much more conscious of X-rays and their possible value.

In France, Marie Curie was much interested in

Röntgen's work and, building on the discovery of radioactivity by Henri Becquerel in 1896, was awarded the Nobel Prize for Physics in 1903. It was shared with Becquerel and her husband, Pierre Curie: *"in recognition of the extraordinary services they have rendered by their joint researches on the radiation phenomena discovered by Professor Henri Becquerel"*. In 1911, she was awarded the Nobel Prize in Chemistry for her work on radium and polonium.

At the outbreak of World War I, Marie Curie, not surprisingly, was very well aware of the potential value of X-rays in saving the lives of soldiers and campaigned the French government to set up military radiology centres. She was made director of the Red Cross Radiology Service and persuaded manufacturers to give equipment and wealthy donors to contribute money. One of these was Winnaretta Singer, Princesse de Polignac, the sewing machine heiress and intimate friend of Nina Hollings' sister, Ethel Smyth. In view of this connection and Helena Gleichen's wide-ranging contacts, it is perhaps surprising that they had the intractable problems with the French authorities described in this book – so serious, in fact, that they were forced to move their endeavours to the Italian theatre of war.

By October 1914, 20 mobile X-ray units – named "petites Curies" – were ready to go to the Western Front. Marie Curie herself learned to drive, use – and mend – X-ray equipment and took courses in anatomy. Choosing her 17 year-old daughter, Irène - later to be winner, with her husband, of the 1935 Nobel Prize for Chemistry - as her assistant, they made their first trip to the front in the late autumn of 1914. Marie Curie quickly realized the desperate need for more trained personnel. She began offering courses and in 1919 summarized her work over the previous five years in *Radiology in War*, besides taking the opportunity to teach American soldiers waiting to be repatriated.

On the English side, Mary Hunter, Nina's eldest sister, and her husband had not only made over their country house for use as a hospital, but were also active in fundraising on behalf of the Red Cross. The problems faced by the Gleichen-Hollings X-ray unit, besides the obvious bureaucratic ones, were probably linked to territorial jealousy: the English were felt to be "poaching" on a French preserve, rather than simply attempting to relieve the plight of the soldiers of both nationalities.

As Helena Gleichen describes, Ethel Smyth came out to Italy to help and Helena found her superabundant energy most trying: "I shall shoot Ethel soon, so kind, so persistent, so damnably energetic," she remarked. Ethel on her side commented:

> *In the year 1919, I published an autobiography called "Impressions That Remained". I wrote that book while doing radioactive work in a French military hospital - locating bits of shell - telling the doctor how deeply embedded they were - and - watching him plunge into an anaesthetised body the knife that shall prove you either an expert or a bungler - is not a music-inspiring job; but writing memoirs in between while was a delightful relief.*

The dangers of radiation were still not fully perceived at this date and, as Helena Gleichen's account makes clear, no precautions of any kind were taken and she mentions casually on their departure: "our hands and our eyes [had] become somewhat affected by them [the X-rays]." Nina Hollings' health was permanently damaged, and Marie and Irène Curie both died as a result of exposure to radiation, from their research, but also from their war work.

Notes

1   See www.hrp.org.uk

2   *Mary Hunter of Hill Hall: Leaves from the Desk of an Edwardian Hostess*, ed. Caroline Stone, forthcoming, 2013.

3   *Dearest Elizabeth: Ethel Smyth's Letters to her Great-Niece*, ed. Caroline Stone, forthcoming, 2013.

4   www.cwgc.org - Commonwealth War Graves Commission website

5   See Daily Mail, March 12th, 2008 as well as the Ewbank's website: where it is recorded that medals fetched £4800.

6   See his obituary in *The Independent*, 22 February, 1997:

7   See www.hellens.com for photographs and history.

8   See Midge Gillies, *Waiting for Hitler, Voices From Britain on the Brink of Invasion*, Hodder & Stoughton, London, 2006

9   A number of descriptions of Caporetto and other of the battles in the region are to be found at: http://www.firstworldwar.com

10 Kipling's articles from the Italian Front are available on line: http://www.kipling.org.uk/rg_mountains_intro.htm

LIST OF ILLUSTRATIONS

	Facing Page
THE AUTHOR . . . . . . Frontispiece	
[Photo Vandyk]	
THE AUTHOR'S PARENTS, PRINCE AND PRINCESS VICTOR OF HOHENLOHE LANGENBURG—THE LATTER IN FANCY DRESS	18/9
THE CROOME HOUNDS *	62
RICHMOND *	100
HUNTING ON THE DAREN ROCKS, BLACK MOUNTAINS, SOUTH WALES, 1921 *	101
MRS. HOLLINGS AND THE AUTHOR AT WORK IN HOSPITAL ON THE ITALIAN FRONT	148
H.M. THE KING OF ITALY	149
ARTILLERY HORSES COME TO THE HELP OF CAR STUCK IN QUICKSANDS IN NATIZONE RIVER *	170
GUNS CROSSING THE PONTOON BRIDGE INTO GORIZIA * .	200
ENTRY OF TROOPS INTO GORIZIA, AUGUST 9TH, 1916 * .	201
[Imperial War Museum, London]	
HORSES STABLED IN THE CHURCH THE NIGHT BEFORE THE BATTLE *	240
AUSTRIAN ATTACK REPULSED BY FIELD GUNS * . .	241
[War Museum, Rome]	
SANT' ANDREA. RELIEF TROOPS TAKING OVER THE TRENCHES UNDER COVER OF DARKNESS, NEAR GORIZIA * . .	282
THE CURVE OF DEATH, NEAR ZAGORA, 1917 * . . .	283
LADY HELENA AND LADY FEODORA GLEICHEN AT WORK IN THEIR STUDIOS	314
MEMORIAL ERECTED AT MONCHY LE PREUX TO THE 37TH DIVISION, COMMANDED BY THE AUTHOR'S BROTHER, MAJOR-GENERAL LORD EDWARD GLEICHEN . .	316
[Sculpsit F. Gleichen]	
HELLENS	334
[Statue of Pan in foreground by F. Gleichen]	
SKETCH MAP OF ITALIAN FRONT	338

* Pinxit H. Gleichen.

INTRODUCTION

IT has often puzzled people why my surname and that of my brothers and sisters is Gleichen, when my father and mother were Prince and Princess Victor of Hohenlohe Langenburg. Count Gleichen is one of the titles belonging to the Hohenlohe family and my father took it when he married my mother, who was a daughter of Admiral of the Fleet Sir George Seymour. My grandfather, the reigning Prince of Hohenlohe Langenburg, had married Princess Feodora of Leiningen, half-sister to Queen Victoria, whose mother had married firstly the Prince of Leiningen. After his death she married the Duke of Kent. My parents had met and made friends when very young and my father was serving on board his future father-in-law's ship as a midshipman. Not until they were twenty-eight was the marriage allowed, and then only if he gave up his name of Hohenlohe and took that of Gleichen. Later on the Queen expressed a wish that they should return to the original name. The family were given the option of doing the same or of keeping the name of Gleichen. My eldest sister and my brother chose to remain as they were, as they had already started on their careers and thought that the change might prove an embarrassment in their work. Valda and I were too young to take much interest in such matters, but when we were of an age to do so heartily endorsed their decision. Then, during the War, when everyone was dropping German-sounding titles, we did the same.

ACKNOWLEDGMENTS

People we have to thank for their invaluable help in our War-work.

H.M. The Queen of Italy
General Badoglio
Contessa Rhodina di Bellegarde, Lary
Marchese Carlo Calabrini
General Capello
General Cattaneo
Professor de Cigna
Prince Corsini
General Sir John Cowans
Sir James Mackenzie Davidson
Colonel Sir E. V. Gabriel
Feo Gleichen
Sir Arthur Lawley
General Lombardi
Valda Machell
Signor de Martino
Lord Monson
Viscount Northcliffe
General Piacentini
General Delmé Radcliffe
Colonel Santucci
Professor Sbrozzi
Professor Solaro
Hon. Sir Arthur Stanley
Sir Courtauld Thomson
Cavaliere Luigi Villari

EARLY YEARS

I

A TRIP ABROAD TO GREECE, TURKEY, ETC.

MY father is the person who looms largest in my early memories. Large, cheery, hot-tempered, one moment the whole world rocking round him, the next the sun was out and we were all basking in the rays of his good humour. His youth was full of good stories—how he bolted from his tutor at school in Germany, and later, how having tried it on again (his idea being to go to sea), he was sent over as a bad bargain to England, to his aunt Queen Victoria, to be put into the British Navy. Most of these stories have been told elsewhere, but there are two or three which I have never forgotten, and which I can tell here.

His first escapade after joining the Navy in 1844 was to slide down a rope which he found trailing astern and to enjoy himself thoroughly as the huge ship moved slowly away from her anchorage. Luckily he was missed almost at once or he would have been drowned as the ship gathered way, and a wet and frightened little boy was hauled before the captain to learn a little discipline.

When he was a full-blown midshipman he had been ashore with the others at Halifax, and they had managed to get into a scrap with the inhabitants. My father had the bones of his hand broken by a blow across the back of it and was in a good deal of pain, when the first lieutenant, who did not love him, ordered him to go up as look-out. There was, of course, no need for a

A TRIP ABROAD TO GREECE, TURKEY, ETC.

look-out in harbour, but my father did not like to draw too much attention to the state of his hand, or there would have been an inquiry as to how it had happened. So he just mentioned that he had hurt his hand and asked if someone else could take his duty. The lieutenant thundered out, "Do as you are told, you young cub." The boy started to climb; up and up he went, getting more and more exhausted, pulling himself up with only one hand and clinging tightly with his legs. Arriving much blown with the extra exertion, he hesitated what to do, when a stentorian voice reached him from down below, where the lieutenant was standing watching him. In panic haste he dropped his hold to snatch at his telescope, which was slung across his back; his legs slipped, a wild grab and he dropped. . . . A seaman was cleaning one of the big guns immediately below, stooping over his work. The boy fell directly on to the man, driving his head down on to the gun and killing him instantly. Victor himself, beyond being very much shaken, was not hurt. Of course there was an inquiry into the tragedy, and the lieutenant was court-martialled and dismissed his ship.

Another story he told me, which is interesting as showing the state of London in those days. He was walking down the Strand still in the uniform of a midshipman, as he had only just arrived on leave, when a man pushed past him and gave him a poke in the ribs. My father swung round to see who had done this and found an obsequious-looking person, who murmured, "If you like good cigars come with me." Always ready for an adventure he followed him down an alley. The alleys off the Strand were dirty squalid places in those days and he owned, when telling me the story, that it did not cross his mind that it might be foolish to go alone and without telling anyone where he was going. However, he had started, so there was nothing

AN ALLEY OFF THE STRAND

to be done about it and he went on. His leader never stopped or turned round, and reaching a small door in a wall, pushed it open and ran up a steep wooden staircase. A door stood open at the top, and my father and he arrived at about the same time. The room was full of people of the most sordid description, drinking, smoking, swearing, and some asleep on the floor dead-drunk. One glimpse was enough and my father turned to bolt, but a woman, blowzy and filthy, had seen him and with a shout made a rush for him. As he fled down the stairs she hurled a fork after him, quickly followed by a knife, but luckily neither of them got him, and pursued by a yelling crowd of half-naked, half-drunken people he reached the alley and bolted for the street. Luck was with him because in his blind rush he might have gone the wrong way, but he had instinctively taken the right turn and rushed straight into the arms of two policemen at the end of the alley, who demanded an explanation of an officer in the uniform of H.M. Navy running for his life from one of the ill-famed alleys off the Strand in the middle of the night. The moment he could get his breath he explained what had happened, but took the blame on himself, saying it was his own fault for having been such a fool as to follow the man. The police did not look at it in the same light, saying they had been searching for that nest of thieves for some time, and they insisted on his showing them the door into their den. He always maintained that he felt rather mean having given them away as they had not actually done anything to him. History does not relate what they would have done had he not been so quick.

Before I leave the subject of my father, I must tell the story of his saving the life of Captain Rowley Lambert. Lambert and he had gone through many adventures together and after leaving the Navy they arranged with the celebrated Captain Shaw of the Fire Brigade

A TRIP ABROAD TO GREECE, TURKEY, ETC.

that each of them should have a bell to his house to tell them when there was any big fire taking place. One night they were both called and hastily grabbing their helmets and axes ran to the nearest fire-station, where they were told that the fire was quite close in a narrow street just off the Strand. One house was already completely gutted. My father and Captain Lambert had climbed to the top of the next house when it, too, fell in with a crash. When the dust cleared away they found that their retreat was cut off. To the right nothing but a gaping mouth of fire, to the left the same, and behind them a roaring furnace many feet below. They were completely isolated on a narrow peak of wall, the only bit left. . . . People in the street were shouting to them, but they could hear nothing and there was no time to think of what to do. Suddenly my father caught sight of a plank sticking up from the brickwork. They both pulled at it and out it came. It was doubtful if it were long enough to reach across the street, but it was the only chance they had. They started to push it out. Would it reach? Yes, just. Now would it bear them? One at a time, my father first as he was the lightest; the plank bent ominously in the middle, but held. He was across. He turned round to shout to his friend that all was well. Lambert had already started, but in the middle he had become hopelessly giddy and sat down with his hands covering his face. The plank, bending under his weight, had only a foot or so to grip on either side. The whole depth of the narrow street was below them, with the tiny figures shouting and gesticulating. There was no time to be lost, and my father, who at the best of times did not like heights, started to go back to him. His words of encouragement had no effect, so stooping, he urged him to try and shuffle along with him. The plank now threatened to give at any moment. Slowly moving backwards, pulling Lambert with him, they got to safety. Then a roar broke out from the street below and cheer after cheer greeted the plucky act. Naturally nothing would induce either of them to face the crowd and they slipped away home as fast as possible.

It can be imagined how thrilled I was as a child to hear this sort of story, and directly I was free of lessons I used to hurry down to my father's smoking-room, where I generally found him busy with some invention or other. He always had a job for me, so my time before bed seemed painfully short. After leaving the Navy he went to work with Theed, the well-known sculptor of those days, eventually becoming himself a professional sculptor. The Queen allowed him to build himself a series of studios and workshops in the garden of St. James's Palace, where she had given him and my mother apartments. These apartments were under the State Rooms, and we children used to be allowed on wet days to go up into the State Rooms to play and could race and tear from one end of the Palace to the other. All our children's parties were held up there, too. Now that they are kept so strictly that permission has to be asked even to go into them, I regret not having taken more notice of the excellent pictures and furniture which are there.

I have often been asked if there are any ghosts in our rooms. There ought to be, for they are the rooms from which Charles the Second, firstly, and afterwards the Duke of Gloucester and his sister Minette escaped; all I have ever heard are footsteps up the long passage which leads past our rooms to what was my mother's bedroom. As I got older and slept by myself in the old night-nursery, I often heard them pass, long after all the lights were out. One night I was feeling more adventurous than usual and jumping out of bed pursued the steps through one swing-door after another. I could hear each door close quietly in front of me, but no one could I see. I reached my mother's door at the end of the passage. . . . No light, only her gentle breathing, and I fled back to my room as fast as my legs would carry me and jumped into bed, only too glad to be safe home again. I remember that Big Ben struck two as I cuddled down, and on many another night I heard the same steps but never worried to pursue them again. The red baize cupboard in the night-nursery, where, when I was naughty I was shut in by my nurse, still haunts me more than any ghost could do. The cupboard had no ventilator or window of any kind, and I could, and did, howl myself sick in it without anyone hearing. I do not know how long I used to be left there, but it seemed to me to be years, and after howling till I could no more, I would go sound asleep, and when eventually the door was opened and my nurse called to me to come out, I would stagger out feeling utterly bemused and far away. I wonder if modern nurses would dare nowadays to shut their charges in perfectly airless dark cupboards for hours at a time.

Whenever my father made some money in the studio he used to give us all some treat or some lovely present. One I remember especially. It was an enormous box of soldiers of the Thirty Years' War. What a lovely thing it was! Gustavus Adolphus on horseback in full armour of the period, without a helmet and with a light blue sash flying behind him, riding a splendid grey charger. Tilly, a sinister figure in black armour, with his visor down, a farm-house on fire, guns, trees, tents, mortars; men with arquebuses and their muskets supported by staves . . . the whole paraphernalia of a big war, even dogs and food-wagons. And to think that it all disappeared one year, when we had been down to the country. I asked for it and was told, "Not to-night," and with one's angelic goodness of those

ST. BRUNO

days, one did not question again that night and after a few more attempts forgot all about it. I often wonder where they all went to. I never had anything else I loved so much, and my father and I used to play with them by the hour together.

Many years after, when I was supposed to be far too old for toys, I joined Alma-Tadema, R.A., Arthur Lemon and Mr. Harry Paget, all painters, in a game of war, nearly as beautiful. In this game we had real bullets and real gunpowder in our cannon. One day Alma-Tadema dodged down just as I fired and the bullet hit his spectacles, breaking them into splinters. His face was pouring with blood and an anxious and angry family took him off at once to the oculist. Luckily no glass had gone into his eyes, but we all thought it wiser that the game should cease.

About 1879 my father built a house down at Sunningdale, in those days a nice countrified place in pine woods. It was built on the site of an old Carthusian monastery, so the house was named after the founder of the Order, St. Bruno. Here we used to be allowed to run wild, dressed, much to the horror of our neighbours, in knickerbockers, and we even had cropped hair. We were allowed to ride astride and climb trees to our hearts' content. When I say we, I mean Valda and I, as the other two, Feo and Eddie, were already grown up—Feo working at her profession of sculptor under Professor Legros at the Slade School and at the studio under my father's head-man, Karl Müller; and Eddie at Sandhurst working up for his exams. to get into the Grenadier Guards.

Lessons, of course, took up a great deal of our time, as we worked six hours a day. In London these long hours did not matter, but in the country it was too much, I now think, for children who were only in the country for three months of the year. I know that

A TRIP ABROAD TO GREECE, TURKEY, ETC.

when at St. Bruno I paid very little attention to any lessons, only longing to get out and catch tadpoles or go and talk to the pig.

Valda was much keener on lessons than I was, even, to my unceasing amazement, staying on in the schoolroom an extra hour or so in the evenings so as to read the history of music, when she might have been out of doors or carpentering with my father in the carpenter's shop, or poking round the stables, where I spent every spare moment I could get, helping or hindering the men in cleaning harness and feeding the horses. I learnt hardly anything in the schoolroom and must have been hopelessly difficult to teach, drawing horses all over the table in every kind of attitude, or sitting staring out of the window at the clouds; anything rather than pay attention to the matter in hand.

When I was about sixteen I went abroad with my father and mother and we went to Corfu. On reaching there we were waiting for a boat to land us when we saw one coming out with a man standing up in it waving frantically. It turned out to be Lord Dunmore who had heard we were on board and had come to meet us. A most cheerful companion he proved to be. My father was ill with his old complaint of dysentery, which had worried him ever since the Crimea, when he had nearly died of cholera, and Mama had to stay and look after him, so Lord Dunmore undertook to amuse me, and we had wonderful expeditions together all over the island, fishing and riding. I shall never forget the beauty of that island, and the intense colouring of the mountains with the wonderful flowery plain which stretched for miles between them and the sea. A great deal of flax is grown there, and the wind blowing across the plain gave the effect of soft grey-blue waves. Up in the hills white Pancratium lilies grew everywhere amidst a carpet of tiny purple irises, and the result was

A DINNER PARTY IN ATHENS

gorgeous. It was amusing, too, seeing English names everywhere on the citadel walls. They had never been altered since our occupation of the island; "Sergeants' Mess," "Officers Only," etc., etc. I wonder why Gladstone gave the island up to the Greeks, and whether the inhabitants liked being handed over to different nations as if they were packages.

Mr. Wood, the Consul at Corfu, told us many stories of the Austrian Empress Elisabeth, who had spent much time at her villa on the island. She used to make him take her out to sea on all the most stormy nights, and many a time he begged her to put back to harbour and she would not—her principal joy being to stand on the bow of the boat, with waves breaking over her, and often he had to tie her in her place for fear she should be washed overboard. He said it was the most anxious time of his life having to look after her.

After Corfu we went on to Athens, and while walking there I was dawdling behind when I was approached by a beggar who showed me a bronze coin which attracted me by its very small size. It was hardly bigger than the head of a pin and had a tiny owl on the obverse, and a sheaf on the reverse. I had already quite a good collection of coins, and bought this one for the equivalent of a franc from the beggar, who seemed overjoyed. Afterwards I found, on taking it to the British Museum to be vetted, that it was a Greek coin of Mycenæ, of which they themselves had no example.[1]

That evening we dined at the Palace with the King and Queen of Greece. The King was a brother of Queen Alexandra, or Princess of Wales as she then

---

[1] Another treasure which I got in Athens was a little Greek tear-jar, given me by Mr. Rennell Rodd (now Lord Rennell), who was at the English Legation then, a treasure which has survived all these years and is much admired by all Greek connoisseurs.

A TRIP ABROAD TO GREECE, TURKEY, ETC.

was, and we had a very nice cheerful evening except when I poured all the soup down my front. One of the horrid children noticed it at once and called out "Pig," being much reproved by his papa for drawing attention to a visitor in distress.

We left the Piræus late that night, encountering a violent storm outside. By the time we reached Constantinople, however, the weather was lovely and we steamed in past the Golden Horn with a heavenly blue sky and all the pink and red Judas trees in full bloom on each bank. We were received by Sir William White, the British Ambassador, who came out in his steam launch to fetch us to luncheon at the Embassy.

This reminds me of a story told me much later by a friend of mine who was staying at the big hotel in Constantinople and saw an attaché of the English Embassy, whom she did not know, put some papers down on the billiard-table near where she was writing. He then went away, and after a few minutes a Turk, who had been sitting in the corner of the room, walked across to the table and picked up the papers, putting them into his pocket. My friend got up and saying, "Excuse me, those papers belong to a friend of mine; I know he did not want them touched," held out her hand for them. The Turk at once apologized and gave them up to her and she took them down to the manager's bureau and had them put into an envelope and sealed, informing him that the attaché would call for them in a few minutes. When the Embassy official returned to the room to look for his papers, my friend told him what had happened. He was intensely grateful and said very seriously that he could never repay her for the service she had done him.

Three or four days after she was dining at the Embassy and was talking to the Ambassador, who was just saying, "I hear you saved some papers that one of my young

A MEETING

idiots had left behind," when the door opened and the would-be robber of the letters, a most magnificent figure in his official garments, was announced. My friend whispered to the Ambassador, "That is the man who tried to pocket the papers," and he answered, "If that man had gained possession of them it would have been a tragedy, as he is a high official in the Turkish Government and no friend to England. Your presence of mind saved more than you will ever realize." [1]

We stayed at Buyukdere some way up the Bosporus, as Constantinople itself was not considered to be very healthy at that time—and the Embassy was just moving to Therapia. The Embassy launch was lent to us most days, and our journeys up and down the Bosporus were a real joy. Once when we were in the public steamboat, my father, who was taking exercise up and down the deck, suddenly came face to face with a big Turk who was travelling in pomp with his suite to Constantinople. For one moment they looked at each other and then the Turk flung his arms round my father's neck. They had known each other in the Crimean War thirty-five years before. Never did I see such delight as on both sides, but an interpreter had to be fetched, as French was not enough for all they had to say to each other.

Just before our arrival a young Macmillan had disappeared in the mountains of Asia Minor and it was feared he had been murdered. In consequence of this we were not allowed to go on any expeditions, a great disappointment, so instead of staying on we settled to go north to Sofia on our way home. However, we were invited to see the Salamnik on the very morning of our departure. The Salamnik was a function attended by all the big officials and many troops, when the Sultan went to the Mosque to say his prayers. Abdul Hamid never told anyone beforehand at what time it would

[1] My friend to whom this happened was Nina Hollings.

A TRIP ABROAD TO GREECE, TURKEY, ETC.

take place nor did he say if he would ride, drive himself, or be driven. We were asked to be in a certain place at ten o'clock and be prepared to wait until four o'clock to see him pass. Then the message came that he would like to see us in the afternoon. My father, in his usual monkey-jacket with a red tie, was quite unsuitably dressed for a visit to the Palace. All our luggage had gone on, so no other garment was available. Friendly Turks offered him frock-coats, not one of which could he get into, and amid shouts of laughter from the good-natured owners he split one after another. At last they gave up trying to make him look smart and he had to go as he was.

The Sultan Abdul Hamid was a furtive, frightened little man in mortal terror of being murdered. While talking to him my father dropped something and made a sudden movement to pick it up. The Sultan jumped to his feet as he did so, pulling out a dagger from his coat, but instantly recovering himself, thrust it back again and resumed his seat with a dead-white face and shaking hands. I was told afterwards that so nervous was he of being assassinated that he never slept twice running in the same room and had the head of his bed raised very high so that he could step out of it in a second in case of an attack. When we left him he presented my mother with the insignia of the Order of the Chefakat and my father with a higher grade of the Turkish Osmanie, which Order he had already been given after the Crimea.

Tired out with our long day, we then left Constantinople for Sofia, where we were to stay two nights. We were met at the station by an invitation to have luncheon the next day with Prince Ferdinand of Bulgaria who had not yet taken unto himself the title of King or Tsar. Sofia in those days was a dirty little Eastern town with cobble-stones and mud in all the streets.

LANGENBURG

There was practically nothing to see, so we were rather bored at having to stay on till next evening. However, my youthful mind was much impressed by the carriage and four very fine horses which was sent to the hotel to fetch us and the beautifully turned-out escort of cavalry, their dolmans flying in the wind and their lovely well-bred little horses bucking and showing off, as they cantered on each side of the carriage; the noise of their hooves on the cobble-stones and the clinking of their accoutrements making conversation impossible.

Prince Ferdinand, who was a Coburg, was a cousin of my father's, and I remember the latter saying, when we got back to the hotel, that being the youngest of his family he was naturally looked upon as a fool, "But," said my father, "for the fool of the family he has not done so badly for himself and I should not be surprised if he did not prove them all to be wrong." He was always mocked at by his relations for covering himself with orders and decorations created by himself, and he was rudely nicknamed "the Christmas-tree."

After Sofia, Belgrade, the Danube, Vienna and then on to Langenburg, my father's old home in Würtemberg, a beautiful old castle where I wished I could have stayed longer as I liked my uncle and aunt very much. I was only to meet them once again, when my mother and I went to stay with them in Strassburg, after my father's death. I remember that one of the things that impressed me greatly at Langenburg was that when we all went to church on Sunday the congregation used to stand and bow, with their backs to the Altar, as we went to the family pew, a huge box, like at the opera, just over the Altar. I thought it a very nice kind of service as when my uncle Hermann got bored with the sermon, which he did very soon, he got up and shut the window which looked down into the

A TRIP ABROAD TO GREECE, TURKEY, ETC.

church, fetched picture-books from a shelf and dealt them round to us all. Before we went to Corfu we stayed a few days at Abbazia and made acquaintance with the Hoyos family who lived at Fiume. Countess Hoyos was a daughter of the inventor of the Whitehead torpedo. This invention had been offered to the British Government but had been refused, so it had been sold to the Austrians, and we had the great excitement of seeing it tried for the first time by the Austrian Navy. We went out in a steam launch, the torpedo was fired and it vanished. Terrific excitement amongst the Austrian naval officers present. It had gone farther than ever before.... Great congratulations all round. They sent their boats everywhere to look for it and it was found close under our launch. It had turned round directly it had been fired and had returned to where it had come from. How everyone laughed! The whole boat rocked with merriment and even the inventor laughed as much as everyone else, though it must have been rather a *rire jaune*. Then we went into tea, leaving the torpedo to be hauled out of the sea and to have its intricate machinery readjusted. I found amongst a lot of old sketch-books the other day, a careful drawing done from memory of the Whitehead torpedo's inside. Very detailed, very careful, but alas, one tiny space a blank, which they would not show even to a small girl. Later I used to go and stay with the Hoyos family, and one of the first evenings I spent at Paddockhurst, I cheerfully challenged Count Hoyos to play chess. He agreed with a smile and we settled down and started our game. Three—four moves and I was checkmated.... "Let us have another game," he said. Again we started and to my fury it happened a second time. The third time, I looked so bewildered that he burst out laughing and called to Countess Hoyos, "You had better tell her." "My dear," she said,

SAFETY IN NUMBERS

"there is nothing to be ashamed of, he happens to be the champion chess player of Austria."

There was a kind elderly person whom I used to meet there who was always seeking my company. I was privately rather flattered, but after a short time I grew nervous of questions such as, "Do you never think of anything serious?" "Whom do you think you would like to marry?" or, "Do you think you could ever like me?" The first was easy to answer with a cheerful "No." The second with "I have not the faintest idea." And the third, in growing terror "Of course I like you," and a hasty change of subject to the dogs or to something that was happening out in the garden. I took refuge in numbers whenever I could and searched for excuses to avoid *tête-à-têtes*. I remember one day, he suggested I should ride with him early the following morning. I could not resist the chance of a ride, so I hurried off to the schoolroom to ask Eddy or Alec Hoyos to ride too. They said they had lessons and could not, so in despair I went in search of their tutor, and begged for the loan of one of the boys. I think he must have suspected why I was so insistent, because with much laughter he consented to let the youngest boy, Alec, come out with me. I enjoyed my ride very much, Alec and I riding races the whole of the time, until my elderly friend lost his temper and saying, "You are impossible," rode off in a huff, and by the time we came in from our ride he had gone to London. His sister interviewed me afterwards to ask my intentions, which were quite defined, so the episode was closed.

2

BALLS VERSUS STUDIO

WHEN I was eighteen I was taken down to Windsor to dine and be presented to the Queen. Being relations we were all of us presented in that way instead of having to go to a Drawing-Room, like other young things of that age. I was quite happy until actually at dinner, when the Queen discussed my personal appearance in loud tones with my father who was sitting next to her. I was next to Sir Henry Ponsonby, the Queen's Private Secretary, who tried to talk loudly to me so that I should not hear what they were saying, but my ears were sharp and I heard " So like poor dear Feo " (my aunt who had died before I was born). " Surely a longer nose; no, I think a little fatter " . . . the Queen meanwhile leaning forward to be able to see me better. I was becoming more and more self-conscious until my father at last managed to distract her attention and the rest of dinner passed off well, except that I did not manage to get enough to eat, my plate being whisked away at the end of every course before I had finished. The moment the Queen had done, everyone was supposed to go on to the next course. As she was naturally helped first, she had finished first and people helped last had very little chance of getting any dinner. My father told me of a former time when he was staying at Windsor. No one was allowed to smoke and anyone wanting to do so went to the stables. (The last place I should have

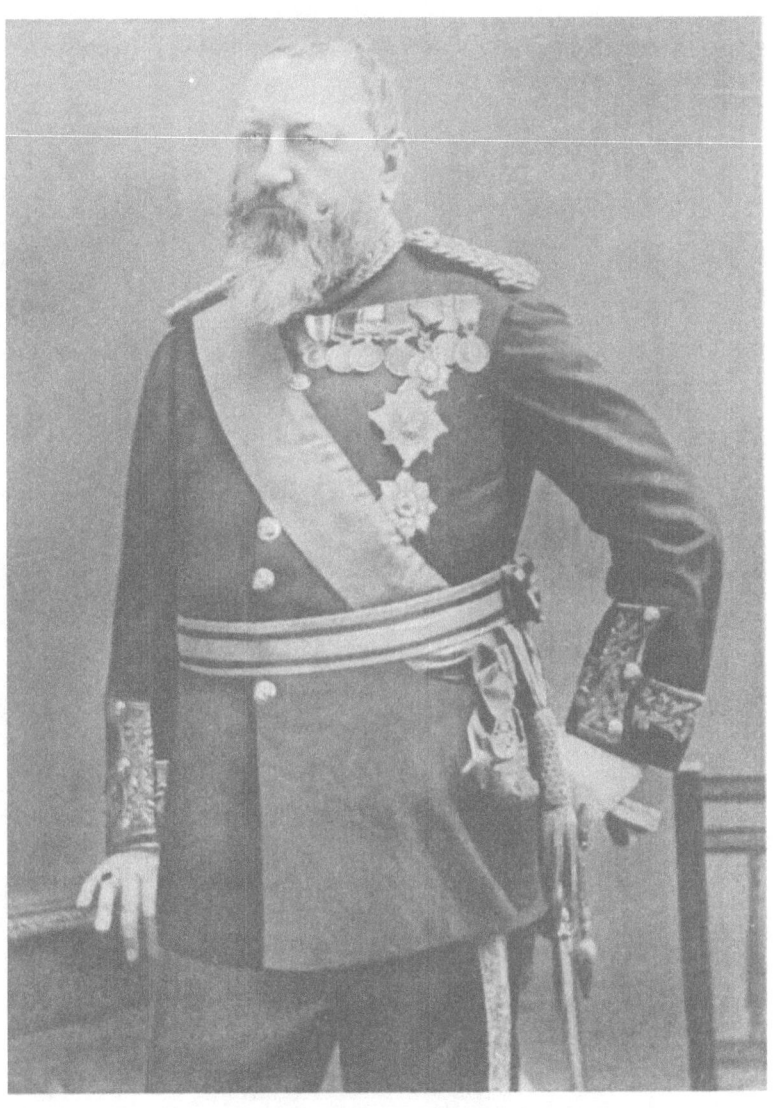

THE AUTHOR'S PARENTS
PRINCE VICTOR OF HOHENLOHE LANGENBURG

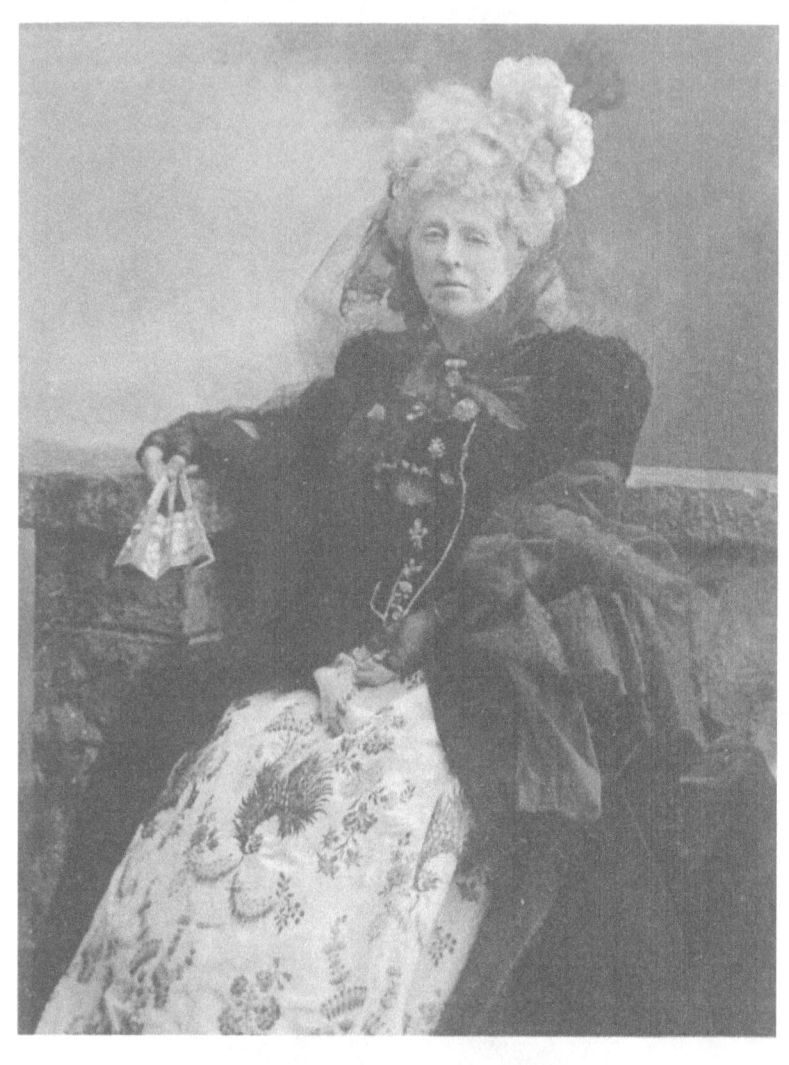

THE AUTHOR'S PARENTS
PRINCESS VICTOR OF HOHENLOHE LANGENBURG— IN FANCY DRESS

THE DEVONSHIRE HOUSE BALL

thought advisable.) Papa, an inveterate smoker, stuck his head up the chimney in his bedroom, hoping the smoke would go straight up and out into the open air. Unfortunately for him his bedroom happened to be immediately under the Queen's room and all the smoke went up her chimney. The Queen sent for him and remonstrated, but the result was that a smoking-room was arranged in another part of the Castle and my father earned the thanks of all who stayed there from then on.

I must have been about twenty when the celebrated Devonshire House fancy-dress ball took place. The family consulted as to which of us three should go, and finally, and most unselfishly, settled that I, as the youngest, should go. My mother went dressed as an ancestress, the Margravine of Anspach, only discovering to her horror afterwards that the lady was not at all respectable. She was dressed in a lovely red velvet gown with hoops and powdered hair. (Incidentally I wore part of the same gown at the jubilee of King George V, and the material looked as fresh as it did forty years before.)

The first idea for me was that I should go as St. Elizabeth of Hungary, the Queen who spent all her money feeding the poor of her realm, much to the annoyance of her husband who feared to become bankrupt. He forbade her to do it any more and threatened her with all sorts of terrible punishments were she to disobey him. The Queen, however, continued her good works in secret, until one day, just as she was going out with her veil filled with loaves of bread for the poor who were waiting at the gate of the Palace, she met the King, who insisted that she should show him what she was carrying in her apron or veil. With both hands the Queen held open her apron, and lo! it was full of roses.

BALLS VERSUS STUDIO

Unfortunately Queen Elizabeth's head-dress did not suit me, and when it was adjusted round my face I looked like an Arab, and rather a disreputable one at that, so it was settled that I should go as Joan of Arc. We took Boutet de Monvel pictures of Joan as our model, and I was fitted with a tabard made of white cloth sprinkled with gold fleurs-de-lis. Sir Guy Laking lent me a small suit of real armour of the period which was unluckily too heavy to wear in its entirety, so I only wore the jambs and sollerets with spurs, and the brassards. These last were agony, as whenever I bent my arm, they took pieces of flesh out. Of course I should have had on a jack, or leather jerkin, underneath as a protection, but I only wore imitation leather which helped not at all. One of the Peels and Victor Corkran were my Esquires, and they walked behind me, dressed in full armour, carrying my banner and big two-handed sword. My sallad (helmet of the period) was carried in front by Sir Arthur Sullivan, the composer, and we made a very imposing cortège clattering up the marble stairs of Devonshire House.

It shows how completely occupied I was with my own importance on that occasion that I remember no one else, only the general effect of brilliance and magnificence, which I have never seen equalled in any other function that I have attended.

My mother had always suffered from shyness and must have gone through agonies marrying into my father's family. The Empress Eugénie told me how sorry she used to be for her when she saw her at the various big functions that she and my father had to attend. She said how pretty she was, with her lovely fair complexion and golden hair and perfectly oval face. But, according to the Empress, nothing would make her talk. We none of us inherited her looks, but all of us, except my eldest sister, inherited her

FEO AND VALDA

shyness. Many people were very sorry for her, too, having such unconventional children, and rudely, if aptly, compared her to a hen with ducklings when we all broke out into our different professions. Feo, the eldest, followed in my father's footsteps and became a sculptor, whose work is to be seen in most quarters of the globe. Even as far as Irak a bronze bust of King Feisal by her stands in the museum of Baghdad. The solemn and beautiful memorial to Lord Kitchener in the Cathedral of Khartoum was modelled by her only two years before her death, and the big group of soldiers, at Monchy le Preux, in memory of the 37th Division, of which there is a reproduction at Sandhurst Military College, is another example of her more important work. Then there is the Memorial to King Edward VII at Windsor, twenty-two feet high, with the King in bronze, supported by four bronze figures (she had won the anonymous competition for this), and the statue of Florence Nightingale at Derby. She was the first woman to be elected a member of the British Sculptors' Society.

My other sister, Valda, who had a very good contralto voice, took up singing professionally and became a well-known Lieder-singer. She studied in Paris under Bouhy and later with the celebrated Russian teacher, Von zur Mühlen. In 1905 she married Percy Machell, Adviser to the Ministry of the Interior in Egypt.

In those days it was a terrible thing for one's daughters to insist on having professions, but my father encouraged us each to go ahead as if we had been boys. Curiously enough, however, when I came along, demanding also to go to art schools to study drawing, I was told that I might go to an animal school if I wished but not to study from the nude. My father, unluckily for me, had died when I was eighteen or I know he would have backed me up; and I had to wait two or three years before my mother would allow me to go to West-

BALLS VERSUS STUDIO

minster School, where at last I persuaded her to let me attend the life-class. I hated balls and parties from the beginning, and always felt that staying up late at night spoilt my chances of doing good work next day. I used to bicycle up to Mr. Calderon's animal school in Baker Street every day from St. James's Palace. At this school we studied anatomy, cast-drawing, etc., being gradually moved up to the life in the form of dogs and horses. The great difficulty in drawing animals is that they often move imperceptibly and you are so busy drawing that you do not find it out, until getting up to rest and looking at your work from afar you find that your animal's hind legs are hind view and his front legs front view! . . . This was despairing at first until one got accustomed to keeping a sharp look out for any movement of the model. Students drawing from human beings do not, of course, have to worry about this as the human model can always put himself back into the correct position if he has left it, but it is very difficult to make a dog or horse understand this unless he is especially clever. I have had several dogs of mine who learnt that they must always return exactly to their pose, if by chance they had moved. One, an Alsatian, whom I modelled with a pheasant in her mouth, would stand by the hour in the same position in my studio in London, holding a cushion which represented the pheasant (pheasants being out of season). Another time I was painting my fox-terrier gazing at the skylight at an imaginary cat, and day after day she would take this pose, and what is more would keep it with her head stretched up and her eyes fixed on the skylight.

I was determined to try and win a scholarship and so pay for my next year's work. We had to pass in anatomy and attend a certain number of lectures and amongst other things had to send up a drawing from life, dog or horse, whichever we liked best. At 9 a.m. we had to

A MIRACLE

be in the school, and very often it was 9 p.m. before I got home. The great day of examination came; we were in the usual state of nerves that I suppose all students are in on examination day. My anatomy, viva voce, was, I knew, shocking. I never could remember Latin words, though I was quite sure of my facts. Then came the most important test, a drawing from the life. I chose a horse for mine—a good-looking beast as far as I remember—but the looks of the animal did not for once interest me, I was only anxious about the result. We were supposed to leave a drawing for competition on the easel and go away. I did two in the time allowed and then could not make up my mind which to leave on the easel. The more I stared the less I knew which was the better. At last, in despair of ever making up my mind, I tossed for it. That settled the knotty point and I went out to the neighbouring bun-shop for luncheon. When I came in after luncheon I found that my drawing had miraculously been changed. The one I had put on my easel had gone, and the other, the one that I had put aside, had taken its place. I was in a great state of agitation; who could have touched it? In vain I asked all the other students; they all swore they knew nothing about it, and at last I had to give up looking, and with a feeling that fate had been too strong for me left it on the easel for competition, and stuffing all my working things into my locker went off home.

A few days after I received a notice to say that I had won the scholarship. The term had still to be finished, and one day on coming into the school after luncheon, I heard a clear voice say, " I call it a beastly shame; if someone hadn't changed her sketch she wouldn't have won." A lot of the students were sitting round the stove in the middle of the school, waiting for the model to be posed. I walked up to them and said, " I suppose you are talking about me." They were all silent except one who answered, "Yes, several of us think it was very unfair." I asked them to come up to Mr. Calderon at once and we all trooped upstairs. I told him what had happened and what I had heard said as I came in, adding that I wished to give up my scholarship, or if he preferred it, I suggested that we should have that test over again. I said that I could not put my original sketch on the easel to be judged as I had never found it since. Mr. Calderon said that he would think it over and come down presently and tell us the result. In the meantime would we please go down and continue our work as the model had been in position for some time. When five o'clock came Mr. Calderon came down into the school and asked all the students to come round and listen to what he had to say. He first asked for a show of hands, and I discovered to my surprise that there were only two against my receiving the scholarship. He laughed and said, "I think that answers itself, there is nothing for me to say, and the scholarship remains in the hands of its present possessor. Many congratulations, Countess Helena, I hope it will be very useful to you," and he departed. All the rest were very nice about it, but I did not for months discover who had changed the drawings, and then I found it was the winner of the scholarship of the year before. I thanked her very much and asked her why she had done it. "You would never have won it with that," she said. "I knew that you were tired out and couldn't judge, so I just threw the first drawing into the stove."

I often wonder if it was fair that I had that scholarship. . . . Anyway, I had to wait for it for some time as I had inadvertently poisoned myself with the paint in my locker, so retired to bed with ptomaine poisoning. I used to keep all my possessions in my locker, but the paint had got mixed with the sandwiches which I often brought for luncheon.

3

ROME AND PAINTING

THE year that my father died was known for the first really serious outbreak of what was called Russian influenza, and he died of it. Everyone in the house had it and every servant was ill. The then Adjutant of the battalion of Grenadiers that was at Wellington Barracks saved the situation for us by sending in several Grenadiers to cook and do housemaid. We have none of us ever forgotten that act of kindness.

One day the following spring my mother came into the room and announced that we were all going to Rome. We were greatly delighted and spent a very happy six months there . . . dancing at every ball that was given and making friends with everyone of both Black and White parties. Our connection with the Black party was through Gustav of Hohenlohe Schillingsfürst, Cardinal and a cousin of my father's—in those days called uncle by the younger generation. We were greatly impressed by him. He was the typical Cardinal, tall, charming and with white hair. He came to visit us in our flat, dressed in his beautiful Cardinal's robes, and the old gentleman was much amused by our admiration of him. He turned round and round for us to see him from all sides and even took off his wonderful Cardinal's ring for us to examine. He was a friend of both the King and the Pope, a very rare thing to be, as

ROME AND PAINTING

the two sides, Black and White, were very heated against each other in those days.

He told us a story that I have never forgotten. When he left his home in Austria as a lad, to go to the German school for priests in Rome, he took with him as his valet the son of the head *Jäger* or keeper. This man stayed on with him throughout the years and they became very great friends. The Jesuits of that time were very jealous of my uncle's influence with both parties and frequently tried to remove him from this sphere. In fact he was obliged to keep a taster, as in medieval times, who tasted all his food before he touched it. One day this taster fell ill, and Uncle Gustav said that as it was so long since anyone had tried to poison him, it was unnecessary to appoint another. The old valet was greatly distressed and begged to be allowed to take the taster's place. He was almost in tears, so at last Uncle Gustav gave in and allowed him to do so, saying, " Very well, taste if it gives you any satisfaction. It is quite safe nowadays or I should not let you do it." The valet put some of the soup which was already on the table into a glass and drank it off. To my uncle's horror he threw up his hands and dropped to the ground stone dead. As the old man told us this story his eyes filled with tears. " He had been with me ever since we were boys together, and he died saving my life; it was all my fault having allowed him to taste my food." We asked how long ago this had happened, and he said about twenty years. This makes the date about 1872.

It was a great advantage to us having a Cardinal uncle, as we were given all the best places in the various Church functions and incidentally made friends with many of the Black party, whom otherwise we should not have known. We attended Mass in the crypt of St. Peter's, which I am told very few Protestants have been allowed

THE CANONIZATION OF A SAINT

to do, and went to a Consistory to see new Cardinals being installed.

Another ceremony which we attended—a very impressive one—was the canonization of some saint. We had our places, but the difficulty was to get to them. I was going alone with my mother that time, and she was always very nervous in a crowd. The crush outside St. Peter's was enormous, and my mother got thoroughly frightened after we had been obliged to leave the carriage and were well in the middle of it. Leaving her to stand near a lamp-post, and asking a kind man to look after her, I started to push my way steadily through the people towards the main entrance, where I could see a lot of the Guardia Nobile [1] standing on the steps. The good-humoured Italian crowd tried to squeeze themselves on one side to let me through, and at last I reached the steps. I explained who we were, "Nipote del Cardinale Hohenlohe," and pointed back towards my mother miles away amongst the sea of heads. At once the man I was speaking to called to the other Guardia Nobile to come, and surrounded by about ten of them, we pushed our way back to my mother, who was still clinging to her lamp-post. With great pomp my first friend gave her his arm, and with me following behind we were safely landed at the entrance. There we were handed over to one of the Pope's Chamberlains who took us to our seats. We were glad not to have arrived any sooner as there had been a horrible accident in full view of all there. A workman, who had been putting some finishing touches above the Pope's canopy, had fallen from a height of about seventy feet on to the pavement in front of all the congregation not two minutes before we came in, and his body was being carried away just as we walked up the aisle.

Before we left Rome, Uncle Gustav offered to lend us

[1] The Pope's personal guard.

ROME AND PAINTING

the Villa d'Este at Tivoli, and I have always regretted that we did not accept his invitation. It would have been wonderful to live in that beautiful place even for a few days, but the weather was treacherous and we were afraid of the cold for my mother. Those old Italian villas are bitter in winter, and the spring winds would have swept through the huge rooms without mercy. It was a great opportunity lost.

The first thing I did when we got back to England after Rome was to go and study painting with Arthur Lemon. A painter little known to the general public, he was very well known among artists both English and foreign. Particularly was he appreciated in Italy, where his work is still remembered and treasured. He had started life by joining the Garibaldians at the age of sixteen. His father naturally did not approve of this at so young an age and made him leave them, so he ran away to America. Here he nearly starved, but was given a job at a baker's shop making sugar figures. Soon tiring of this he became a cowboy, and while watching the big herds under his charge would spend his time making studies of them. So intent was he on his work, that one day a bull came up behind him without his finding it out, and before he could grasp what had happened, he found himself flying through the air over a big wire fence and his paint-box and sketch were being trampled on by the infuriated beast, whose rage was increased by being unable to get at him again. Lemon stayed in America until he had collected enough money to return to Europe, when he went to study at Barbizon. There, to inspire him, he had the example of Jean François Millet, Rousseau, Corot and all the other great masters.

After spending some time in France he went to Italy, where he met and made friends with the Cecconi brothers and others, and where he finally settled down until his marriage. He married a daughter of a well-known English banker in Italy, and it is told of him that at the time he should have been being married he was lost in painting a picture on the Campagna. So late was it before he was found that the poor lady waiting at the Embassy melted into tears and went home. The next day his friends did not lose sight of him, so the marriage duly took place.

Having seen his paintings, I much wanted to work with him. How this came to his ears I do not know, but he asked John Sargent if I should be likely to be of any use as a pupil. Sargent's answer was that the rest of my family knew what serious work meant, so he supposed I should be the same, and I was determined to prove that Sargent was right in my case also.

I went down to Brockham Green to make acquaintance and to see if Arthur Lemon would take me on. I was terrified lest I should not come up to the mark. He solemnly inspected the things I had brought down for him to look at. The studies of animals—some done alone, some done at Calderon's school of animal painting—all, as I now know, tight, uninspired work, but terribly in earnest. Dead silence, while he sat smoking, holding his pipe in his hand, and I humbly bringing one thing out after another and propping them up in front of him. He never made one remark, but at last got up and said, "Let's go for a walk." My knees were shaking beneath me, and we walked silently away into the fields. He began talking in his quiet slow way—of his life as a painter, of animals and their ways, of tones, of the difference between shadows and shade, of the many ways of getting effects of light. Very soon I had quite forgotten my nervousness and we were sitting on a gate watching sheep and cattle without a thought, except painting, in our minds. He told me long after that he had been as frightened as I was; not for the same reason, but for fear he should not be able to make me understand his theories or be able to be of any use to me. I was his first pupil, and he said he had no idea how to begin. He could not have begun better, and everything in painting that I have ever succeeded in, I owe to his patient teaching. Truth of vision, no trickery, sound composition, each object balancing the other; that was what he tried to teach, a very good complement to what my father had always taught.

The walk was often repeated, and I think he taught me more in those walks than in any other way, as he would very seldom touch or alter his pupils' work. He always wished them to go their own way and not to be dependent on their master. I remember being deeply hurt later on when I was more advanced, because for more than a year nothing would induce him to come into my studio or help me with any of my work. Afterwards, he explained why: it was because he thought that I was following him too closely. Then I understood, but I still think he might have explained first and not last. When he did explain his seeming indifference, he also explained that the danger was past, so he could now come whenever I wanted him. But by now I had grown quite independent, and if he touched or painted on anything of mine, I almost invariably altered it back again after he had gone. I asked him once if he had minded this, and with a smile he said that that was what he had hoped!

I think my time working at Brockham was the happiest time in my very happy existence. Up and out painting by 8.30 a.m.—he would not let us go earlier, always saying that painting was exhausting enough. "Why go so early? You won't be fit to work again later in the day." In to luncheon at 1 p.m., sleep or read till four, out painting again till 9 p.m. What a nice way to spend your life! . . . I had in the very beginning taken a cottage of my own, much to my mother's horror; it was 1892 and the female young were still supposed, at the age of eighteen, to be under their parents' orders. However, when she found that I had signed the agreement and that the cottage was mine for the time being, for the sum of £20 a year, she gave in with a good grace and like an angel supplied me with blankets and linen and an armchair. My uncle, Wilfred Seymour,[1] had given or lent me everything else that I wanted as he was always very kind to me. I did not need very much as the cottage had only two rooms upstairs and one down, with a kitchen and lean-to outside. The kitchen I turned into a dining-room and relegated the cooking to the lean-to. I then hired a charlady to come and look after me and sleep in the cottage, as my mother had put her foot down at the idea of my sleeping there alone. The first charlady that I had was a nice round little dumpling of a woman, with bright-red apple cheeks and white hair, who always wore her husband's cap over one eye. She was rather a trial to me, as if she thought I was dull or had nothing to do on a rainy day would insist on coming into the sitting-room and standing very upright (about four feet nothing), with her hands behind her, would recite " The Mistletoe Bough." If I spoke or moved she had to begin all over again from the beginning, and it took so long that I soon learnt not to stir so as to get it over. I could never refuse this kindness, because once I did so and the old lady burst into tears. My next one was an equal success in her own way. She was the bad-hat of the village, but looked after me quite passably, giving me raw black-currants and sardines for every meal, until Mrs. Lemon found it out and insisted on doing my catering for me. Mrs. Brooker was the old-fashioned sort of charwoman, slatternly and

[1] General Lord William Seymour.

down at heel. She always forgot to clean the front doorstep, until one morning she found me kneeling outside cleaning it and whitening it myself. Instead of the gratitude I expected, her fury was unbounded. . . . She said I should give her a bad name in the village and that she would never hear the last of it. I believe she never did, but my doorstep was spotless from that day on. One memorable day she was going to her home, having left my black-currants and sardines out on the table for me. I had been out painting, and we met on the road. We exchanged greetings, and as she passed me I saw sticking out of her pocket some wax candles. My candles had been vanishing very quickly lately, so I said mildly, " By the way, Mrs. Brooker, if you happen to want any candles, you have only to ask me and I shall be only too glad to let you have some." She clapped her hands to her pocket and became inarticulate and purple in the face. I hastened to assure her that I had already seen them and was glad to know that she would not need any more for some time. Without answering she hurried away down the road muttering to herself, but I never had to complain again of my candles or anything else disappearing.

Mr. Lemon and I had many amusing expeditions together, one being on bicycles to the Derby (the only time I have ever been to the Derby). We started very early so as to get there before the crowd began to arrive. We had a gipsy friend whose encampment near Brockham we had often raided for sketching subjects. We wandered about amongst the gipsy caravans searching for him, as we knew he would take care of our bicycles for us for the day. We knew personally a good many of the Romanies, who all greeted us, some wishing us luck on the day, but none bothering us to let them tell our fortunes. They were all too busy on their own jobs, and clever enough to know that we had not much

THE DERBY

cash to spare. They knew that painters were seldom full of spare cash. We had an exceptionally pleasant day, dawdling about from one show to another, occasionally looking up as a lot of horses galloped past; shooting in the shooting-gallery, throwing at coco-nuts, talking to the Fat Lady who invited us to see her show without paying for it. Mr. Lemon's gentle smile fetched them all. Then we nearly bought a blind horse; luckily, at the last moment, just as we were wondering what on earth we could do with him, someone else stepped in and bought him over our heads and we thankfully slunk away into the crowd. At last it penetrated our obtuse minds that it was getting late. Most of the crowd had dispersed, and we went to collect our bicycles from the friendly gipsy. In those days no telephone, no wireless, and as we bicycled across the village green everyone came running out to ask who had won the Derby. We looked at each other. . . . " Who had ? " . . . We didn't know ! We never felt such fools in all our lives. We had been to the Derby and didn't know who had won it.

We always went out after our work on fine nights, and once were dawdling about in the fields when I fell heavily over a large object which turned out to be the farmer's bull turned out for the night. He lumbered to his feet, and we fled for the gate, but he was too bewildered to know which way we had gone or perhaps he was too lazy, but we were lucky as he was well known to be very bad-tempered. Another episode I remember well. It had been raining hard and we were coming down a chalky lane which had streams of water running down it. Mr. Lemon suggested damming the water to form a lake. I joined in with enthusiasm and we made bridges, dams, locks and channels galore until interrupted by an infuriated old lady who came running up the lane. One of our dams had burst and all the

ROME AND PAINTING

water had been turned by our best canal into the door of her cottage, which we had not noticed was some yards below where we were playing. Our regrets were of no avail, and I shall never forget Mr. Lemon's woebegone appearance as, covered with chalk and clay, hat in hand, he bowed with an archducal bow before her in deep apology. Nothing appeased her until one of us produced a half-crown, when without saying " Thank you " she went off grumbling to herself that people of our age should be ashamed to behave like babies at the seaside.

That reminds me of a sight that greeted me one morning when I came down rather late for breakfast at Berrydown, a house my mother had taken for the autumn. Mr. Lemon was staying with us at the time and either he or Feo had upset the coffee all over the clean tablecloth, and a fine mess they had made. Feo had suggested salt to prevent staining the cloth, and they had emptied all the salt-cellars into the coffee. This had obviously suggested the passage of the Beresina to them, and when I came in they were busy with forks making wheelmarks through the dirty snow, arranging the bed of the river in a sluggish stream of coffee and making retreating troops out of lumps of sugar and brown bread squeezed into the required shapes. It was a truly beautiful game. (When asked which was Napoleon Mr. Lemon quickly answered he had already gone on.) The staff, I remember, was made with curls of bacon—red coats on white horses or white coats on red horses—so I had to go without bacon that morning. My mother appeared in the middle and, highly amused, joined in with fresh suggestions. Mr. Lemon could do no wrong in her eyes, and she was as fond of him as all the rest of us were.

I started very early in life having bad accidents. The first—a fall in Hyde Park off a lent horse, when I

FRIENDS

damaged my back—I was pulling up my girths when the horse suddenly bucked, sending me flying. This was followed by another to the same unfortunate back, when a kind friend offered me a chair at the shooting luncheon in a farm kitchen. I accepted the chair but sat down before it was there . . . and the stone floor proved to be very hard. This last accident kept me in bed for over a year. After the first few weeks I settled down and enjoyed myself immensely, as people were extraordinarily kind to me . . . and the flowers and books that were given me, as well as the constant company I had, were enough to gladden anyone's heart. My cousin, John Fortescue, was one of my most regular visitors, and he came to read his *Story of the Red Deer* as he wrote it, chapter by chapter. Later, when they moved me on to a sofa in the next room, Maurice Baring, Albert Mensdorff (an Austrian cousin who was attached to the Austrian Embassy in London and later on became Ambassador to the Court of St. James's), and the Gordons—these latter grandchildren of Mrs. Siddons—arranged plays for my benefit, and great fun they were.

Mentioning Maurice Baring reminds me of one of my best friends, Tom Baring, an uncle of Maurice's. Tom and I made friends in very early days. He was quite old when I first met him, or at least I thought so. I had gone down with my mother to stay with Lord and Lady Mount Stephen at Brocket in Hertfordshire. Lord Mount Stephen had been a great friend of my father's and his story had always fascinated me because he had started life as a butcher-boy in Aberdeen. He always used to swagger about this beginning in front of his pompous and enormous footmen. He said he liked to shock them. From a butcher-boy he had gone on to sweeping out an office, and gradually had worked up to being chairman of the Canadian Pacific Railway, and

ROME AND PAINTING

one of the richest men in England. (An anecdote about him and his wife in later years always gave me great pleasure. They were sitting in the drawing-room at Brocket one evening during the War when an enemy aeroplane came over and dropped a bomb on the lawn, smashing all the windows. Later Valda asked Lady Mount Stephen what they did in this crisis. "Why, rang the bell, of course," said Gian, "and much to our annoyance no one came. I can't think what had happened to everybody.")

Tom Baring was staying at Brocket, and I discovered that there was nothing this old gentleman did not know about birds and their songs, so I set myself to learn all I could from him. This started a friendship which continued for years. We used to spend many an afternoon poking about in antiquity dealers' shops, where he sat talking to the dealers while I was shown all the treasures which were usually kept locked up. For me, it was an ideal friendship and I learnt a great deal from him. His presents, too, were an unending joy. An early Ming Dynasty bronze horse, a lovely cane with an old Dresden china top, a large comfy sofa for my cottage, and a salmon-rod, were among the treasures he gave me and which I still look upon as most precious possessions. Though he loved china he did not often give me any because he realised that I was not worthy of it. I always argued that *pâte* alone did not make an object beautiful and that it must be well-modelled, of good colour and good composition, to make a work of art. I have often thought since that he, as well as other china collectors, forgot the artistic side completely in their pleasure over the feeling of the *pâte* or the quality of the glaze. I was sad when our friendship ceased after his marriage. It just died a natural death.

When Queen Victoria died my mother and Valda were away abroad, so Feo and I had to represent the

THE QUEEN'S FUNERAL

family at the funeral at Windsor, Eddie of course having gone to Osborne. Our orders were to be at Paddington Station by a certain time. We should there find a special train with seats reserved in it for us. A mounted policeman was at the front door waiting to precede our carriage through the streets. Smothered from head to foot in crape with long crape veils reaching down to the ground we started for the station with plenty of time to spare. All went well until we reached the middle of Hyde Park when the policeman's horse suddenly shied violently and sat down. Our horse followed suit; the coachman was unable to pull him up in time, and he climbed on to the other horse's back, and breaking one shaft. The crowd, very solemn up to that moment, were delighted and surged forward with offers of help and pieces of string which were gratefully accepted. Five or ten minutes later, tied up with string like a parcel, we continued our drive to Paddington. Arrived there we were greeted by officials who put us into a train waiting by the platform and told us that we should be starting almost immediately. The whole station was hung with mourning drapery and a guard of honour was drawn up opposite our carriage. Mounted police rode in, gave messages and rode out again; time went on, our train did not move. We sent our footman to ask officials if there had been a mistake and if we were in the wrong train. "No, it's all right, your train will go presently." We grew more and more anxious as we knew that by that time we ought to have been sitting in our places in St. George's Chapel. There was nothing to be done, so we gave ourselves up to watching what was going on. The feeling of expectancy grew stronger and stronger. The train which was to carry the bier was drawn up opposite to ours. Then we heard the notes of the Dead March . . . first far away, gradually coming closer and closer. Arms were reversed, the men's heads were bowed and the wail of the bagpipes echoed through the arches of the big station, making an almost unendurable noise, followed by dead silence only broken by the sound of the horses' feet as they came to a stand with the gun-carriage in front of the funeral train. Then all was bustle and hurry, hundreds of different-coloured uniforms hastening to take their places in the trains reserved for them. Red, scarlet, white, gold, every nation represented, the picturesque Hungarians in their Hussar tunics with fur capes thrown over their shoulders, Indians, gorgeous in pale blue, scarlet and gold with white turbans decorated with marvellous jewels, all hurrying to and fro with anxious faces. An order to the guard of honour, and as the train bearing the coffin moved out of the station, our train, crowded with officers, pulled slowly out behind it. No one recognized the two little black figures in the corner of the carriage reserved for foreign guests. What were we to do when the train arrived at Windsor! I remember hating two of the foreigners, who did nothing but laugh as they tidied themselves up for their next appearance. They did not mind a bit and we all minded so much.

The train drew into Windsor station . . . already the coffin had been put on the gun-carriage ready to draw it up to St. George's Chapel. There was a clattering of swords and spurs as the foreign representatives ran to take their places in the procession, but it was drowned by the noise of the team in the gun-carriage; they had been kept waiting too long, they were fresh and it was cold. A great many reasons have been given, but the fact remains that one swingle-hook had broken and the horses kicked over the traces and generally misbehaved themselves, becoming totally unmanageable. With a good deal of difficulty they were unhooked, and no other team being at hand, the naval guard of honour took

THE QUEEN'S FUNERAL

their place, and drawn by sailors the gun-carriage moved slowly away into the streets of Windsor.

Fritz Ponsonby at that moment caught sight of us and called a corporal of Grenadiers, telling him to escort us through the crowd and up to the Chapel as quickly as possible. Stumbling at every step over our long veils, which were not meant for walking in, we hurried after him through the crowd, who parted to let us through. Never did I know a man walk so fast, and we were both completely blown by the time we reached the door of the Chapel, only just in time, one minute before the head of the procession came in sight. Old Spencer Ponsonby was there to meet us, and whispering, "I thought you had missed your train and have put someone else into your seats," he hurried us up to the Altar and turned the other unhappy people out to make room for us. Even then our troubles were not quite over, as thinking we were not coming our places had been filled for luncheon, too, and we went back to London without having had any food of any kind, arriving at home more dead than alive about 5 p.m., having started out at 8.30 a.m.

What a horrid day.

4

IN FRANCE

IN 1903 my fox-terrier died, and I was so sad that my family urged me to go away somewhere and find something else to occupy my attention. My brother was at that time military attaché in Berlin (see *A Guardsman's Memories*). I have rather forgotten my stay there. The parties I went to were very stiff; even the ones in my brother's house were not exciting, though I suppose the guests enjoyed themselves as I remember that we had privately to order their carriages to be announced because they stayed so late. From Berlin I went on to stay at Potsdam with a charming cousin named Feo Holstein, daughter of my father's youngest sister, Ada, who had married the Duke of Schleswig-Holstein. She was very nice and very intelligent, a poet and a painter, but terribly hampered by being sister-in-law to the German Emperor who interfered with everything she wanted to do. He would not let her go to an Art School or study from the life; he would not let her go anywhere she wanted to. Her independent spirit was stamping and fuming over all her restrictions, and she envied us for our independence and freedom from all regulations. Considering how little training she had, her writings and drawings were really good and full of imagination. Feo Holstein and I had some very happy times painting out in the lovely Potsdam woods, which were in places quite wild and untouched, with wide marshes full of birds of all sorts.

MY NEW FRIEND

We only met once again, when she came to stay with us at Ebrington, a house my mother had rented from the Fortescues, near that lovely old town, Chipping Campden. There she was happy for a short space and loved the old Cotswold houses, but she had a bad heart-attack which took away part of her pleasure. She wouldn't let her old lady-in-waiting go near her, so I went up to her room and found her leaning out of the window struggling for breath. As I leant out next to her, she whispered, "How I wish I need never go away from here. I'm not going to live long so I shouldn't bore you too much." Later, when she was better, we talked it over, but she said she must return to Germany as it was her home. She died only a few months later, alone as she always was, when she felt an attack coming on.

About that time I made friends with Nina Hollings, Dame Ethel Smyth's sister, a friendship which has nearly equalled that of the Ladies of Llangollen as it has lasted ever since. The attraction at first was horses and hunting, Nina being a wonderful rider to hounds. She was also a first-rate companion, always good-tempered and cheerful, very quick in the uptake, very energetic and highly amused at everything. So we arranged that when I left Eddie she should meet me in Munich and we would go together to France for me to paint.

The first place we stopped at was Vesoul, where we had a strange adventure.

We had left the train at a small wayside station and were driving to Vézelay, where we intended to stay. A tremendous thunderstorm came on and we were soaked to the skin, so our driver suggested that we should stay the night in Vesoul, a small town on our road. It was already past nine when we arrived there and we drove through a *porte-cochère* up to an old-fashioned inn to ask for beds for the night. The innkeeper came out to inspect us and was quite firm that his hotel was full and that he had no room for us. In vain we showed him how wet we were. He was quite obstinate, and we were sadly turning away to continue our wet drive to the next village when the *femme de chambre* suggested loudly that we should have the rooms over the *porte-cochère*. The inn-keeper shook his head with decision. " Mais non," he repeated and turned back to go into his kitchen, with the *femme de chambre* running alongside him talking rapidly all the time.

In a moment she returned to us saying, " Come quickly, I will light a fire, and you will be quite comfortable; hurry, in case he changes his mind." We hastened after her up some steps in the courtyard which led to a balcony running along the wall over the archway that we had entered by. There were bedrooms opening off this balcony, and the balcony ended in a blank wall; the only means of getting to the rooms or away from them being by the steps that we went up.

In the first room she dumped all our soaking rugs and bags, slopping off down the steps to fetch sticks and paper and dry blankets. Once we had got our dripping garments off and were sitting wrapped in blankets in front of a roaring fire, we felt more normal beings again and received Louise and hot supper with joy. While eating we heard rather a strange sound coming from the corner of the room. Squeak—squeak —squeak, and the popping of a cork being drawn. We knew we were over the archway and there were no rooms or cellars under us. These squeaks happened two or three times, but we were so happy and warm that nothing bothered us.

Louise pushed her very ugly but kind face in, to tell us that our bedrooms were ready, and off we went along the balcony, I to the end room against the wall, and

AN UNPLEASANT NIGHT

Nina to the next one. This left one empty room between our rooms and the room where we had supper. Both, very tired, went to sleep at once. I was awakened by heavy steps coming along the balcony. My door slowly opened and in one second Nina dashed in shouting to know who it was that had come into my room. I had by that time found the matches and lit a candle. My door was wide open and I could see Nina standing in the doorway silhouetted against the cold blue of the night sky. No one else was on the balcony and there was no wind to account for the door opening. We agreed to spend the rest of the night in the same room, neither of us having liked the episode. So Nina settled herself in the armchair with one candle and I got into bed again with the other on a chair beside me, after we had first locked the door and pushed an enormously heavy table against it, jamming it under the handle.

Nina was already asleep, and I was getting sleepy when suddenly I heard a sound and saw the handle of my door turning and the table moving slowly back into the room as the door opened. Out on to the balcony we both rushed, Nina first as she was nearest the door. . . . Nothing there, only the cold air just before dawn. We stood on the balcony for some time, but saw and heard nothing, and then returned, this time to Nina's room, where we both sat up and talked until broad daylight . . . hearing and seeing nothing further.

Louise asked us many questions as to how we had slept, had we heard anyone about, had we seen anything to disturb us. The funny thing was that we never told her a word about our unpleasant adventure, although she told us that during the French Revolution the local Marquis and Marquise had been murdered in those rooms. (She gave us a white cockade, which she said had been found there and must have belonged to them.) Since they had been done to death in those rooms,

IN FRANCE

no one had been able to sleep in them. She added that the rooms had never been used since the last traveller who occupied them had committed suicide there. Even then we had some curious instinct which kept us silent and we never told her of our disturbing experience—I wonder why.

We were quite glad to leave Vesoul and pursue our way to Vézelay, a fascinating little town, high up upon a rock overlooking the valley of the Cur. Here we settled ourselves in a small unsophisticated inn. I can't say we were comfortable, two rooms with tiled floors the size of cabins, *soupe maigre* every day and very little else. We had one excitement, the post-office caught fire. No one knew what to do, so Nina and I, who had turned out to see the blaze, suggested buckets from hand to hand from the village pump. This idea was received with enthusiasm. They thought it a very good idea, but by the time the bucket reached the fire most of its contents had been spilt. Someone then remarked that the post-office dog, who had given warning of the fire by barking, was nowhere to be found, so we left the villagers and went round to the back. There, after we had forced our way in, we found the dog lying on the ground amid swirls of smoke, quite unconscious. We hastily dragged him out and started artificial breathing. After a bit he began wheezing, so one of us rushed back to the inn for our brandy flask and gave him a good dose. This seemed to pull him together very quickly. By this time, having put out the fire, some of the villagers came round to look for us and were astounded to find us dosing a dog with cognac. The news spread over the country, not of the fire, but of the fact that the lunatic English gave their best cognac to a dog, that did not even belong to them!

We went miles away sketching one day, and on going to a farm to ask if they could give us some luncheon,

THE BULL

they said "No" very crossly. As we turned away the farmer called after us, "Are you the two English ladies who gave the post-office dog cognac?" When we said "Yes," he urged us to return saying that everything he had was ours and that his wife would at once cook us some *déjeuner*. He said we ought to have told them who we were, as they would never have refused had they known. After *déjeuner* they asked if we would like to see the boy who had been tossed by the bull in the morning, it would give him so much pleasure. So we were ushered up to his room in the attic He had been badly trampled on and had a broken thigh, but seemed quite cheerful and much excited at our appearance, wanting to know all about the much-talked-of dog. Then the farmer's wife said that surely we could not leave without seeing the bull which had tossed the boy. Of course we agreed, so the daughter of the house, with a baby in her arms, said she would show him to us. Followed by the farm dog, we started off across the fields to see him. We thought to look safely at him from behind a gate. . . . Not at all. The girl tramped across a field in front of us, and when we reached the middle, stopped and pointed, saying, "There he is " . . . and there he stood, in the same field with us, his horns covered with mud and grass, which he had just torn up, and making a horrid grumbling noise in his throat, being thoroughly upset from his morning's adventure, when the farm men had had to beat him off his victim. As she showed him to us with pride, he again began tossing his huge head and pawing up the ground. Nina seized the baby and I grabbed the dog and we fled for the nearest gate, getting through just before he reached it. And then, much to our fury the girl would go up and down the hedge calling to him and throwing sticks and stones over at him, so that, thoroughly angry by now, he tried to get at

IN FRANCE

her through the hedge, which luckily was fairly tough. It was with the utmost difficulty that we made her put another couple of hedges between him and us. She seemed quite mesmerized by him and obviously thought Nina and me very cowardly for insisting on leaving his vicinity as quickly as possible.

I spent the afternoon painting lovely creamy oxen in a blue wagon.

We stayed some time in Vézelay, notwithstanding the discomfort, as there was always something interesting to see or paint. The weekly market was enough to fill an animal-painter's soul with delight . . . although not perhaps an animal-lover's . . . the animals being roughly handled as in all markets. Nina was always struggling with the peasants to persuade them to milk their unhappy cows brought to market unmilked, and consequently in agony; or she would argue with a pig-owner whose pigs were packed in wagons in four tiers, and when unloaded, pig after pig was slung with tied legs, screaming, down a slanting board, to arrive with a heavy bump on the hard ground. I was meanwhile trying to paint the constantly moving mass of delicious white and cream-coloured cattle, with their long horns and large liquid eyes, together with their black-and-blue-clad owners who moved about continually in their midst. How enjoyable it all was, and how nice all the people were to us.

We had a wonderful experience at Vézelay. On the top of the rock jutting out over the valley there is a very beautiful church, built on the site from which Peter the Hermit preached his first crusade. One lovely night we thought we would walk up to this *Abbaye*. It was in full moonlight, and the heavy old yew-trees were casting black shadows across the half-cemetery, half-garden which surrounds it. We were leaning over the parapet looking down into the misty valleys below

A WONDERFUL EXPERIENCE

and feeling the solemnity and silence surrounding us, when suddenly a hound bayed far away to our right, a deep hound's bay, not a dog's bark. Then another hound took it up, and yet another, and the hitherto silent valleys took up the echo, as hound after hound joined in, not baying at the moon, but a savage sound as if a great pack were after blood. So savage that you felt your hair rise and your gullet contract with fear. We leant over the parapet in breathless silence, while the great sound rolled round us from valley to valley, the echo no doubt increased by the mist below. Then it died away as suddenly as it had begun and was succeeded by dead silence.

. . . The mist by this time had climbed the steep rock to the church, so we left and went down to the town, arriving about 2 a.m. and having taken about a quarter of an hour to get back. Next morning the inn-keeper's wife asked us where we had been so late, and when we told her, asked how we could go to such a place at night, as it was known to be full of *revenants*. We mentioned having heard hounds and asked who kept them. Her answer was that no one kept them now, but that a certain Comte de —— had kept bloodhounds in the seventeenth century to hunt his serfs when they ran away. He was known to have been very brutal and cruel to his dependants, and many were the men those hounds had pulled down and torn to pieces at his orders. Finally, the country people had turned against his rule and had murdered him, his family and his hounds. She added that the hounds had many times been heard since by persons who went up to the church late at night, but only strangers ventured there now, as the Vézelay people did not dare to do so. We went once more while staying at Vézelay in hopes of hearing them again, but it was of no use.

After a bit we tired of our uncomfortable lodging

and bad and insufficient food, so having discovered a little inn down in the valley in the tiny village of St. Père, we moved down there, bag and baggage.

We had discovered this inn in rather an odd way. I had been sketching near the river Cur, which made a lovely foreground to the purple and lilac towers of the old Vézelay church standing out against the setting sun. The mayor of St. Père, who had been ploughing, was standing behind me watching silently, when there burst out a screaming and shouting from the direction of the village. I jumped up to go and see what had occurred when the old mayor said quietly, "*Que Madame ne s'inquiète pas*, it is only Monsieur and Madame Drouin of the hotel quarrelling. *Quel* animal, he knocks her about shamefully. Only last week he was drunk and carried her out in her *chemise de nuit* and held her by one foot over the river bridge. He is very strong, *c'est un homme de taille*, but if she had not stayed very still, he would have dropped her into the river. *La pauvre*, she has a terrible life. Formerly she had many clients at her hotel and she did them well, but now everyone is afraid and no one goes there." This sounded just what we should like, so we went off to see madame and see if she would care to take us in. Our interview did not begin well: "Non, mais non," and she tried to shut the door, but Nina with great foresight had inserted her foot, so the conversation continued. "You do not know what it is like here, it is impossible for me to take in anyone." We assured her that we had heard all about her troubles. . . . "And you still want to come?" and she burst into tears, and flung the door open, crying, "*Dieu merci*, I shall have someone to speak to."

She took us upstairs saying, "You shall have the whole of the first floor for the price of two rooms, as long as you will allow me to come up here to sleep

MADAME DROUIN

when my husband is drunk. Here is your dining-room, here your salon, here a room for Madame la Comtesse to keep all her painting things, and you have the balcony to sit on in the evening to watch the sunsets behind Vézelay." It was truly a lovely place with the river running immediately under the windows, the great *colombier* opposite and the old stone bridge with the constantly crossing traffic of slow-moving ox-carts, with their drivers clad in the usual blue or black blouse of the peasant. There was always something to look at.

One day a week the village drummer would drum to all who would listen, " Come and hear the news of the outside world." He mentioned the South African war as " *La Guerre des Anglais,*" and bowed towards us. A very old lady standing near turned to us saying, " I thought Queen Victoria had insisted on the war between France and England being stopped. Surely our Napoleon is now a prisoner ? " We didn't explain, it was too difficult and would have taken too long.

As it happened we were not much troubled by the rows between our host and hostess. Sometimes we would hear an occasional swear-word and china would go crashing to the floor; and once she came upstairs to sleep, locking and bolting all communicating doors. That night there was certainly a good deal of noise below stairs and she was very hysterical and difficult to soothe, but once made to laugh—and Nina was very good at that—she would quickly recover. I think she loved our being there, and we stopped nearly two months, withstanding all appeals from our families to return. The weather was heavenly, with lovely clear skies, fields of delicious lush grass and the river a constant joy to bathe in, and also to fish in. We caught lots of strange fish called blancs, quite good to eat; they took a home-made fly quite contentedly, but did not play much. Our bathing-gear was simple and comfortable, a shirt and knickers and a large straw hat, and many heavenly days we spent letting the current carry us downstream, and when we judged we had gone far enough, we got out and walked back under the poplars, to sit against the hay-stooks for the sun to dry us. Then sleep and into the river again and again until bedtime, when we would dawdle back to Madame Drouin who always had something excellently well cooked for our supper.

As July arrived the weather grew hotter and hotter and the people in the fields had less and less on. In fact, most of them worked in a shirt and hat only, their skin gradually burning the colour of mahogany. One stifling day we thought that we should never be able to bear the heat of the house to sleep in, so arranged to sling our home-made hammocks on some trees down by the river. *Drunki-bus* Monsieur Drouin helped us. He had been a sergeant in a crack regiment and when sober was always obliging, though somewhat silent and morose. All was prepared, books, coats, food, all taken down there, even a blanket each, in case it turned cold in the early morning, a most unlikely contingency. We were finishing our supper in the house before starting for our hammocks, when a far-away grumble of thunder made itself heard. Madame, with her usual anxiety for our welfare, begged us not to start. She declared that a big storm was coming. So agitated was she that we gave in, thinking sadly of our books a mile away. The storm was a long while coming, and we settled down to try and sleep in the balcony, quite useless as the lightning was by now playing all round, hardly ceasing for a second. At one moment, the huge *colombier* and the lovely lace tower of the church were floodlit against a black sky and all the white and grey pigeons, terrified out of their wits, were whirling and tumbling in the glare, the next minute *colombier* and tower were standing out black against vivid sheets of lightning,

THE STORM

quivering in the sky. By now three storms were meeting overhead and the unceasing crash and glare were very impressive, not to say frightening. Our trembling hostess had come to join us, begging us to shut the shutters. But just that we would not do . . . and I am glad we did not do so or we should have missed a sight I have never forgotten. We could hear a tremendous roar approaching, getting louder and louder; what could it be? Wind? A hurricane? We were craning out of the window trying to see what it was, when suddenly we saw coming down the river a huge wall of water apparently at least forty feet high. We could see by the light of the lightning that it was pale coffee colour, and borne along in the wall were gigantic trees with their branches, poor dead cattle and many other things indistinguishable in the half-light. The vast volume of water hurled itself against the great stone bridge, pouring over, through and round it. The noise as it hit the bridge was even more terrifying than what had gone before, and one large tree jammed itself across one of the arches. Would the bridge hold? Part of the parapet toppled over and disappeared in the rolling, rushing torrent of water which fled away downstream, leaving a heaving, weltering mass behind it, and we heard its passage as it tore its way down between the banks, spreading its waves out over the peaceful fields. Poor Papillon and Rose, two beautiful white cows, much prized by their owner—their bodies were found high in some trees many miles down the river. Many poor beasts were drowned that night. We should have been amongst them, had it not been for Madame Drouin. Next morning the river was nearly its peaceful self again; the sun was out, but the fields were strewn with dead trees and branches, the roofs of sheds, dead animals. What a sad sight! No work was done for quite twenty-four hours; everyone had something to relate to whoever would listen, and the crowd on the bridge never ceased to look, stare and talk.

I consider that Nina saved my life one day. It had been very hot and we dawdled up the river to look for a place that the townspeople had recommended to us for bathing. We must have misunderstood them, as when I jumped in to what looked like an ideal pool, I was instantly caught by an undercurrent and swept under the bank; there my legs became entangled amongst some strong roots and I was perfectly helpless and hardly able to keep my head above water, the current being so fast. Luckily Nina was very strong, and throwing herself down on the ground managed to catch hold of my arms. Even so it was not easy to get out and we were two very exhausted people by the time she hauled me up on to the bank.

Amongst our other amusements at St. Père was driving a young horse which Drouin was trying to break to harness. He let us have him whenever we liked and we drove him in a frighteningly high dog-cart. He was very green at first, drifting all over the road, apparently never having been mouthed at all, but he soon improved and was marvellously quiet except for occasional shying at obstacles which we could never see, and consequently were not prepared for; and many a time we both bumped off the seat into the bottom of the cart. The only condition made was that we should fetch Drouin home after market-day in the neighbouring town. We had to go to the *estaminet* to fetch him, and it was not always an easy job. However, his friends usually lifted him on to the back seat where he slept peacefully till we got him home, when Madame Drouin would pull him out like a sack of potatoes on to the cobble-stones of the stable-yard. I never knew how she did it as he was an enormous man. The village

PURPLE SNAKES

congratulated us much on the improvement of his morals and manners while we were there, but from all I hear, he returned to his evil ways the moment we left, and Madame Drouin eventually made a bolt and went to Paris. Her affection for us had become rather trying at times, and it showed itself in odd ways. One day we had settled not to come home for luncheon because I was painting some oxen ploughing, and the only moment they stood still was when their master went for his meal. Madame Drouin couldn't bear to think of us starving, so she walked out all the way carrying our food to us. She waited about for ages to see us eat it, but I had peeped under the cover and had seen a lot of purple snakes! so painted steadily on until at last her patience was worn out and she departed. Then we turned and buried the disgusting objects as quickly as possible, so that when she saw the platter she should find it empty. We couldn't bear to think her feelings should be hurt, after taking so much trouble. Alas, we hadn't waited long enough before burying the things; when we came home she asked us if we had made a good *déjeuner*. With oleaginous smiles we assured her that we had eaten well. "Ah," she screamed, "I have you, I waited behind a bush to see you eat and you buried in the *sale* earth my lovely food. It was the inside of a calf. Never again will I give you treats. You are only English savages after all. Rice *poudings* shall you have and *rosbif*, nothing else while you are under my roof." We at last appeased her wrath by explaining that we had not wanted to hurt her feelings by leaving it, and that we were not hungry. "Not hungry," she grumbled. "Why, you have eaten enough for four men this evening, and no wonder (here her voice rose to a shrill scream) you wouldn't eat my beautiful *entrailles*, never again," and she grumbled away into her back-yard.

Even our departure was amusing. There was only

IN FRANCE

one train a day going to Paris, at 6 a.m., and the station was about thirty kilometres away. The horse was harnessed, the luggage loaded, but Drouin, who had to drive it back, was nowhere to be seen. Madame came rushing in. "You will miss your train, I can't get him up, you must come and help me." Nina and I hurried up to the bedroom, to find Drouin, the ex-sergeant, sitting tousle-headed in his shirt on the edge of the bed lifting first one leg, then the other and urging them to hurry. "Courage, *mes amis*, courage," he kept saying. When he saw us at the door he changed to saying, "Courage, *mesdames*, courage," but our appearance had an effect and he got swaying up on to his legs. Madame would not let him finish dressing, nor would she let him eat, notwithstanding his wails. She threw his great-coat over his shoulders, hauled up his trousers and buckled a belt round him, stuffed half a loaf into his hand and, aided by the farm-boy, heaved and pushed him up behind, where he clung precariously as we swung out of the yard and started our journey at a smart canter which very soon dwindled to a slow trot. His whimpering reached our ears for some time and then ceased. He had returned to his interrupted slumbers, which he kept up until we reached the station. The train was already there waiting for us, and all the passengers got out to help us in and to put Drouin into the front seat, as he was still quite incapable of getting there himself. The last we saw of him was sound asleep again, while the horse progressed at a slow walk the thirty kilometres home.

5

PLEASANT DAYS

LADY WANTAGE was one of the best friends the family ever had. Somewhat stiff in manner as she was, and consequently rather difficult to talk to, I was very fond of her, and she was extraordinarily kind to all of us equally. She lent my mother a house close to Lockinge in Ardington village, date about William and Mary, with a lovely staircase in it. We all of us revelled in the downs which surround Ardington. A heavenly painting country and delightful for hacking. I got little riding that summer having had an operation for appendicitis. About that time appendicitis was very fashionable, and Nina and I both had it. She had no luck because we had just taken a house for hunting in the V.W.H. and she had very little fun there. My appendix had been removed just before I went to Lockinge and I remember well the first day I was allowed out of bed. Nina prepared a great treat for me and had arranged that Tommy de Burgh should ride a young horse we had just broken in. He was to take him under my window so that I could see him. Our new purchase, I regret to say, was not very well ribbed up. His girths had not been pulled up tight enough, and saddle and all slipped back. The horse was, of course, terrified and started kicking and bucking for all he was worth, decanting Tommy— a beautiful rider—on to the ground; he then proceeded to jump back and forth in a panic over some iron railings with the saddle draped round his hindquarters. Foreseeing tragedy, Nina (her family with the usual brutality of one's relations always said that her brain only worked in an emergency) ran in under the horse as he jumped the railings for the fourth time, caught the dangling reins and jerked him off his balance, seating herself firmly on his head as he fell to the ground. The quickest thing I ever saw.

To return to Lockinge, I used to take the pony-cart with the Argentine cob out painting for the whole day. I took oats for him and sandwiches for myself, and we enjoyed ourselves thoroughly. I usually picked out the most lonely places I could find, where I knew I should be undisturbed. One day I had taken the pony out of the shafts, and having tied him to the wheel, settled down to paint. I was deep in my work when suddenly I was made to jump sky-high by a man's voice in my very ear, asking if I was not afraid to be there all alone. I looked round and there, seated close behind me on the ground, was a most disreputable tramp. I did not fancy him so close, and answered that no one had ever been disagreeable or unpleasant in any way, and I went on painting, hoping he would leave. He did not speak again for nearly half an hour, sitting smoking the most filthy-smelling pipe the whole time, when suddenly he began telling me his life history. It was not particularly interesting in itself, but I was curious as to what could have made him start telling it to my unresponsive back. He had been a boy in various small coasting ships, then had signed on in the Navy, only to return to his wandering life after a few years' service. He had been all over the world and now was on the tramp back to Southampton to try and get to sea again. After talking for some time he said, "I suppose you know your pony has gone?" Sure

FEO AS A WATER COLOURIST

enough, the brute had slipped his halter and departed. I pretended not to mind and said that someone would soon come and bring him back, that the house was quite close and they knew where I was. A flat lie, but I thought a good one met the case better on that occasion than a half one, the house being quite three miles away, and as I had not made up my mind when I started where I was going to, no one knew where I was. I tried to go on painting as if it was quite usual to lose one's means of conveyance home. Apparently it succeeded, as the tramp got up and saying, " Well, you are a cool one, so long," went off across the downs. I watched his tall figure striding away until he disappeared over the Ridgeway, and then, stuffing my things into the cart for safety, hurried off towards home, to find that Porter, the coachman, was just starting out to look for me, the Argentine having only just come in. Next day we saw in the local paper that a tramp was being searched for, who had stolen some things out of a shop in Wantage. By the description I recognized my friend of the day before.

Another year Lady Wantage lent us Overstone, a huge place with a house much too big for us, so we only lived in a corner of it. There was a large lake and a mere or marsh there, and many crested grebe and different kinds of wildfowl made their home there. I loved the park and found a lot to paint. Feo, too, used to paint when she had time to spare from her studio in London, and we had great fun together, she painting in water-colour or tempera as the spirit moved her, and I nearly always in oils. Being a skilled draughtsman she had not the difficulties that assail many water-colourists and her water-colours and tempera sketches, only looked on by her as a relaxation from her professional work as a sculptor, will hold their own as real works of art in years to come.

PLEASANT DAYS

A sad thing happened during those otherwise pleasant months at Overstone. We had a particularly nice butler at that time called Atkins, and the men used to go and bathe in the lake in the early mornings before we were about. Atkins was no swimmer, but was being taught by one of the footmen who had been in the Navy. One morning at about 7 a.m. my sister Feo was awakened by shouts and yells coming from the direction of the lake. Her bedroom looked out that way. She at once grasped that something was wrong and ran to Eddie's room to call him. Having dug him out she went to call the servants to help. Meanwhile Eddie, who had had nearly half a mile to run, had found the two footmen in a terrible state of distress; they had left Atkins hanging on to the boat resting after his lesson and they had gone off for a swim, racing each other. When they looked round the butler had disappeared and the boat was drifting in the middle of the lake; they neither of them could dive, and had not the faintest idea what to do. My brother tore off his coat and jumped in at the place indicated by the men as where they had last seen the butler. He dived and dived repeatedly, and at last had to give it up from sheer exhaustion and cold. He said that the water, though warm above, was intensely cold when he got down deep and it was not possible to keep on. All that day and the next they dragged the lake, and only when they let the water out at one end did they find the poor man's body deep down at the bottom of the grating against the lock fifteen feet down. Of course Eddie could never have reached that depth with no height to jump from.

While still at Overstone, Nina and I went for a day's hunting with the Pytchley. I was riding a mare called Indigo, and Nina, who was coming down from London for the day, had asked me to get her a hireling. A

good-looking, well-bred chestnut appeared at the meet
... and we had a very pleasant hunt, Nina enthusiastic
over her mount who had gone like a bird. I was
feeling rather flush of money at the moment, having
just sold a picture, so went up to his owner and asked
what he wanted for him. Seventy guineas was his
answer. I then went to Lord Annaly, who was the
Master at that time, and asked him if he knew the
horse, telling him what the dealer had asked. "Be
careful," he said, "if he is only asking seventy there
must be something wrong with him. I know Bertie
Sheriff gave four hundred for him two seasons ago." I
went to the stable to look at the horse before he was sent
home. The groom who was strapping him snatched
up a foreleg as I went up to him in the stall. "Why
do you do that?" I asked. "Is he ill-tempered?"—
"Oh, no, miss, only he doesn't care for strangers."
I went out and telegraphed to the dealer: "I will
give you twenty-five pounds and ask no questions,"
R. P. The answer came: "You can have him for
thirty pounds." So Senator, son of Tacitus and grandson of the great Hermit, out of Roman Bee, came to
Nina as her horse. We were inordinately proud of
him. A bright golden chestnut, well up to fifteen
stone. A beautiful rein, a wonderful shoulder and long
sloping quarters with very big but fine bone. Nina
and I were breathless with excitement. What a horse!
The first thing he did was to turn the groom out of
his box. He came at him with open mouth, breathing
fire like Faffner, the dragon in Wagner's opera. He
had not been cleaned underneath for weeks, and what
is more he did not intend that anyone should clean him.

The day after he arrived we had a board on him.
Old Colonel Longhurst, the well-known Aldershot vet.,
came and ran over him for us. He was as enthusiastic
about him as we were, and the verdict was that he

should be laid up and fired, both tendons in front being dicky. This was done, with great difficulty, as he had to be thrown before they could do anything to him, and we thought of him no more for some long time. When he came up from his rest after being fired he was looking splendid, and Nina took to hacking him a good deal. We had been warned that he always tried to savage people if he got them off, and he had a most unseating way of bucking like a whiting with his tail almost in his mouth. Worse for a man than for a woman. He was much quieter and a more happily dispositioned horse now and perfectly devoted to Nina. She could do anything with him, and although he tipped her off by standing and bucking instead of jumping properly over one of the Staff College jumps, there was no question of his savaging her; he just stood poking her with his nose asking why she had tumbled off. The first day he had to be clipped she went to the stables to see how they were getting on. There was a terrific noise, shouting, kicking, stamping. Six men all trying to hold him, and he wild with irritation and nerves. Nina walked in and told all to leave the stable except Goodyer, the old stud groom. Once they had gone she went into Senator's box where he was crouching up in the corner shaking from head to foot and showing all the whites of his eyes, a little trick of his. She began to fondle him, and his terrified eye grew soft and he put his head on her shoulder. " Now, Goodyer," she said, " go on." Goodyer moved quietly up to him, laid a hand on his shoulder, and then the clippers. Senator trembled and shook, and Nina went on whispering in his ear; the clipping machine began—in those days only a hand machine—and he stood still as long as she remained without movement, but the moment she shifted her position he grew frightened, so she had to stay. Eventually he even allowed another man to come in and start on the other side. This proceeding had to be gone through every time he was clipped for some years, but eventually he lost his fear of humans, and although he hated the tickling on his sensitive skin, would stand still and allow the grooms to do their work.

He was always funny-tempered; some days the best hunter you could find, fast, and a big, steady jumper, taking everything as it came; other days he would suddenly refuse the smallest obstacle and nothing would persuade him to jump it. Whichever of us was riding him would at first waste hours trying to make him jump, but we soon learnt that nothing would make him once he had refused, and that it was only waste of valuable time trying to persuade him, so we had to give in and jump the fence in another place. But I must say this did not happen very often.

Nina rode him for some years, and when he was getting on in age I took to riding him as I rode lighter. But he never cared for me as he cared for her, although he carried me very well.

Although not his fault in any way, Senator was the cause of a good deal of trouble to me. I came to rather a hairy fence out hunting and, thinking it looked fairly breakable, sent Senator at it. One of the young branches, however, proved too tough to break and it caught me across the chest and pushed me over backwards on to his quarters as he jumped. I broke one of the vertebræ of my spine, with the muscles attached, and also tore all the fibres of my sciatic nerve. This made a hopeless crock of me for six years, and practically finished my hunting. I tried once or twice, but the pain was more than the pleasure and I was forced to give up riding from then on. Painting, too, was very difficult as I always stood at my work, and it so happened, as bad luck would have it, that I had

PLEASANT DAYS

quite a lot of important commissions to carry out during those six years. One, a subscription picture, given by the Croome Hunt to Mr. Dudley Smith, M.F.H., was especially hard work, as it was a big canvas, about seven feet by five feet, with many portraits of hounds as well as portraits of the Master and Lady Barbara, and the huntsman, also their horses, and entailed an enormous lot of work doing studies for it; and well I remember the misery I went through standing at my easel. I would paint for five minutes and lie down for fifteen, and so on all through the many months until I finished it and it got quite a good place in the R.A.

We eventually gave Senator to Lady Craven, the old lady M.F.H., so well known and loved in the down country above Shrivenham. She kept him for a couple of years and then had him shot.

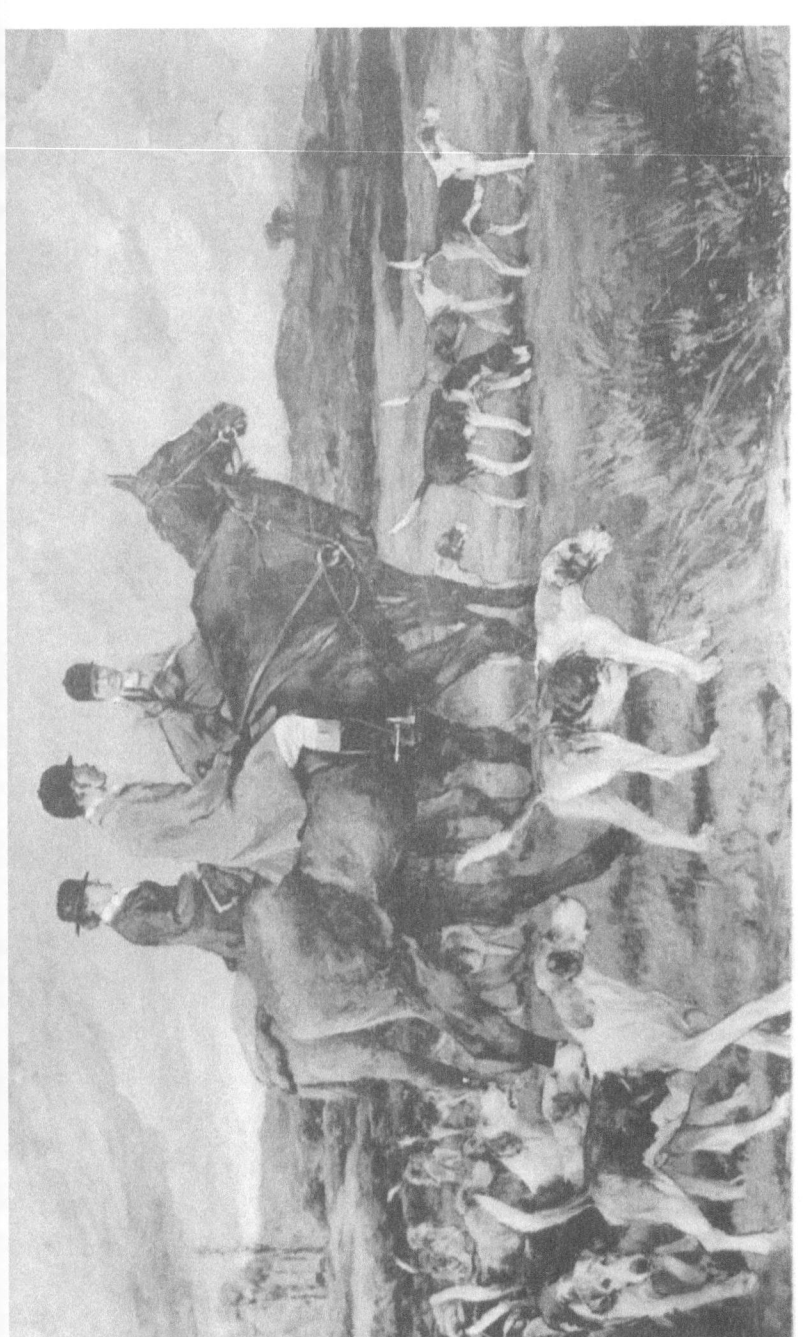

Hunting on the Daren Rocks, Black Mountains, South Wales, 1921

6

YACHTING WITH THE EMPRESS EUGÉNIE

IN 1904 Nina and Hilda (Nina's girl) had been asked by the Empress Eugénie to go yachting with her to Copenhagen and Stockholm, and she invited me to come too. The party on board, besides ourselves, consisted of the Empress, old Monsieur Francesco Pietri, her private secretary, and General Kelly-Kenny. I had always been seasick when I even looked through a telescope at the sea, so it was a very rash experiment on my part to go yachting; but I could not resist such an attractive expedition. I made up my mind that the best way not to be ill was to be so occupied that I should forget I was on the sea; a form of Christian Science, in fact. So directly we left harbour I began making a sketch of the man at the wheel. I knew that if I was painting I should think of nothing else. Alas for my hopes, Christian Science proved useless in my case. One moment the horizon line would be above the man at the wheel, the next far below him; nothing remained the same for two minutes together, and presently, giddy and clinging to my head, I fled to my cabin, already beaten in my firm determination not to be seasick. I cannot imagine why I enjoyed that trip because whenever it was the least bit rough I had to bolt for my cabin. The Empress was marvellously kind, and when we had meals on deck, used to have a screen rigged up, so that I could not see the sea. She also made large thick sandwiches of cold mutton with her own fair hands and handed them down through the skylight of my cabin just when I felt a little better; the sight of them always started me off again. She said, " Comtesse Éléna would die if she did not eat." Much more likely she would die if she did.

When the *Thistle* was lying at anchor off Kiel, some German midshipmen thought they would have a lark and would board the English yacht. So without asking permission, five or six cheerful noisy boys swarmed up on deck. The Captain was furious and ordered them off, without the slightest effect; they only laughed at him.

The Empress retired to her cabin and told me to go and explain the situation to the boys. My German was never very good, and the Empress, who was listening through her skylight, made much mock afterwards of my efforts. She said she could have done it better herself. The boys were quite certain that I was making it all up and howled with laughter; they thought it a splendid joke that the yacht should belong to the Empress of the French. There was no such person; let them see her: they would soon know if she was a genuine Empress.

At last the eldest, who was about seventeen, grasped that I was trying to talk sense and smacked and kicked the others into paying attention and listening. You should have seen their faces when they began to understand what a *gaffe* they had made. Their one idea was to get hold of their boat, which had meanwhile disappeared. So the Captain of the *Thistle* had to order out one of his boats; with this, manned by Britishers, the crestfallen and terrified midshipmen returned to their man-of-war. Of course, coming back in a strange boat they were spotted by their own officers and reported to their Captain. Half an hour afterwards the Captain

A REVIEW OF GERMAN TROOPS

himself, a very stiff personage with a scarlet face and bottle-brush hair, come on board, accompanied by several other officers, to ask permission to apologize in person to the Empress. The Empress appeared most gracious and kindly, begging that the boys should not be punished for their little joke, but I did not care for the look in their Captain's eye. Of course I was had in to translate again, and I felt like the Beaver in the *Hunting of the Snark* who " wished he had taken more pains with his sums "; I had always had to say what I could and not what I wanted to, in German, that most difficult of languages.

When I stayed in Strassburg with my Uncle Hermann Hohenlohe, who was Stadthalter of Alsace-Lorraine at the time, I had the same trouble, for although my relations were polite to me about my pronunciation, they soon found out my weakness and chaffed me unmercifully. I wished I had known some good swearwords in German, when my mount ran away with me right in front of the whole German Army. Uncle Hermann had asked me if I would like to ride with him to a big review that he was going to hold of all the troops belonging to his command. . . . Of course I was delighted, but little knew the agonies which awaited me. They gave me a fine big charger up to three times my weight, chosen for being thoroughly well trained to troops; the saddle which was put on his unhappy back was at least thirty years old (and I was accustomed to a Mayhew). It had three pommels, all shaped like butcher's hooks, all equally pointed, and you sat with your knee well above your head at the most painful angle. It was torture, but there was nothing to be said, as apparently there were no other side-saddles in Strassburg. So I tried to sit upright as we rode solemnly through the town, although all the time I felt as if I should topple over backwards. We reached the parade

YACHTING WITH THE EMPRESS EUGÉNIE

ground, and with much pomp and ceremony my uncle took up his position at the saluting-point. My orders were to stand next to him; here began my first struggle. My horse said that it was not seemly that I should stand next to the Stadthalter. It simply was not done—so every time I got him into the place which had been pointed out to me as mine, he backed firmly into the staff, which was immediately behind, and scattered all their horses. Result, chaos. The real trouble was that he had been properly *manèged* and trained to obey signals, and I had never been taught what those signals were. At last I gave it up and let him stay amongst the staff. The crisis came when my uncle turned round to make some remark to me, and finding I was not where he thought, half-turned his horse to see what had happened; at the same time he spoke quickly in German to one of the staff. My horse took this as an order for him and started forth immediately at a fast and shaking trot for the far end of the huge parade-ground, which was completely surrounded by troops. Nothing I could do would stop him or even turn him. He was convinced that he had been told to take a message to every corps present. If I could have turned him to the right or left I might have looked less of a fool, but his head only came round when I pulled with my full strength, and his body continued at that shattering trot in a straight line for the troops. As I passed down the lines I caught a glimpse of many bespectacled faces, mostly with their mouths wide open. At long last, to my intense relief, a large man ranged up alongside and seized my bridle, and I was ignominiously led back at the same agonizing trot to the saluting-point. The kind man who had retrieved me—a major—was grumbling under his moustache that it was a beastly shame to have given me a horse like that. This comforted me a little, and I was thankful that he kept close enough to me for the rest

STOCKHOLM: THE RIDDARSHOLM

of the time to be able to catch the brute, if he had started off again. My uncle's gentle gibe was, "I thought all you English prided yourselves on being able to ride."

To return to the *Thistle* (or "Distelle" as Pietri called her). We went on up the Kiel Canal, a dreary long business, and so to Stockholm, arriving late one evening to anchor opposite the Riddarsholm. The colouring was most impressive: the old castle and other masses of buildings belonging to the town standing out a cold hard black against the pale sky and the waters of the harbour looking like a sheet of molten metal long after the sky had turned into sombre reds and browns.

We all enjoyed our stay at Stockholm. The Empress was thoroughly happy with the Swedes, and they did all they could to entertain her in their pleasant way. The first morning after our arrival there, the Empress, with her usual spirit of adventure, said, "Quick, before anyone hears of my arrival we will sight-see round the town." So off we went in a tram to see all we could of that attractive place before entertainments and functions began. The King was a most beautiful, enormously tall old man, and he and the Empress were quite delighted to see each other; so much had happened since their last meeting, and both were very *émotionnés*, kissing each other repeatedly on both cheeks. We were taken to the Riddarsholm that afternoon, where the King showed me my father's banner hanging amongst those of the other knights of the Order of St. Lazaar. He had evidently known him well and had liked him as much as everybody else did. We all went out to the Palace of Drottningholm for luncheon, a lovely old palace on an island some way from Stockholm. We went there in steam launches, threading our way in and out of the islands.

Nina and I went the following day as well to Drottningholm, as the keeper of antiquities, M. Böttiger, wanted to show us some things he thought we should like. Things that Gustavus Adolphus had asked for from Louis XIV when he went to Paris, and the French King had not liked to refuse . . . the most gorgeous tapestries, Aubusson carpets, china, etc. Apparently Gustavus Adolphus had had no shyness about asking for what he wanted and Drottningholm was full of the treasures he had collected. Böttiger told us that his great-grandfather had been head of the Sèvres factory when the Swedish King had asked for all the best pieces, so he felt that he had every right to have them in his care now. There were quite a lot of modern things there, too, and several very good pictures—one of the King by Anders Zorn, a fine portrait.

One day we were taken out to an island that belonged to Prince Eugén, the Empress's godson. The first thing we saw on approaching the island was a huge Victory of Samothrace up on a high rock, and very effective it looked from some points of view, but it was rather spoilt when you got the cream-coloured villa behind it. He took me into his nice big studio and showed me a lot of interesting studies and paintings by himself, mostly landscapes. He had plenty of imagination and I liked his arrangement of things. While there he showed me some very attractive pictures by a man called Lilliefors who painted birds in the wild. Many people do this now, but he was one of the first I had seen who followed them to their haunts to paint them there. Ducks amongst the reeds, chaffinches and tits quarrelling in the bushes, a big horn owl being mobbed by little birds, ravens in their nests high up in the rocks, etc., etc.

While at Stockholm the Empress received news that the Tsar might have to flee for his life from Russia,[1]

[1] This was towards the end of the Russo-Japanese War (1904).

AN ISLAND NEAR DENMARK

and she told us that arrangements were being made that the *Thistle* should go to Russia and wait for him to embark. She meant to take him back to England, so we were all to pack and be ready to leave the yacht at a moment's notice, to go home by steamer and train. Nothing, however, came of it; in the light of what happened later I wish it had. We left Stockholm in the yacht to go to an island near Denmark called Laaland to see a Count and Countess—the latter had been born a Bonaparte. It was a dreary island to live in. We went to luncheon with them, and the house and garden were like a rather neglected French château. Before leaving we were taken a melancholy drive round the island, in three carriages, which progressed slowly behind each other. The only things I remember clearly about that visit were the lovely old glass beakers in the dining-room and the way the peasants tethered their cattle. There were no hedges or fences to the fields, so the cows and bulls were tethered side by side in long lines. I asked if it was very safe as I noticed that they tethered two or three bulls in the same line, but they assured me they never broke loose or fought each other or went for people.[1] On our way home from our drive we passed a huge bull about eight years old, ridden by a tiny boy leading all the rest of the cattle home along the public road. I counted eleven loose bulls wandering along alone, all of a certain age and size and by no means pleasant looking.

From Laaland we went on to Copenhagen, and while there went shopping with the Empress. While she was in one of the shops the people suddenly realized who she was and came crowding round the windows, cheering her and shouting, " Vive l'Impératrice." She turned

[1] Dr. Axel Munthe told me later that there are more people killed by cattle in Denmark and Sweden than die from any other cause.

to us, with her eyes filled with tears and said, " Ah, que je suis à fond canaille, comme j'adore ça ! " What a long time it was since she had been cheered like that. No wonder she was pleased that they remembered her.

The King and Queen of Denmark were away; so we had no functions to attend, but the explorer, Fridtjof Nansen, came to luncheon on the yacht, and we then proceeded to Hamburg on our way home.

The Hamburg docks were very interesting with their mass of shipping. The tiny white and green *Thistle* threaded her delicate way in and out of the great crowing, hooting steamers, which stood high up above her, their sides running in red rust.

The first thing we did on landing was to go to Hagenbeck's Zoo. The great Hagenbeck himself met us at the gate and took us all round, showing us everything. The Empress had been provided with a pony-chair as it was rather a long walk for her. He showed us a huge boa-constrictor and quietly remarked, "I was nearly killed by one of those; it was one of my closest escapes." It appears that the boa was not well and Hagenbeck went in alone to dose him. As he stooped to give the beast medicine he swung his tail round, catching Hagenbeck in the back, and the next thing he knew was that he had the coils round him pressing his chest tighter and tighter. His shouts for help brought his son with a gun, but he could not shoot for fear the death-agony would tighten the grip still more. So an axe was hurriedly brought and the great snake was literally hacked into small pieces. Hagenbeck was quite unconscious when pulled out of the cage and had many ribs broken . . . but he said he was very hardy and soon recovered. He added that had he not had a very big strong son he could not have been saved.

As we were walking back to the yacht, General Kelly-Kenny, who had been missing for some time, came running round a corner calling to the Empress, "Your Majesty must come quickly; I have something wonderful to show you." The Empress, always ready for any excitement, hurried round the corner with him, only to come back in two or three minutes in a state almost of hysteria. With tears trickling down her cheeks and little chokes of semi-laughter she cried, "Only imagine what he wanted me to look at—all the Eagles of France which the Germans had taken from us at Sedan." She added, "And he thought it would please me!" *A propos* of this story about the Empress, there is another I remember being told by an eye-witness some years later.

During the World War (which I suppose we must now call the First World War), the Empress gave up a large part of her house near Farnborough for convalescing officers. One day she received a message that if she would go to the gate on the Farnborough road, she would see something that would interest her. The Empress, although well over eighty years of age, was always keen for something new, so accompanied by her lady-in-waiting she was at the gate punctually at the time mentioned. There she saw a company of soldiers marching past and in their midst a large number of the Prussian Guard who had been taken prisoners in the War and were on their way to the prison camp. The Empress turned away with tears in her eyes, saying, "At last I feel that I have not lived in vain."

On the way back to England we met a tremendous storm. The Captain sent in to ask, was he to proceed, as the weather looked so bad. The Empress's answer was "Certainly," so we steamed out of Kiel harbour in a dead calm. The sea was a curious black leaden colour and the sky a dull green. As we moved out we met many boats running for harbour, but the Empress was still bent on keeping on. Presently we met the gale,

YACHTING WITH THE EMPRESS EUGÉNIE

and a full gale it was. The little *Thistle* was a wonderful sea-boat, but even so she shivered and shook as we met sea after sea. I need not have been ashamed of being ill, all the officers and most of the men were sea-sick. Only the Empress and Nina held their heads up, and they enjoyed the storm thoroughly. The Empress was eighty-one then, and as gay and keen as a two-year-old. I often regret that I did not make notes of all she told us of her former life. How she was born in the middle of an earthquake and her mother was carried out of the house and laid under a tree, her family ever after used to mock at her saying, " The mountain was in travail and it brought forth a mouse." Then she told us about her Scots relations and her affection for the Duke of Hamilton, and how shocked the French Court was when one day he had damaged himself and could not come out hunting with them, and the Empress had said quite simply, " Yes, I saw the bruise on his leg; it looked very bad." The French had quite forgotten that the Duke wore a kilt and that his legs were visible to everyone. She had to ask him to come to dinner next day in his kilt so that they should see the bruise for themselves.

She told us, too, of the time when she offended Bismarck past all forgiveness. The French Court were going on some expedition, and Bismarck had been staying with them on business. He, with regrettably bad manners, was late, so after having waited some time she gave the word for the train to start without him. As the train moved out of the station, he hastened on to the platform. The Empress just caught sight of his face of fury as the train gathered speed; she told us that she knew that all his personal enmity for her started from that moment.

She then went on to say how when the Emperor was a prisoner in Germany, she had been determined to see

IRELAND IN 1913

him about some important State matter. Accompanied by one of her gentlemen—Count Clary, I think—she went disguised to the place where he was imprisoned and by bribes managed to get in and have an interview with him. As they were leaving the station to go home a big German Polizei-diener suddenly put his hand on her shoulder. She thought that all was over and that she had been discovered, but the policeman only wanted to see their tickets, and Count Clary thrust them before him while the Empress, with her face well covered by her cloak, jumped into the train and all was well. She said if it had not been for her stupidity in having offended Bismarck's *amour-propre* she would have been able to have done so much more for her country.

On coming into Southampton we found the whole of the French fleet lying in the Roads; they had come in to visit the English fleet. As the *Thistle* steamed down the line of French ships, dipping her ensign to each ship in turn, the Empress stood on the deck looking inexpressibly sad, and I heard her murmur, as to herself, " The last time I went down the French lines it was they who dipped to me, *et me voilà*."

In 1913 Eddie was commanding in Belfast, and my sister-in-law being away, he asked me to come over and keep him company. Soon I got to know quite a lot of amusing people. Amongst others a man named Bigger, anti-British but a great Irish patriot. I was busy doing designs at that time for a new illustrated edition of Lady Gregory's book on Cuchullain, and both Mr. Bigger and a Major Berry, who was on my brother's staff, were most helpful in finding me old manuscripts that showed the costumes of the period.

Of course everyone realized that Ireland was in a very shaky state at that time, and Eddie and I had quite an amusing little expedition once in the middle of the night. I was awakened by the persistent blowing of a police

YACHTING WITH THE EMPRESS EUGÉNIE

whistle and scrambled out of bed to go and call my brother, who was out in two minutes. We got on some shoes and coats, and Eddie, taking a revolver for himself, pushed another into my hand, and we ran as fast as we could towards the sound. The whistle was still blowing frantically, and on turning a corner we found an R.I.C. calmly standing blowing his whistle just because he was bored, and had no one to talk to. His apologies were profuse when he found that he had turned the General out in the middle of the night. I then understood why my brother was so popular with his men as, instead of blustering with annoyance at being disturbed, or even reproving the man, he just roared with laughter, and saying good night we turned for home and bed.

I saw something of the same kind at Doullens during the War. Eddie was commanding the 15th Brigade, and Nina and I had paid him a visit when we were with the French Red Cross on our way to St. Pol. We were all three standing watching an aerial fight between a German and one of our own machines when a private, not looking where he was going, ran straight into Eddie, nearly knocking him off his legs. His only remark was a mild " Mind where you are going, or you will hurt yourself." The man, with horror on his face at having nearly knocked over a brass hat, rushed away, covered with confusion, while Eddie calmly brushed himself down and resumed his sentence where he had been interrupted.

This calmness seems to have been well known, as one of his Brigade told me that during the retreat from Mons he was invaluable; although everyone was hurried and agitated almost to the point of panic, Eddie was standing at the cross-roads for hours directing troops quite calmly, with his eyeglass firmly in his eye and a laugh and remark for each lot which passed him. Another man

EDDIE

told me that the said eyeglass was supposed never to have left his eye for three days and nights, and that his inveterate imperturbability had reassured all ranks in turn. Rather a pleasant remark to have made about one's brother.

7

INDIGO AND MABBOT'S FARM

WHILE I was at Eaton painting various horses and some spotted dogs which the Duke of Westminster was very fond of, I saw the tragic and celebrated Orme, whose son, Simon Dale, I was afterwards to paint. I went to his paddock meaning to do a sketch of him and was warned to be ready to run at any moment, as he used to attack people without any provocation. He was in an enclosure with high wooden palings all round, and I sat just inside the door which the groom held half open for me. The horse was standing in the middle of the enclosure swinging his head from side to side. He had a very sulky, brutal expression which was not improved by his lop ears. I settled down with my sketching things, and hardly had I begun when there was a shout from the groom and Orme, throwing his head sideways, started to gallop straight for us, at the same time making the oddest noise, something between a grunt and a scream. I bolted through the door which the groom slammed, only just in time as the horse came crash up against it with his hoofs. The man told me that he was quite mad, and no one could do anything with him. He said that when young they had hoped to cure him of his fits of temper and had tied him down, and six men had beaten him with rods! Is it a wonder that he had looked upon man as his worst enemy ever since? I

"A FUNKER'S PARADISE"

remember hearing afterwards that an Australian horse-breaker had recommended this brutal treatment and that the Duke of Westminster had never forgiven himself for having allowed him to try it.

I had quite a narrow escape when painting Simon Dale too, as he suddenly let out with both heels when I was sitting in his box. There was plenty of room as the box was a big one, but one of his hind shoes flew off and whizzing over my head, embedded itself in the wood of the door. He was a dark brown horse, long and low with rather lop ears; they had hoped much of him, but I do not think he ever did much. Bend Or was another celebrated horse I did a painting of in my youth. I wish I had known more about painting when I did him, as the result was rather feeble, but I have never forgotten what a beautiful horse he was, with the wonderful copper sheen on his coat and the dark patch on his quarters which repeated itself so often in his progeny.

The Duke of Westminster very seldom mounted people for hunting, generally hiring for them, but for some reason while I was staying there he very kindly gave me a mount, a big, strong, good-looking horse, a wonderful hunter but inclined to take hold. We had a very pleasant day with plenty of galloping and lots of small clean fences. Cheshire is, I believe, called the funker's paradise, and certainly this funker enjoyed herself very much until the end. Just as hounds were running into their fox we came to rather a hairy place; I did not think it worth jumping so pushed through a gap into the field where hounds were already breaking up their fox. I slid off my horse to rest his back before going home and suddenly noticed a small yellow stream of an oily substance oozing out of a tiny hole at the side of his hock. I had no idea what it was, so asked a man near me what it could be. He got down at once to examine it, and looking up with a face of horror said,

INDIGO AND MABBOT'S FARM

"It is joint oil, he must have staked himself somewhere. Take him home quickly before he gets stiff or you won't get him home at all." I was in despair, he was such a fine hunter. I walked him home nearly seven miles, he becoming lamer and lamer, me the same, as my hunting boots were agony to walk in. At last we got back, and I sent at once for the stud groom, who shook his head. "I doubt he will ever come out again," he said, and I could have sobbed. Then as the horse was led away, he added, "Our usual luck." I did not know what he meant, I was too miserable to ask. I crept into the house and up to my bath, feeling that I dared not meet the family. After I had changed I asked for the Duke, and was told he was in his own sitting-room. There I went, and he came to meet me saying, "I know all about it, you couldn't help it; it is just my fault for having lent a horse when I had made a rule never to do so. I have never lent a horse to anyone without having had some bad thing happen. I had not done it for so long that I thought my luck might have changed, but it obviously has not." I was very grateful to him for the way he had taken it, but I never ceased blaming myself for that last gap; if I had jumped the horse over a fair fence he would have taken the trouble to clear it, but as it was he had slacked through the gap anyhow. I never liked gaps from then on and always tried to avoid them.

I was always extremely lucky in any horse I bought. Bonus was my first purchase, a good-looking cob found for me by old John Porter, the well-known trainer, whom I had made friends with when we took a house near the training stable of Kingsclere. I kept him for some time at Mr. Gerald Buxton's house in Epping Forest and used to go down from London to hunt with the Essex hounds. It meant starting from St. James's at eight o'clock in the morning and arriving home about

MY FIRST SALE

9 p.m. twice a week, a tiring job but well worth it. How much more tired one gets when young; I remember everything used to go black and one used to see objects as if looking through water. I found that the best years for work and play were from the age of thirty to forty, and incidentally we found that our assistants in the War were much the most useful when of that age.

To return to Bonus, he was quite a good-looker as I have said, a good safe jumper but slow as a man, so I settled to sell him. Here I got into difficulties at once. I told many people that I wanted to sell him, and two ladies whose names I luckily forget both wanted to buy him. How it happened I cannot think, but I nearly sold him to both. They both came to see him so often, and both talked so much, that I became muddled and despatched him cheerfully with the first groom who was sent to fetch him. Half an hour after he had gone the other lady turned up, saying she had settled to buy him. Her face, when I said that he had already gone, was a sight to see. "But," she cried, "I would have given you anything you had asked, I did not mind what I paid, I wanted him particularly." I said that the price was not the point, I had sold him for what I had asked and was quite satisfied. She went away swearing vengeance on the other lady, and I believe never spoke to her again.

The next horse in our stable was Indigo, a black mare by Dunvagan, out of Black Pearl, a hunter mare belonging to Will Goodall, the celebrated huntsman of the Pytchley. I was staying at Althorp and happened to be driving through Brampton when I saw an extremely nice-looking animal in a field. She took my eye at once, and I sent the groom who was with me to the farmhouse to enquire who she belonged to. When he came back, he said, touching his hat, "She is the mare I thought. No one has been able to break her; she is by his Lordship's horse Dunvagan and a perfect little fury.

INDIGO AND MABBOT'S FARM

She is six years old and they have tried to break her over and over again, and she always gets the better of them." I asked what she did that they could do nothing with her, and was told that she threw herself on the ground and nothing would make her get up. I left word asking the farmer, her owner, to send her down to Althorp for me to look at. How they caught her I did not ask, but she appeared with four men walking as her body-guard next day. Dunkley, Lord Spencer's head groom, and I looked her over, and I liked her better than ever.

Suddenly Dunkley swung round and said to some other stableman who was standing about looking on, " Look sharp and get out the lungeing tackle." The farmer very anxiously asked, " What are you going to do ? She is very nervous, do be careful." Dunkley merely asked him if he wanted to sell the mare, and at the same time said, " If you say she has been in harness you can't mind her being lunged in the open park." I had meanwhile asked the farmer what he wanted for her, and he had said a hundred pounds, which I laughed at, and Dunkley said, " We will talk about the price when we have seen her in harness."

The lungeing tackle arrived, also a pad and breeching with plenty of loose straps flopping about. Dunkley, a short, fattish, elderly man, walked up to the mare from in front, holding a hand out and talking to her in a low voice. She backed snorting away from him into the breeching and harness which the men were holding behind her ; a spring forward and she was in the lungeing bridle which Dunkley had been holding behind his back. It was the neatest thing I ever saw, and the mare stood snorting and puffing between them all for one second ; then they let her go and she started to kick and rear and plunge. Two men at the lungeing rein had all they could do to keep her from breaking away. Feeling the loose straps, breeching and tugs banging

HORSE-BREAKING

about her drove her nearly crazy and she kicked for nearly three-quarters of an hour without a stop. Instead of being black, she was now white with sweat and foam. She stopped, tired out, but the minute she was urged on, it began again. The farmer was terribly agitated, repeating over and over again, " She will hurt herself, I know she will." Dunkley, however, was quite adamant and kept steadily on till she gave in, and with eyes starting out of her head, scarlet dilated nostrils, tail sweeping the ground and dripping with sweat, she walked quietly into a loose-box where two men at once set about her to wipe her over, giving her some hay to occupy her attention. She stood still enough, but would not eat for three or four hours, and Dunkley himself took her in some corn and chop which she graciously accepted . . . she was terribly tired.

After she had gone in we had a slight discussion about the price, and I finally said that I would give £30 for her as she stood. The farmer thankfully agreed, and I wired to Feo, who was abroad, to ask her if she would share her with me. " Seen wonderful unbroken mare, thirty pounds, pure spec. Will you share ? " The answer came back immediately : " What fun, certainly." So Indigo became ours. Dunkley broke her splendidly. I do not say she was not excitable—that of course he could not cure—but she was very intelligent and once she understood what was wanted, very wishful to oblige. Of course the first few lessons were difficult, but she got on very quickly. He even broke her to harness, a wicked thing for such a beautiful beast, and we took her to London for a few weeks to drive in a dog-cart. But good as she was, she was so nervous she could neither eat nor sleep, and she ended her career in London by charging with the cart into Sand's shop in Sloane Street, Valda falling over the splash-board on to her back. Even that did not make her kick, but we thought it a

INDIGO AND MABBOT'S FARM

shame to keep her in London and sent her back to Althorp, until we went to the country for the autumn, when she joined us again ready for jumping lessons across country.

I used to take her for long walks and taught her to stand still while I climbed through the hedge, calling to her to come when I got over the far side. She was very good and never jumped on top of me. After we took to hunting her I will own she got a bit hot, shutting her eyes and jumping where she last saw the fence. But she was like a cat and saved herself and us over and over again by her quick-wittedness.

Her quickness was rather upsetting sometimes as she would see which way hounds were swinging more quickly than I could, and without any warning would swing at a right or left angle immediately on landing over a fence—most unseating; and I remember, much to Lord Ribblesdale's amusement, making my nose bleed on her off shoulder as I landed over a fence. He told me afterwards that he could not imagine how I got back into the saddle at all, saying I must have climbed back up my own leg. Another time we were standing talking in the road while hounds were feathering about in the next field. Indigo was watching them—I was not and she suddenly bucked from a stand over a hedge into the field, without giving me the slightest warning. Bless her, she was keen. Feo loved her even more than I did, their temperaments were so alike.

One day when we were hunting with Lady Craven's, I saw them jump a hedge down into a lane and arrive up the opposite side on Indigo's nose and knees. I asked afterwards what had happened, and Feo pantingly explained, "I wanted to turn down the lane and she wanted to go straight across; she won." Those deep chalk lanes on the Berkshire Downs are not very suitable for a difference of opinion with your horse.

MABBOT'S

Enough about Indigo, I could write volumes about her. She went when she got older to the stud farm at Hampton Court where King George V said she might stay to have her foals. She had two lovely ones, but too much carriage type to be of any use to us, and Feo had her back to the cottage when Nina and I were at the War. My sister's trust in her was such that, without any previous exercise, she got her in from the field and saddled her, intending to go for a nice little hack. But Indigo had forgotten how to behave in her two years at the stud, put her head between her legs and bucked Feo clean off on to her back on the cobble-stones, Feo being very badly hurt having damaged her spine. As we had no one to look after Indigo, all grooms being away at the War (and she being over twenty years old), we thought it better to have her shot, the best end for a good horse.

Nina and I took Mabbot's Farm about this time, a delicious little cottage set on a high bank with a lovely view of beechwoods and rounded hills, not far from Petersfield in Hampshire. The house, farm-buildings and a small extra cottage were thatched, the latter housing a couple who were our servants; the cooking was all done there and the meals carried through the garden, no matter what the weather. As may be imagined the food generally arrived on the table cold, but in those days we did not mind small discomforts. Our cottage was not in any way windproof, and in windy weather the carpet in the sitting-room used to belly up and down like the sails of a ship. The bedrooms had no fireplaces, so at night we used to take turns to have a hot bath in the sitting-room in front of the huge fireplace, and then rush to bed while still warm.

We started Mabbot's with some difficulties. We had arranged that our luggage and furniture should meet us on a certain date—we arrived all right, but the luggage and furniture did not. We had brought a cold chicken and some bread with us, luckily, and found that the old village woman who looked after the cottage had put some wood in the kitchen (afterwards to become the dining-room), so we made a fire and settled down on two logs to await our belongings. Presently the old woman appeared and said, "You won't see the van to-night," and on our asking what made her so positive, she said that no wagon might pass down the lane after dark; asked why, she went on to explain that ghosts haunted the lane and prevented anyone coming down. She added, "I must go now, or I shall be caught." It was useless asking her to get us rugs or blankets: she said it was too late. By this time, seeing that she was really frightened, we said, "All right, you may go, but please get us a drop of water from the well before leaving."—"Oh, I couldn't do that," she said. By this time we were getting a little irritated, so said, "Very well then, help us lift the bucket, and then you can go." Her eyes started from her head as she exclaimed, "You can't go to the well after dark. It isn't that I am afraid of falling down, it is *What May Come Up* that I am afraid of!" And she went off up the lane as fast as her legs would carry her, leaving us without water, food or bedding, and with only a narrow oak table to sit or lie on for the night. Meanwhile a stray cat had eaten the cold chicken, so we made our meal of bread toasted at the roaring fire, which we heaped up in the hopes that it would last all night, and help to chase away the eerie feeling which the old lady and her ghostly hints had engendered. I can't say that our night was comfortable as the oak table was but three foot wide, whilst Nina and I were both fairly hefty people; I forget how many times each of us fell, or kicked the other off on to the stone floor, but we kept the fire up all night and saw no ghosts.

EVIL

We soon heard the story of Mabbot's Farm. It appears that the former owner drank very heavily and used, when in his cups, to bully the meek sister who lived with him; he terrified her by lighting huge fires in the kitchen and heaping bavins (bundles of light wood) half-way up the chimney, which made red sparks pour out at the top and light on the thatch; he also had an unpleasant habit of asking his lady friends down from London to drink and make merry with him. The poor sister, who apparently was not convivially inclined, was pushed out and made to sleep in the lean-to below the cottage. One night, unable to bear her existence any more, she threw herself down the well, which was in the lean-to. Ever since, her ghost had walked in the yard and down the lane, wailing and crying. Once, a brave man had followed the weeping figure and, to his horror, having followed her to the back door of the house, had seen her disappear down the well in the back kitchen. Since then no villager would come down the lane at night. The village was so angry with the disreputable brother that he found life unendurable and packed up all his luggage, engaging wagons from far away to take it to London. When the horses tried to pull the load up the lane they found that they were unable to move it; nothing would make the wheels turn. They had to leave it till next morning stuck in the lane, when four more horses were hitched on and they were able to haul the wagon, but with the wheels still jammed, to the top of the hill. There, the wheels at last turned, and the furniture began its journey to London. But when they got to Woolmer Ponds, a very evil spot, the wheels stuck again, being held back by the spirits that are known to inhabit those ponds. Again more horses had to be brought, but this time nothing would move the wagon, and it was left to the spirits who had claimed it.

The spirits did not worry us very much, but there

INDIGO AND MABBOT'S FARM

undoubtedly was a ghostly feeling about the house. There were only three rooms upstairs in our cottage, one on each side of the tiny staircase, and a very small dressing-room leading out of the room that Nina had taken for herself. She many a time felt strange and ghostly hands touching her while lying in bed. I took this with a grain of salt, until one night, when she was away, I slept in her room, and woke covered with a cold sweat to find the same thing happening to me.

Another night I was disturbed by Thor, our great bull-mastiff, whining in the most piteous way in the farmyard. There was a bright moon, and when I looked out of my window into the yard below I could see every detail. The loose-boxes, each one with a contented chumping sound coming from it, the straw in the middle of the yard, Thor's kennel in the corner, and Thor crouching up behind it, whining and crying softly to himself; as I looked and called gently to him, I became aware of a white misty figure crossing the yard, coming from the direction of the well room, where it was said that the poor lady had drowned herself. As I looked, the white figure, more like a calf than like a human figure, slipped across the yard, over the five-barred gate and away down the lane. I shouted to Thor to follow. "Hi, after it. Quick, man. Loo, loo, loo," and he rushed out from where he had been hiding, jumped the gate and went off down the lane in the moonlight as hard as he could go. I could hear him giving tongue for miles in the silent night, and I listened till I could hear him no more. Nina was listening too, she had put her head out of her window, wakened by the noise of my shouting and by Thor giving tongue, but she had been too late to see the misty figure. I have often wondered since if the poor lady had taken the shape of a calf in her next incarnation. Thor came back next morning, very muddy and tired; I wish he could have told us what he had seen, but he sulked in his kennel most of that day, and only seemed to have really recovered his cheerful, good-humoured self by the next day.

When we had a guest I used to move into the little dressing-room. One morning when I had been sleeping there because Valda was staying with us, I got up fairly early to go and see to the horses, and on coming in to tidy up for breakfast I found my bed black with bees, which had swarmed through a hole in the ceiling. The whole bed was a moving mass, and the only way to get rid of them was to shut the room and burn a sulphur candle in it. We swept them up in thousands afterwards. Fancy if I had been in my bed! We had, of course, known that bees were in the roof as we could always hear a steady hum. We sent for the best bee man we could hear of. He arrived, dressed in a leather coat and trousers, gloves, a hat and veil, and demanded to be taken to where we thought the bees were. The only way into the roof was through my bedroom, so we took him to the little door and ushered him through it, shutting him in. In one minute he was out again, and tearing the veil from his face said, " Nothing would induce me to go in there. The whole of the interior of the roof is solid with bees, and great combs of honey are hanging from every beam; anyone interfering with those bees would be stung to death in one moment." He added, " No, I don't want to be paid. I haven't done my job, and I don't mean to," and nothing would make him accept any money, though he had come a long way. We insisted on his having a glass of beer which brought the colour back into his cheeks, and before leaving he begged us to give up the cottage, saying the bees were not safe, they might break through at any minute. We did leave soon after, not thinking it was worth risking either for ourselves or the animals.

8

ABOUT HORSES

SENATOR, mentioned earlier, and Indigo are the horses which loom largest in my hunting days, but many others passed through our hands—most of them much loved and very few, I think, really disliked.

Cocksure, the short, compact horse of over sixteen hands, up to seventeen stone and over, able to buck over anything from a stand; quick and nippy with his feet and always a fifth leg ready for emergencies, but slow and piggish of temperament when hounds were not running, ended as a gun horse in the War. Torpedo, supposed to be up to sixteen stone, but long in the back and slack in the loins, his colour, a beautiful iron-grey, his only merit. I think he was born tired. Rory, a nasty underbred brute who got grease (we found out afterwards he got it every winter). These last three were sent over from Ireland by a friend of Nina's, old Captain Dick Kerr, who used to send us six at a time and tell us to ride them all and sell them at Tattersall's when we didn't want them any more. Cimba we bought at Tattersall's, a bright chestnut with light mane and legs, a nice-looking beast up to fourteen stone, but always in a state of terror; I think he must have been very badly treated as he would hide in the corner of his box shaking from head to foot, he never seemed to use his brain to save himself and always obeyed in a fluster. One day when I happened to be standing on a railway bridge with him it suddenly entered his head that I wanted him to jump down on to the line, and he very nearly did so, only being hauled off after he had got his forelegs and most of his body on to the parapet. We sold him to the V.W.H. to carry one of their whips, and he proved very useful. The same year that we had Cimba we bought Bacchus at Tattersall's, a fine, big, upstanding horse. Oddly enough, very few people seemed to be bidding for him and he was knocked down to us for £100. Rather a lot for us to give, but he looked worth every bit of it. 16·2, up to sixteen stone, by " Lord Fitzwilliam," he was rather more the stamp of a charger than of a hunter. An odd-tempered horse, as he would always try to rub us off against a wall or tree if he got the chance, but charming otherwise. We handed him over to a hard-riding gentleman farmer in hopes of taming him down a bit before hunting began. I met him out one day and changed on to him—my goodness, he did feel big under one! (I rode 13·7 in those days.) He at once began trying to get rid of me against a wall when, luckily, hounds found, and from that moment on he thought of nothing else. We had a very good run in which I was a complete passenger the whole time, never getting a pull from beginning to end, and rousing the wrath of a little man who had tried to cut in in front of me at a post and rails . . . Bacchus and I jumped him as well as the post and rails!

Alas, the first time Nina had him out he collapsed badly. Old Will Dale, the Duke's former huntsman, galloped up to me saying, " You had better go back quickly. Something has happened to that fine horse of Mrs. Hollings's. I am afraid he has broken his back. I am going for your second horseman." There he was sitting up in the middle of the field like a great big dog with Nina standing alongside and many others watching him. Nina's only explanation was that he must have dropped his hind legs into a little grip crossing the field. In vain we tried to make him get up, he was quite unable to do so, and four or five men got round him and lifted him on to his feet, where he stood swaying to and fro, every minute nearly losing his balance. At last our man came up with Nina's second horse and we left him to be taken home, propped up on both sides by the men.

For the rest of the season he was laid up and blistered, and by the time the summer shows came round he was looking his best. Only those who knew could detect a slight swaying movement in his hind-quarters. We sent him up to the Bath Show, and he won second in the heavyweight open class. Then we sent him up to Tattersall's, and we had the luck to sell him for exactly the sum we had given for him, to go to Germany as a charger; he was lucky, too, as that sort of life ought to have suited him well.

Our selling was not always as lucky as that. Cocksure, whom I mentioned earlier as a good jumper but rather slow, had a curious accident when being shown off to a prospective buyer. A Captain C., belonging to a cavalry regiment stationed not far off, came over to look at him and asked permission to try him over some jumps. We agreed at once, saying he could take him anywhere he liked across country. But that was not what he meant, he wanted jumps put up in our own field. Knowing our Cocky, and that he never turned his head at anything, we again agreed and, telling our man to put up a hurdle or two in the field, we went in to luncheon.

When we came out all was ready . . . two hurdles propped up on one side of the field, each with a wing hurdle, and a hairy concoction made up of some spare posts and rails and cut furze bushes; like fools we

A CURIOUS ACCIDENT

never went and examined it closely. A builder who had been working near by had helped put the jumps up and, without mentioning it to anybody, had supported the fence with a scaffold pole, stuck at an angle into the ground on the far side of the jump so that it was hidden from everybody. Captain C., who was not a great rider, rode at the place in a very half-hearted manner and Cocky, not seeing why he should jump in his own field, just outside his own stable, ran out at the corner of the wing straight into, and against, the point of the scaffold pole. The pole went into his chest and right through, breaking the girths, snapping short off in the chest. He crashed down, emptying Captain C. on to the ground, who took the bridle over his head with him. It broke, and Cocky was loose, saddleless and bridleless, with the great scaffold pole sticking out behind his shoulder. Luckily Nina was quick-witted; she got to him before he had time to get away and seizing him by the nostrils choked him into submission. I was there nearly as soon, tearing my shirt off to fill the hole, the moment the groom could pull the pole through. It was a ghastly moment, Cocky choking for breath as Nina squeezed his nostrils, the groom pulling and tugging to get the pole through. Having broken off right inside the chest it was quite impossible to pull it back the way it had gone in. Three foot of pole, four inches in diameter! We did not care what had happened to Captain C., and I do not know to this day if he hurt himself, but I do know that he never offered to help us, and that when we next looked round he and his motor had gone. We never heard another word from him. Meanwhile, having stuffed up the two gigantic holes so that the air could not get in, with slow, painful steps, we got the horse to his box. Poor little man, he was so good, but his one idea was to lie down and that could not be allowed, so Nina and I and the groom took turns propping him up against the side of his box while waiting for the vet., who had many miles to come. When he did, he found by probing that the pole had not gone into the chest cavity, but had hit the breast bone and slanted off under the muscles of the shoulder, coming out through the girths. Tetanus was, of course, the principal danger, as the pole was filthy, covered with earth and a green sort of mildew, but Cocksure recovered and was as good a hunter as ever. We kept him until the War, when he was taken with several other of our horses to do his duty for his country.

Our attempts to sell Paddy, too, were not happy. Paddy was a huge brown horse with a fiddle head, up to any weight, a fine performer, if you were strong enough to hold him together, which I was not. How curiously some people behave! A Mr. L. came down from London to look at him, and asked if he might just get on him for an hour to feel what he was like with hounds. We knew the said man was accustomed to hunting in good countries, so agreed cheerfully, but said, " Not more than an hour please, as Nina wants to ride him second horse herself."

Later on, the Master came up to one of us and said, " I don't know if that fellow has bought your horse or not, but I saw him deliberately put him at a barbed-wire fence just now; he cleared it with lots to spare, but I think you had better go and see what he is up to." Nina and I searched for him everywhere, but were told that the last people had seen of him was on the high road to Swindon, miles away. Not having another horse out we were obliged to go home, expecting Paddy to come back every moment.

At last the horse appeared about 9 p.m., covered with scratches and dried blood, and led by a tramp who said that a gentleman had given him five shillings to bring the horse home from the railway station, ten miles away, and he had partly ridden and partly led him back. The horse was quite worn out, and dazed with fatigue, besides having lost a shoe. The tramp said that the gent was covered with mud and his coat torn to ribbons. Three days after we had a letter, quite short, " I would not have him at a gift, he is a dangerous brute and no woman should ride him."

Various people who had been out that day told us afterwards that this man had ridden Paddy at every fence, possible and impossible, ending up with the barbed-wire one we had already heard of which he had jumped splendidly, while everyone's heart had been in their mouths to see what would happen. We both hunted him for the rest of that season and sold him at the end, to the Master of the Pytchley. He won the Pytchley Heavyweight on him the following season.

Nina's horses were rather big for me, but we had to share, and the result was that I was nearly always riding horses well over my weight.

There is one episode connected with Paddy of which I am not proud. We were hunting with the V.W.H. from Cricklade one day, and had planned to go out with the Cirencester hounds the following day. My partner was to come down from London for it and was to ride Paddy. My own horse was too lame to come out the first day, so I hired a chestnut from a neighbouring farmer-horse-dealer, which turned out to be blind of one eye. He was so nervous and slow about his jumping that when I caught a sight of Nina's horse, Paddy, being exercised as we passed near Cricklade, I hastily changed on to him and hurried after the hounds who had just found in a neighbouring copse. We had a lovely run, at the end of which Paddy was so tired that I had to carry his head for him, and very heavy it was. We were miles from home and I only got in about eight o'clock. The groom, for some reason that I have forgotten, was out, so the cook and I had a long and weary business, each standing on a kitchen chair trying to dry Paddy's back and ears and throat. He would keep on breaking out, and I did not dare leave him. At last he was dry, and I went in to my bath and to eat and sleep the sleep of the just.

Next morning, before I was up, in walked Nina dressed in her best, top-hat and all. "What is the idea?" she said. "What am I to ride? I hear you had Paddy out until midnight last night. Torpedo is lame. What have you done about it?" I looked at her in horror; my mouth dropped open and I had nothing to say. I had clean forgotten her very existence ... I had never thought of her or her horse at all. I think it says a good deal for our friendship that it did not end there and then. She was marvellously forgiving, and has hardly ever alluded to it since. That day a shutter had closed on my brain; I wonder if it happens to other people's brains too.

In 1910 Nina and I bought a small farmhouse in the Duke of Beaufort's country and kept it till after the War. We built on ten loose-boxes and an extra two rooms, besides a cottage-bungalow for the servants, with the proceeds of an exhibition of paintings I had held in London. Our money affairs were always precarious, but somehow we generally managed to find the means to do what we wanted. We bought the farmhouse for £300 with some money left me by an aunt, spent £2,000 on it, and eventually, when the bank became insistent about our returning the loan, sold it for £3,000, so did not do so badly.

We started enjoying ourselves at once—Captain Dick Kerr, Nina's friend, sending us over three or four horses from Ireland, as he had before, to ride and send up to Tattersall's for him, and we had two or three of

SAFETY FIRST?

our own besides. Feo had her own two, and Hilda a wonderful horse called Trojan who had been given to her by a Spanish friend, the Duke of Peñeranda, who had hunted him for several seasons in the Quorn country. As the last two were often unable to come down, I had the run of their horses as well as my own and we had great fun. The meets were near as a rule; we had very nice neighbours and grew to know the country as the palm of our hands. That last is a thing I do not really appreciate, as I think it teaches one to ride cunning. In a new country you must follow hounds or you get lost, in a country which you know too well you learn to know the line your fox will take as well as the unpleasant places and are liable to take short cuts and so get lazy. People who do not hunt themselves will never understand the point of view of those who do. I remember one Sunday walking a point with a man who did not hunt; we came to a really nasty place, a hairy fence with a steep drop into some marshy ground which had been the scene of plain funking on my part some time before. The blessed Senator, more sensible than I, had refused it point-blank. Again and again I had taken him at it with my heart in my mouth; this, of course, he knew quite well and took advantage of. After struggling with him for some time I became aware that hounds had swung round and gone straight back behind us. Much relieved, but rather ashamed, we left our bone of contention and went after them, but I always had conscience pricks when I saw the place ever after. I pointed out the fence to the man I was walking with that Sunday, and he could not understand my point of view. "I thought you hunted for pleasure; why jump anything you are frightened of?"—"But that is the very reason I should have jumped it," I said. "Surely you can see that. Also it was very bad for the horse to have

ABOUT HORSES

been master." No, he could not see it, and he only said that he thought hunting people must be mad, especially me.

My theory in life has always been, if you dislike doing a thing, make yourself do it, although I must own it has not always worked. Many a time I have hurt myself and gone on with the job in hand, having had to pay for it afterwards . . . such as insisting on going out hunting after I had broken a vertebra in my spine, and going out shooting with two ribs unseated. I must say in self-defence that in neither case did I know what had happened, only that I was sure that if I was amused enough I should forget the pain. Stupid perhaps, but better than giving in unnecessarily. Think what fun in life I should have lost if I had given in and stayed at home when I thought that I was frightened. Once out, all that is forgotten in the excitement. Besides, what pictures there were at every turn: early morning cubbing with the dew on the grass, the silver cobwebs shining and the low light slanting behind them. The long shadows grey upon the ground, and the cheerful yowl of hound after hound as they pop in and out of the low cover under the trees . . . appearing and disappearing as they bustle the cubs round in the cover and across the rides. The lovely purple colour of the Whip's coat as he comes galloping down the ride towards you with the light behind him, the true pink of his jacket only showing on the edges. What mornings those were. One especially stands out in my memory. On the downs. In the sky-blue patches, and a golden light on the edges of the clouds, but down near the ground a white wispy mist, one minute you could see, the next everything blotted out. Hounds and huntsman mere wraiths of soft colour, appearing and disappearing, and every sound magnified (I painted a picture of it and sold it to one of the Rothschilds in

A GREAT DRAG-HUNT

Paris). And again, what lovely things were to be seen in the evening when all the world was purple and brown, with great slashes of colour across the sky reflected in the puddles in the road. Hounds, huntsmen, whips, horses, all with a golden halo round them as they jogged along homewards.

Here is a story *not* of the Duke's country!

We had been having very indifferent sport with a provincial pack and one of the members came up to me one day and said, " I hope you are all coming out on Saturday." I was rather uncertain, as, to tell the truth, we were getting rather tired of never finding, and of the eternal jogging along the roads from cover to cover, and we had planned to do something else that day. My friend, a cheerful soul with a sense of humour, pressed the subject, saying, " I can promise you you will not regret it." So out we went. Feo, Nina and I. We were rather short of horses as one of them was ill, so Nina rode a pink roan hireling, an odd-looking animal, Feo was on Indigo and I was on Ballet Girl, Hilda's polo pony, about 14·3, a charming pony and a very fine fencer, but who could never be persuaded to walk. When hounds were put into cover my friend, L. G. (not Lloyd George), signed to us to keep close to him, and he cantered off to a corner the far side of the wood. Hounds had not been in a moment before one, and then another, lifted up their voices, and out they came with a crash of sound, closely packed together and running for all they were worth. We all three got away with a wonderful start, and as L. G. galloped on, close behind the Master, I heard him say, " They are running as if it were a drag, sir."—" Nonsense," shouted the Master, " do you suppose I don't know when my hounds are running a fox!"

On they went over the very best bit of country we

had there, running as hard as they could go. It was curious that at almost every jump there were people standing watching. How, I wonder, did they know which way that fox would go ? . . . The fact remains that they did. At one place where you had to jump into a lane and out the other side, there were a lot of carts and motors drawn up, and as Nina on her strange pink animal jumped down and up again, one spectator was heard to ejaculate, " Pretty leap, that." The horse went by the name of Pretty Leap ever after. For me the straightest and fastest run I ever took part in ended rather soon. Ballet Girl, not in her first youth, was getting rather blown with the pace we had been going. As we came to a post and rails running across the middle of a field my sister shouted to me to go on and give her a lead, and the next thing I knew I was flat on my back and Feo saying politely, " Thank you," as she galloped past and disappeared after hounds. Ballet Girl had made her first mistake, catching the top rail with her chest she had turned a neat somersault, flattening the obstacle for my sister. For ever after I was able to raise a blush of shame from her when I referred to that moment. She said, in excuse, that she knew I was not hurt; now, how could she have known that! Anyway, it gave me a good handle against her for many a long year after.

The whole story of that hunt came out, of course; L. G. had laid the drag himself that morning, and the result was that the luckless youth had to leave the country for quite a long time. The horrified members of the Hunt, headed by his elder brother, would have no more to do with him.

There is no possible doubt whatever that far and away the best rider to hounds of our party was Nina Hollings. Brought up with horses from her earliest babyhood, accustomed to being put on any horse by

THE BEST RIDER

her father, to make it and to mouth it, there was little that Nina did not know about riding or about how to get across a country. One of the stories she has often told was how, at the age of sixteen, having had a violent difference of opinion with her mother, her father had asked her to come out with him and try a young horse he had just bought. She had a very rough ride, but after an hour or so he settled down and was going so nicely that she asked permission to take him over some steeplechase jumps which were near her home. The horse jumped them perfectly, and on their way home her father said to her, "If you had as much tact with your mother as you have with a horse you would get into less trouble."

She was big built and needed big horses, but she would always turn up at the right place at the right moment. When we joined forces, she had a very good horse called the Squire . . . a short-backed, strong black horse who had carried her very well up in the Zetland country where she used to hunt regularly every season till I knew her. One day, out with the South Berks when all the field were trying to negotiate some rails in a nasty, poached bit of ground, I saw Nina on Squire quietly canter up to one of the posts and buck him over it from a stand. Of course it was the only sound take-off and the only sound landing, but other people had not thought of it and she had. Lord Spencer had always told me whenever I had a horse that I wasn't quite sure of at timber, to jump him at a post, as he said horses saw vertical lines better than horizontal ones.

Neither Feo nor I had had enough hunting to make us really good. I had fairly decent hands, not over light, a firm seat, and could make a horse gallop, so always enjoyed myself. Feo's hands were too light, if anything, and she was not determined enough with

ABOUT HORSES

her horses to show them who was master, but she had no knowledge of fear and enjoyed herself wildly; always well up and bustling along with tears of excitement streaming down her cheeks. It was interesting to see what a good horsewoman she became latterly, improving every season in judgment and knowledge.

The other member of our party, Hilda, Nina's girl, was very good on a horse, quiet and businesslike, and always there; one cannot say more for a person than that. She was a nice light weight and could ride anything that was up to thirteen stone.

I don't know why in telling of our horses, I never mentioned Richmond, son of Hampton. I got him cheap one day when I had gone into Tattersall's to see if there was anything exciting on. A very big horse, aged, well-bred looking, rather leggy, and not up to much weight though he was 16·2, a fine leaper and a good hunter on the days he did not pull my arms out, the other days I only wanted to get off and shoot him; no bit made any difference to his pulling and many a day I came home long before hounds because I was worn out. I believe all, or nearly all, Hampton's progeny had the same habit. He was a very good horse, and I kept him till he died of old age . . . or rather, earned his bullet.

St. Govan was a little mistake as we had never meant to buy him. He was only up to twelve stone and could not carry our boots. We had happened to go to Cheltenham to sell one of our horses, and we were just making up our minds to start for home when into the ring came a beautifully shaped little thoroughbred. Nearly everyone had left, and there were only two or three rough-looking customers dawdling about who stopped their conversation to look at what was being brought into the ring. No one bid at first, then someone said " Ten guineas " . . . long silence, and

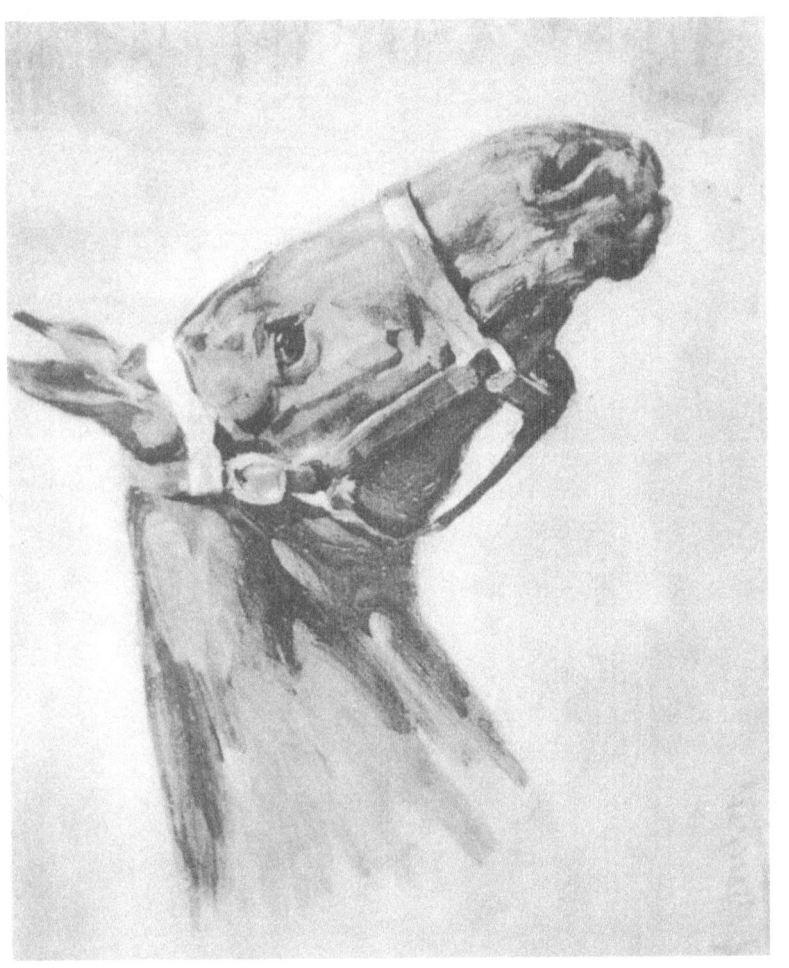

RICHMOND

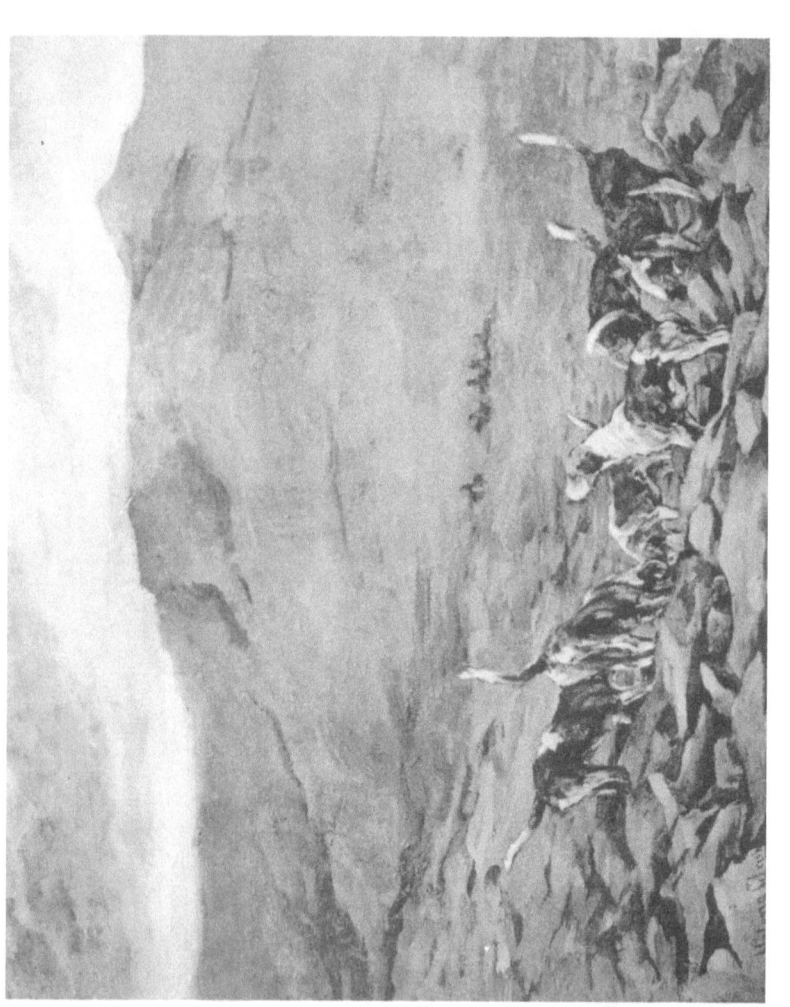

Hunting on the Daren Rocks, Black Mountains, South Wales

another said "Eleven." We said "Twelve," and no one else spoke. The hammer came down and he was ours. We did not want him in the least, but we could not see him thrown away. We went round and questioned the groom, who had he belonged to? Why had he been sold? The answer was that the gentleman had taken a dislike to the little horse, and had said that he was to be sold without reserve; anything, as long as he didn't ever see him again. He was too much for the young ladies, and he, the groom, was miserable, as he was very fond of the horse. He was six years old and was by Gold Medallist out of Penitent Queen. No, he had never been entered for any races yet, but he had a good turn of speed and should do well. We let Hilda ride him for a bit, but he did not understand hunting, and was all over the place, not a pleasant mount for a woman, so we sold him to a man in the R.A. who ran him in the Grand Military and came in second. He and his master then went to the War and were both killed in their first action.

Trojan, although not ours, was with us a great deal. Wise as Solomon, with curiously sunken eyes, up to 13·7 or fourteen stone, the picture of a hunter, his performance was as perfect as his appearance. In common with many another good horse he always stood with his forelegs bent; I do not call it standing over because there is a difference, and several well-known racehorses, St. Simon amongst others, did the same. Often when Hilda could not get away to hunt, I had a day on him, and I always enjoyed it enormously if hounds ran. If, by chance, we had a blank day, then I hated Trojan. He would never walk—I don't think he knew how to—and he would jigget and jog all day; he could never stand still either, his idea of standing being to turn round and round, first one way, then the other; but let hounds run, then he was quite a different horse and you could not ask for a better hunter.

Montana, my last buy, I got at Tattersall's. I was just getting about again after being laid by for more than a year with a damaged spine, and suggested to Nina to go into Tattersall's and see what was going on.

It was spring-time and a lot of good horses were going up for sale. Suddenly a very good-looking grey caught my eye and I went in to his box to look at him; he was a picture of a horse, apparently clean bred, and well up to my weight. I enquired who he belonged to, and was told Major Pigot Moodie, Scots Greys. Nina had wandered off looking at other horses, but I could look at nothing except the grey. Major Pigot Moodie came in while I was in the box and asked me to come outside to speak to him; then he said in a low voice, "Don't bid for my horse, he isn't sound in front, besides which he makes a noise. It doesn't stop him now, but it may get worse. I am selling him because he won't last the season." I thanked him much and moved away, still determined in my inside to see what happened to him when he came up to the rostrum.

Nina and I were in a good place when the moment came and the grey was led out. There was a murmur of admiration as he showed off in front of the crowd, but evidently something was known against him, for the bidding went up quickly to thirty guineas and then stopped. We waited. Fifty-five ... sixty ... sixty-eight. Nothing more. Sixty-nine from me, dead silence, down went the hammer, he was mine, and he was led back to his box with his beautiful long tail swinging above his hocks and his tiny ears pricking first in this direction, then in that. What a horse to look at. Worth buying for that alone. Up came Major Pigot Moodie. " Well, you got him after all. Don't say I didn't warn you. What are you going to do with him?" I answered, "I am going to lay him up and fire him to get those tendons right, and then turn him out, and by next season, when I hope my back will be fit to hunt again, he will be fit too. As to his wind, he will go quite fast enough for me. Now tell me what he has done and all about him." So his former master proceeded to tell me that the horse was a Canadian thoroughbred; he had won the "Gentleman's Steeplechase" over there and had then come over here to win again at Aldershot; his worst fault was that he was a bad feeder and nervous. That did not worry me as he would have all the quiet he needed, and all the cosseting too, at our cottage.

When the time came, and I took him out hunting, I found that the slight noise that he made did not stop him at all. I was late for the meet the first day I took him out, and hounds had already found (I had had to go to the doctor at Tetbury to have my back strapped up before hunting, and he had taken an unconscionable time over it); I could hear them the far side of the valley running fast, so turned Montana in at the nearest gate to take a short cut to join them. There were two small fences to get over, and then a fair-sized brook. He never hesitated, and took me straight as they came, with a lovely long stride, as smooth and comfortable as could be, and never pulling an ounce. How delighted I was with him; and when I found later that he could out-gallop anything that was out my joy was redoubled. Everyone came up to ask his history and where I had got him, and we were both as pleased as Punch with ourselves. Alas! this joy was not to be repeated often. My back soon struck work again and I had very little more hunting at all, and then only in great discomfort, and I had to give up riding altogether.

ABOUT HORSES

Soon the War broke out, and Montana was shot as being too nervous and too bad a feeder to be of any use as a charger. He would only eat at night, and if there was any sound of men or horses about, he was completely put off his food.

9

DOGS

WHAT about dogs? . . . We have possessed many, or rather they have possessed us. I knew a man once who said he would not have a dog because his life would not be worth living. He would have to go out when he wanted to stay at home, he would have to be sure his dog was comfortable before he sat down himself, and if his dog wanted his particular armchair he would have to sit in another. No, he said it was not good enough, it was ten years' penal servitude to own a dog. Another man I knew, an Italian, took his dog with him to Macedonia and he told me that no one, not even the General himself, dared sit down until they knew which chair Bomba wanted.

We have never suffered in that way because our dogs have always had comfortable beds in every room. We have had fox-terriers, bull-terriers, mastiffs, spaniels, Alsatians, Labradors, each and all with their different characters, each and all wishful to do all they could to make life agreeable for us and to bring us into all their amusements and excitements.

One, with no particular label to her, we only had for a few weeks, but I have never forgotten her, we named her Squash.

I was working in the studio at St. James's Palace, and was disturbed by shrieks outside in Marlborough Gate; running out into the road to see what had occurred I met a policeman carrying what looked like a bundle of black and white rags. I asked what had happened and he told me that it was a dog that had been run over by a car, and he was taking it to the police station. I asked him to take the dog into my studio and there we examined her carefully. She howled whenever touched, so I went to the telephone and called up the vet., asking him to come at once . . . the poor little black and white bundle settled herself in the corner of the sofa where we had put her, sobbing to herself. When the vet. came he declared no bones were broken although she was evidently much bruised and was suffering severely from shock. The nice policeman left, saying he would let me know if anyone claimed her. No one ever did, and Squash slowly got better. The vet. kept her under drugs for several days to give her inside a chance of healing, and one day when I went down to the studio I found a cheerful, bounding little person awaiting me at the door, to all outward appearances quite recovered. She proved to be marvellously intelligent and there was nothing you could not teach her, but she had strange attacks of screaming which came on for no apparent cause. I took her down to our cottage in Wiltshire, and she ran about happily with all the other dogs, enjoying life vastly, even climbing apple-trees to amuse herself and us, but the screaming fits increased, and as no vet. could tell us what was wrong with the poor little dog, we had sadly to consent to having her put down.

Dogs' characters have always interested me enormously. Why do some people's dogs love me dearly while their owners are there, but directly they are left in my charge they treat me as if I were the greatest brute on earth? They cringe before me, hide in corners or under beds, refuse utterly to come out for walks, and, in fact, send me to Coventry, no matter what pleasures

MITRA, SHORT FOR MITRAILLEUSE

I plan for them. When their owners return they become charming to me again. What is their theory? If they were people the reverse would be the case. Humans know which side their bread is buttered and are charming to you when there is no one they like better, but dogs, No.

People often say that dogs have no sense of humour. I do not agree. I have seen Mitra, my Malinoise, roaring with laughter many a time, and she would roll over and over downhill if she thought I was bored or depressed. I took her, and another Alsatian bitch, to see a trainer working on Wimbledon Common. After the usual show was finished he came up to me and asked, pointing at Mitra, if she had ever been trained as a police dog. I had bought her the last year of the War, in France, and, except for her excitement at seeing the battlefields, had never had any suspicion that she knew anything about training. It is true that I had once said " Attaques " when some people were bear-fighting in a garden, and she had promptly torn a man's trousers from off him, but that might have been merely anxiety to please.

I told the trainer that I didn't think she knew much about it, and he said, " We shall soon see. Have you anything you could give her to guard ? " I produced my cigarette-case, and he put it down in front of her, having first chained her to a post stuck into the ground. Mitra never took her eyes off mine and paid not the slightest attention to what the trainer or his assistant were doing. Remarking with contempt that she evidently knew nothing, the trainer told his man, who was dressed in leather from head to foot, to creep up behind Mitra and take the cigarette-case away from her. Meanwhile, she sat with her forelegs wide apart, her ears flat, and her fat sides wobbling with amusement, staring at me while the assistant crept closer and closer to her. Suddenly, without any warning, she spun round and caught the man by the leg, fastening on him and worrying him in a way that made me quite glad that his legs were well protected. She succeeded in giving him a good pinch as it was, and when I called her off the man went away grumbling and rubbing his leg. Mitra was extremely pleased with herself and the trainer was delighted, saying there was no possible doubt that she knew all about guarding property, and about attacking too. She congratulated herself and me all the way home, panting and smiling and washing my face whenever she got the chance.

I think perhaps that sometimes a dog's sense of humour is somewhat mistaken; as, for instance, when my huge Clumber spaniel, Cherry, on being taken out shooting, waded into a pond and pursued, caught and killed a prize Aylesbury duck that she brought to me with pride. The same dog, if she thinks she has done something she should not, will shut one eye, twist her face all on one side and limp helplessly along, falling to the ground every few steps. Many a time when out shooting I have heard people calling, " Your spaniel has hurt herself very badly, do come," and they think I am very unsympathetic because I only laugh. I know my Cherry. Once I have laughed at her, her lameness goes, her face becomes straight and she comes waddling up to me to scrape my shin with her enormous paw, her principal sign of love and affection.

Another of our spaniels, Gypsy by name, also had a great sense of humour. We bought her from the *Exchange and Mart*, and the first time we took her out with a gun she was so offended at going shooting with women, and she thought it so unseemly, that she would do nothing but catch butterflies and bring them to us. She considered it more suitable to our sex. Gypsy did a very clever thing when we first had her. We had taken her up the Table Mountain at the back of our house on

SPANIELS

the Black Mountains in Wales, where we were living at that time, and on the way down Nina dropped her silver cigarette-case. She had no idea where she had dropped it and the walk had been a long and rough one. Gypsy was new to both of us and we had but little hope that she could help us. However, we showed her other things out of Nina's pocket, and saying, "Hi lost, good dog, fetch it," we sent her off back on our tracks. Off she went, and we saw her no more for at least an hour when she appeared with the case in her mouth. She did not know Nina's scent too well, and also dogs do not like carrying anything made of metal, so I think it was a fine performance.

I never think that a spaniel's character is as genuine as that of other dogs. They are so much inclined to play-act and to watch your face and see how you are taking it. Affectionate to sentimentality, their affections, as a rule, are easily shifted to another person. Other dogs are usually simple and direct, but spaniels never, maybe they think along more human lines.

One we had, who when ferreting, would never stay with the gun, but would creep on her stomach all round the field until she reached the place she thought the rabbit would bolt to, and there she would lie hidden in grass, or behind a bush, to catch the rabbit as it entered its hole. No one dared shoot because no one knew exactly where the spaniel had hidden herself, but she would appear, rabbit in mouth, time after time, and you could not scold her, because, after all, we were trying to get rabbits, and she knew it.

We had dogs at the War, of course. They used to come and give themselves to us when they lost their owners, but foreign dogs are very different of temperament to English dogs. Here, for generations, they have been taught to expect kindness, but abroad I have always found them suspicious.

DOGS

Once we had, as a family, taken to Alsatians, other dogs, much as we loved them, seemed to fade into the background. I bought my Malinoise (Belgian drover's dog) in France, but all the others were English bred. Hopeful of making my fortune over them I bought a puppy when they were at their highest value in this country. Alas, by the time she was grown up and had puppies ready to see, someone had managed to persuade the English public that Alsatians were nasty, dangerous brutes, and that Airedales were the only watchdogs to buy.

I sold two of my fourteen puppies for £40 each, far beyond my wildest expectations, the others I had to give away, because they had already gone out of fashion. All my money-making schemes have ended in this fashion. I have always been very good at buying, but when it comes to selling ! ! !

Talking of Alsatians, of course they are nervous, all sheep-dogs are, and they are only European sheep-dogs after all, and have been so from the beginning of all time. Everyone is careful how they touch a strange sheep-dog, at least I know I am. Press your attentions on him, there follows a snap, not necessarily meaning to get your hand but a warning. One has to be careful with Alsatians in the same way, that is all. At one time when collies were the fashion they were too much inbred; result, they became nervy and quick-tempered. In the same way Alsatians over here were at first too much bred for looks; result, the same, but now that so many are used to lead the blind they are breeding much more for brains. Only once have I been bitten, and that was entirely by accident. One of my puppies, Grey Brother by name, had been playing with his sister, and the game had changed, as games suddenly will, into a fight. I rushed to separate the puppies before they could hurt each other, as I pulled Grey Brother away he caught hold of me quite by accident, thinking I was his sister; finding that he had hold of me he tried to back away, but it was impossible as his tooth was securely hooked into the fleshy part of my finger. Then he got frightened, and the more I tried to reach him with my left hand, the more he backed away. At last I managed to grab him and pull him towards me and unhook my finger. Poor lamb, he could not understand that he had done nothing wrong, and had to be much comforted before he was satisfied, but . . . my finger was very sore and throbbed quite a lot for some time.

A game the Alsatians liked was for me to place them all according to speed at long distances apart; they were not allowed to move until the word was given, though one or two of them would lie down, and the moment my back was turned they would begin to creep on their tummies till I looked round, when they would instantly sit up in the position I had left them in and pretend they had never moved. The farthest point reached, I would turn and shout, and the whole lot would race to see who would get to me first. It usually ended in a general rough and tumble. It was very amusing teaching them, but I had to have much tact and not overdo it or they became bored, and a bored dog is hopeless.

I had one Alsatian, very nervous, but quite willing to learn when I could get her attention, which was generally centred on some far away sound; she became a wonderful retriever and although she had teeth like sabres, could retrieve a partridge without ruffling a feather.

Her name was Risk, and when young she showed rather too much interest in sheep; the little mountain sheep in Wales ask for trouble as, directly they see a dog, they start running. I took her into a field with a large flock of sheep feeding in it; I had put on a broad leather slip collar and had attached to it a ploughline about twenty feet long, the other end of which I tied round my middle. Holding the slack of the line in my hand we went quietly into the field. Directly we showed ourselves, the sheep rushed off and Risk, thinking she was loose, started off after them at top speed. When she came to the end of the lead the jerk threw her clean over backwards and pulled me on to my face. There was no need ever to do this painful thing again—she never looked at another sheep, nor did she ever attempt to chase them again on her own. At first she used to be afraid to go into a field where there were any sheep, but later I could trust her to drive them out of the garden, and the slightest whistle fetched her back.

After consultation with several breeders I decided to send her to a regular Alsatian trainer. The man was English but had been to the Germans to learn their methods. I took Risk down from London by car and left her with him, making him promise not to let her loose until he had got her confidence. He had quite a lot of dogs there, all in different stages of training, and when called upon to show off, they all did their work well. He had a habit of shutting each dog up in a little hutch alone in the dark for half an hour before, and half an hour after, work. He said he put them there to think. The hutches were all over the training ground so that the dogs could listen to the others being taught but could see nothing to take their attention. I hated leaving my dog in strange hands, but had been told so much about this man that I hoped all would be well.

Three days after, while attending a committee meeting at the Royal Academy, a telegram was brought to me, saying that Risk had got away soon after I had left and that, although she had been seen, no one could get near her. Would I come down and see if I could catch her.

I left the committee, got my car and went down to

A LOST DOG

Sussex as fast as I could go. The trainer was very distressed (as well he might be). He owned that he had let her loose directly I had gone, thinking that she would be quite safe with him in a big enclosure, which was surrounded by a seven-foot fence. But to his horror she had cleared the wire at once and had vanished into Ashdown Forest. He had been out day and night looking for her, had sighted her once or twice but could get nowhere near her, and the villagers in the neighbourhood were terrified, saying there was a grey wolf loose in the Forest. He had no excuse ready, either for not having kept his promise to me, not to let her off a lead, or for not having let me know at once when it happened.

I took a room at the neighbouring hotel and at once got on to the telephone to the Chief Constable of that part of Sussex who, I discovered, was a Captain Williams, whom we had known well during the War. He had been in the Gunners in Italy. He at once answered that he would do all he could to help, and besides sending some police over to help in combing out the coverts near Horsham, he gave orders to every policeman in the county to report immediately if the dog were seen.

I had brought my old dog, Mitra, with me, because I knew that even if Risk had so far lost her head that she would not come to me, that she would come to Mitra at once.

There ensued three days and nights of great anxiety . . . reports came in from all sides, and from miles apart . . . a grey wolf-dog had been seen galloping in front of the train down the Horsham and Brighton line. An Alsatian was seen to bolt through all the traffic on the London main road at the same hour, forty miles in the opposite direction, etc., etc. Accompanied by two stalwart policemen I motored from place to place, always too late. Yes, the blacksmith had seen her five miles away, an old lady hanging up clothes had seen a wolf looking out of a bush . . . two children had played with a strange big grey dog, and so it went on. You might think that Sussex was peopled with big, grey dogs.

At last, one evening, just as I was sitting down to a belated meal, a boy was shown into the dining-room of the hotel. "Quick," he said, "if you come at once you will see her, she is feeding on the rubbish heap outside the town of Horsham."

We hurried off together, and there, in the half dark, I could just see her outline against the sky. I made the boy sit down behind a bush, impressing on him that he was not on any account to move or show himself, and then, calling Mitra and whistling my usual call, I went boldly towards her. On hearing my call up went Risk's head and big ears and she came tearing across the rubbish heaps, falling upon Mitra first, and then on me, and sobbing with excitement and joy. I need not have been afraid that she would not know me. There was no doubt of her jubilation at finding us again, and we went off home, devoutly thankful that all had ended well. The boy, too, was very content, having a good tip added to the reward already offered.

I was much interested to see that Risk had not lost flesh at all during the whole week that she had had to fend for herself, and her coat was in perfect condition.

Risk was a great sadness to me as she grew more and more nervous as she grew older, and I had eventually to have her shot. She was the most beautiful and graceful thing alive; to see her jump a five-barred gate was a joy, and to see her gallop across a field was like watching a thoroughbred horse move. But she was always listening, listening to far-away, terrifying sounds which we could not hear. If a visitor came she would burst into a torrent of barking and rush behind the sofa or out into the garden, anywhere to hide, and then you would see a couple of large ears appear above

A TRAGEDY

the window-sill and duck down again the minute she saw a stranger. After she had her family she grew worse instead of better, as I had hoped. She rushed at the Rector one day, and with her sabre tooth gave him a nasty scratch (not bite) on the arm; but that I felt he deserved as he had come up to the house hatless and in his shirt-sleeves; she naturally thought he was a tramp and that she had to defend the house. She would make a great fuss of me one minute, and then be staring over my head at imaginary enemies; she was a real example of the evils of inbreeding.

We had one terrible tragedy with her. Busy, my eldest sister's little Sealyham, who was in my charge, would defy Risk at every opportunity; she was one of the very small old-fashioned Sealyhams and had no fear. Once or twice I saw a look in Risk's eye which I did not like, but a word from me and her eye would soften and her tail wave a reassurance that all was well.

Busy continued to insult her and I gave orders that they were never to be let out together, as, in the excitement of rushing out, they might start fighting. One night Valda and I went to the cinema, leaving the dogs in charge of the housemaid with strict injunctions not to let the little dog out until the big ones were in again. She forgot . . . and we came back to find Busy with her throat cut from ear to ear, the jugular vein was hanging out and the whole of the interior of the gullet was exposed. The housemaid had let them all out together. Busy, in her excitement, must have snapped at Risk, who had returned it, catching her by the throat with those huge teeth. Then followed the most curious thing. Busy calmly went on out into the garden, did her duty and returned to the house as usual, then only did the horrified housemaid see what had happened. Busy was fourteen years old and as brave as a lion.

The vet. was already there when we got back from the

cinema and said he could do nothing. "If the huge gash were to be sewn up the little dog would be sure to die of shock." So, we gave the order and he brought out his morphia and chloroform. We assured her that she was going to be all right, and her poor little terrified eyes got quite quiet and soothed, and then the vet. gave her the morphia injection as she lay in her own basket. Soon she was asleep and he began giving the chloroform. He did it beautifully, just giving her little sniffs at first from quite far away, gradually approaching closer and closer till he put a cloth over her head and I got a tumbler to put over her nose with cotton-wool, soaked in chloroform, placed at the bottom. She slipped away into the other world without a sigh.

I have given every detail of this putting to sleep of Busy to help other people do the same for their beloved dogs. It takes a long time, painful perhaps for the owners or onlookers, but quite comfortable for the dog.[1]

Risk had no idea that she had done anything wrong, and my own feeling was that, let out in a bunch, as they had been, meaning to rush at the sentry and shriek round his heels (a pleasure they gave themselves every evening), Risk had tumbled over Busy in the dark and just mistaken her for a rabbit.

Valda had also a beautiful Alsatian, a daughter of the famous dog who tracked a murderer across the city of Liverpool at the busiest time of day, and caught him in a public-house. I took her as payment for a picture I had painted of a celebrated champion. She had not yet been named; I heard our cook calling her Tara. "What a nice name," I exclaimed, "but what made you call her that?" The cook answered with a sigh, "Because she tires me so." So Tara she remained.

[1] I have since taken to using nembutol to send them to sleep, and then the chloroform, and in the case of big dogs an injection of hydro-cyanic acid *when unconscious*.

A GLORIOUS SCRAP

She was a marvellous guard, as was proved when a clergyman's wife came to see my sister one day. For some reason or other Tara did not trust this lady; she was icily polite to her caresses but did not return them. When the time came for Mrs. W—— to leave she stopped on her way out and picked up a little piece of old silver lying on the table, meaning to ask what it was. In one second Tara streaked down the room and had seized her by the wrist, holding her tightly, and turning to Valda for orders. Luckily Mrs. W—— was fond of dogs, but she had rather a white face. "Please call her quickly, she is not hurting me at all but her teeth are very hard." Tara had made no mark and came away at once when my sister called her.

Our three Alsatians were very great friends, so I cannot account for the following episode, except that it was just a children's squabble. I was ill in bed, and not supposed to move as I had gastric trouble. My own two dogs were a great joy to me as they never left me unless they were literally dragged out, and then, if left in the garden, would try and climb in through the window to get back to me. I think they thought that my nurse had some ulterior motive and they liked to keep an eye on her. One evening after dinner they had all been let out and I heard a terrific noise in the drawing-room, which was next to my bedroom. I waited a bit, thinking the growling and snarling would stop in a minute; but it didn't, it grew worse, and I heard my sister shouting for help. I leapt out of bed and rushed, in my nightgown, down the passage and into the drawing-room. There were the three Alsatians fighting like Titans, Valda in the midst, trying in vain to drag Risk off Tara. Risk had her by the neck, and Tara had Risk by the cheek, I believe, but it was difficult to distinguish them, and it was Risk's eye and lip that suffered most, and Tara's neck. Mitra, meanwhile, who never fought herself, had got Tara by the hindquarters and was tugging for all she was worth, enjoying it all thoroughly; Mitra always used to try and separate fighting dogs and was quite aggrieved when I hauled her off, hustled her into the hall and shut the door on her. Valda and I then managed to get Tara and Risk apart, hurled them into different rooms and threw ourselves into chairs to pant. Valda had got bitten, she always did somehow; I was much too cautious ever to get hurt. Suddenly I became aware that my nurse with a scared face had been scolding for quite a long time; she seemed to think that it would finish my duodenal ulcer altogether helping to separate fighting dogs, instead of which it did it good, which I think proves that the diagnosis of my disease had been wrong. Anyway, no one was really hurt and the dogs had had a thoroughly enjoyable evening.

Totally different in character to other dogs, our Alsatians soon taught us how to look after them. We expected instant obedience and always got it, no wink of the eye and disappearance round the corner like you get from a terrier, no deliberate deafness like from an old spaniel or retriever, their one idea is to please their owner, that is my experience of them. If they are quicker to attack it is from the eternal idea of the defence of their master or of his property which has been instilled into them for centuries on the continent. Alsatians think and reason more definitely than do other dogs, there is no doubt, and if you take the trouble you can always follow out their line of reasoning.

I was going out one afternoon in London to a place where I could not take Mitra. Valda asked me, without mentioning a name, what I was going to do with her. I asked my sister if she would keep her with her and we did not refer to it again. Mitra had been lying by me while we were talking, and, on looking round

TELEPATHY

to tell her to stay with Valda, I found she had gone. This was very unlike her as she never left my heel, and I searched all over the house for her. No one had seen her. As a last resource I went into Valda's room and there she was established under the bed, a place she had never been to before, and nothing would make her move.

This proves that they listen and understand conversations not even directly addressed to them, and I think people ought to be much more careful what they speak about in front of dogs, as they may often give them great distress by things they say. Even what we think about seems to penetrate a dog's consciousness sometimes. Many a time I have thought, "I will give that to Hebe when she wakes up," and instantly my Labrador, who seemed to be sound asleep in her basket, has got up and come to ask me what I wanted. There is no doubt that there is more telepathy between people and their dogs than between most human beings.

At one time we had a big fawn bull-mastiff which we bought from a photograph in the *Exchange and Mart*. I went to meet him at Waterloo Station; the train had come in but there was no sign of him on the platform. At last I heard loud barking and saw some men backing out of the guard's van at the other end of the train. I asked a porter, and he said that there was a very savage dog in the van and no one dared go in and get him out. I went down and there, muzzled and chained, I saw the dog we had bought, with a large label and my name on it. He was standing at the length of his chain, barking at the top of his voice—a bark with a pathetic whine in it; not a bit savage, only begging to be let out. I went in to a chorus of "Don't go near him, ma'am, he will bite you." Every man Jack of them afraid of him. Poor old man, how pleased he was to have his muzzle off and be taken out of the van. I took him, or rather he took me, down the platform to a taxi that I had waiting; I do not think that he had ever been in a shut vehicle before, and before we had left the station he was hanging half out of the window, much to the amusement of people in the street. He was altogether too heavy for me and I could not pull him back and had to call to the driver to stop and help me get him in; then, with all the windows shut, we progressed more comfortably. His joy at being let loose in the garden at St. James's can be imagined. He never forgot that I had been the one to rescue him from the train and he attached himself to me for ever after. In another place I have told the tale of his behaviour when I looed him after the ghost at Mabbot's Farm.

The end of old man Thor was sad. One day I came in from motoring, put my car away and walked to meet Thor who was coming across the yard. To my astonishment, instead of greeting me effusively as was his habit he looked at me as if he had never seen me before. His yellow eyes were hard as stones and his gait was as stiff as could be. I called to him and he jumped straight for my throat. Luckily I had on a leather coat, and I got my arm up in time to knock him off; at the same time I roared his name at him, " Thor, what are you doing? Down." He crouched before me, and I walked past him to my studio, thinking that if he came there, where he was accustomed to spend most of his time while I was working, that he would remember where he was and become himself again. So, taking off my leather coat and picking up my palette and brushes, I started to work, telling him to go and lie down in his usual place. He obeyed me, but in quite a different way to usual, slinking across the studio with his tail between his legs, and crouching low to the floor; rather a frightening sight in such a big, powerful dog, who, as

THOR BEHAVES ODDLY

a rule, looked you full in the face with the happiest, best-tempered eyes possible.

After painting, or pretending to paint, for about ten minutes, I turned round and spoke very gently to him, holding out my hand. His answer was to crouch yet closer to the ground and show all his teeth, at the same time growling low. I then perhaps made a mistake; I shouted at him, scolding and rating him, at which he bolted from the room and fled to the loose-box where he usually slept. I followed, shut him in, and told the groom that we would give him a big dose of castor oil that evening and that no one was to go near him until then. The groom then told me that Thor had behaved somewhat in the same manner to him that morning; he had not flown at him as he had at me, but had growled at him every time he spoke to him and had not been at all himself.

We dosed him and he seemed all right next day, or at least nearly so, but there was obviously still something wrong with him. Then I heard that the school children were afraid to pass our gate as, instead of greeting them cheerfully as he usually did, he now growled at them. Then he was in the drawing-room one day and my sister, who was lying on the sofa, called to him to speak to her. He came, but pushed against her, growling and using his full strength, with all his hackles up. She called out to me, "Helena, please call Thor, I don't like him, he is behaving so oddly and doesn't look like his usual self at all." I called him, but he would not move, so I had to go and fetch him, catching hold of his collar and pulling him along. He was very sulky and silent. People who have studied dogs will know what I mean when a dog is silent; they are either ill or cross, it always means that something is very wrong.

Several other small incidents were reported to us and we made up our minds that he had better go to his ancestors. We were very sad because we had loved him much, but he was too big to run any risks with, and could have killed a grown man with perfect ease.

That reminds me that one day I was working in my studio alone and looked up to find a big disreputable tramp standing in the doorway. I asked him what he wanted and he answered, "Money." I said that I hadn't any, and he asked me if I expected him to believe that. I said, "Yes. Do you suppose I am fool enough to keep what I have got out here?" In a grumpy voice he said he supposed not, and if he let me pass would I get him some? I had to agree as he had me cornered, and he stood aside to let me go to the cottage. I told him to wait while I went up to get a shilling. At that moment Thor came tearing round the corner, and I heard a piercing yell from the tramp, followed by a torrent of oaths. Thor had driven him to the end of the hall when I got down, not touching him, but standing in front of him, threatening him. I handed him the shilling, as I had promised it, at the same time putting my hand on Thor's neck. The tramp stood in front of me telling me exactly what he thought of me for keeping a dog like that "to bully and frighten a poor man." I told him to leave, but he would not, so I let Thor go, and I never saw anyone clear out so quickly. I whistled and Thor came back, sitting in front of me with his tongue hanging out, shouting with laughter. We never saw that tramp again nor, odd to say, any other, while we lived in that cottage, although it was on a much-used road. He must have passed his experience on to other tramps.

WAR

10

EXPLANATION

IN 1914 my friend, Nina Hollings, went over to France to look for a suitable spot for Lady Eva Wemyss to start an English hospital. The French authorities had offered several châteaux for the purpose, and eventually one near Compiègne was chosen, the Château du Fayel.

Nina and I worked in this hospital from February to May, 1915, fetching wounded from the centre of Compiègne, translating between the English doctors and nurses and their French patients, running a dispensary for the village at the gates and making ourselves generally useful as well as a general nuisance, as our ideas of discipline were considerably stricter than those of the hospital.

The well-known orthopædic surgeon, Mencières by name, who visited the hospital, suggested to us to leave our work of driving ambulances and take up radiography, which he said was very badly needed on the French as well as on the English front.

Armed with an introduction from him, we went to the Panthéon Military Hospital in Paris and studied there for six months, obtaining first-class certificates in radiography. Then we went to London to work under Sir James Mackenzie Davidson, the celebrated X-ray specialist, as we wanted to learn his method as well as the French method of localization of foreign bodies.

EXPLANATION

Meanwhile, our relations were working hard collecting money to enable us to put together a portable X-ray apparatus which could be carried from place to place as required at the front.

Naturally we offered ourselves first to England, but the surgeon who asked the War Office to employ us was told that as no women had ever been known to be radiographers, we could not be employed as such. The French, on the contrary, accepted our offer of help with enthusiasm.

We wasted much time waiting for orders and kicking our heels at the French War Office. Job after job was promised, but permits to start were not forthcoming. It is true that the big officials, who shall be nameless, suggested that we should go up to the Front without permits, but this we refused to do. Many amateurs had been caught in this way and had had their hospitals taken from them and been sent home themselves.

At last we were asked by the French Red Cross to go to St. Pol, and we left Paris with a semi-military convoy led by Count Étienne de Beaumont. Many adventures followed.

Military drivers had been provided for the convoy. I drove a 70-h.p. Berliet given us by Sir James Mackenzie Davidson, the soldiers driving a Mércèdes which had been sent to us by the Red Cross in London, and we had an Austin which we had fitted out as an X-ray car. There were about fifteen cars in all in the convoy, and the men were a very cheery lot, all as keen as possible to do their best in the work to come. Paul Adam, the writer, was one, M. Paul de Boulongne, a poet, another, with several others whose names I have forgotten. Two of the convoy were going as radiographers and begged us to teach them all we could and show them all the details of our apparatus, so that they might be useful when they got to their destinations. We fell completely into the

A NASTY SHOCK

trap, and spent our time teaching them all we had learnt and letting them practise on our machine.

Arrived at St. Pol, again a long pause. We were asked not to leave our hotel, as orders might come at any moment. So patiently we stayed there gazing out of window, a very interesting occupation as troops were constantly passing, both British and French. Officers with a few moments to spare from their regiments rushed in and out of the hotel demanding water to wash in and food or drink. One, a very young Frenchman, told us that he was quite worn out by the noise in the trenches and asked if he might come up to our room for a few moments' peace. We discovered that he was a son of a friend of Nina Hollings, and when he found that she knew his people and that he could talk of them to us he very nearly broke down altogether. But after a bit we managed to cheer him up and he went back to duty quite gay and soothed. He was killed next day.

A little after, in came an English officer of the 21st Lancers, the regiment that Nina's son, Jack, had belonged to (he had been killed at Messines in October, 1914, when attached to the 9th Lancers). This man had actually got Jack's polo pony with him, and had much to tell us before he went on.

Still no orders for us. They had taken our cars and apparatus to the military park, where we were unable to get at them. Then in came de Beaumont, in despair, with the news that the army had seized our cars and apparatus and the orders were that we were to leave them all and go back immediately by lorry to Paris ! . . . This was a nasty jar. We hastily thought it over and demanded to see the general in command. How sorry they were, he was not in St. Pol, and no one knew when he would be back. Then might we see the next in command ? They couldn't very well refuse that request so we were taken to headquarters by de Beaumont;

EXPLANATION

there we found a commandant surrounded by a few junior officers. The commandant was very polite, said how much he regretted the trouble to which we had been put, but our permits not being *en règle*, he had no alternative but to send us back to Paris. No doubt the War Office would arrange the matter and they would soon see us back again. We, equally polite, said that of course orders were orders, and we quite saw that nothing could be done about it, but what were we to tell the many people in England who had subscribed to the cars and X-ray plant, if we went away and left them at St. Pol ? I then had the brilliant idea of mentioning all the most important names I could think of, names that any Frenchman would be likely to know. The Commandant looked rather nervously at the other officers present and saying hastily, " Will you excuse us ? We must talk this over," he left the room followed by all the others, including M. de Beaumont. Shouts of laughter arose from the next room to which they had retreated, and presently back came M. de Beaumont alone, to say that the commandant had agreed to our taking the cars and plant back with us to Paris. Would we please be ready to start in half an hour.

So back we went. We stopped at the Hôtel du Rhin Amiens, for luncheon, and de Beaumont told us, with crocodile's tears in his eyes, how sorry he was, but the order had come through that we were to leave our cars in Amiens and go on to Paris without them, and that they would follow us on to Paris next day. We were debating privately how to counter this last move and feeling rather desperate, when in came General Sir Henry Wilson, together with several staff officers. Nina had known him very well, so she sent him a note asking him to come and have coffee with us after luncheon. He waved a greeting and called out, " Certainly, with pleasure." De Beaumont, looking very anxious, asked

ANOTHER ATTEMPTED HOLD-UP

me if I could tell him what Mrs. Hollings had said to the General in her note. I replied that I was not sure but I expected she was asking him to help us get our cars back safely to Paris, and that he would want to know what had happened to us, as he was a great friend of hers. This was merely a shot in the dark, as I hadn't the least idea what she had said, but I hoped it might frighten de Beaumont. As it turned out, it did frighten him; he made some excuse and left the table hurriedly. After a few minutes he returned to say that he had persuaded the authorities to allow us to take our cars back with us.

We had yet more adventures on our way back to Paris. M. de Beaumont stopped the cars on the road and said that he would like to talk matters over with us. He then begged that we should not tell anyone what had occurred. Why he asked this he would not explain. I am afraid we were not very sympathetic, and laughingly said that we could not possibly agree to this as we intended to make a good story out of our adventures to amuse both English and French friends. He became so distressed at this that we relented and promised not to tell anyone for twenty-four hours. To our astonishment he instantly accepted this compromise, and jumping into his car, dashed off to Paris as hard as he could go. We did not see him again.

He left his secretary to accompany us back with several other cars which were returning to Paris. After a few miles the secretary suggested that we should stop and have some tea in an *estaminet* by the roadside. This we did, and Nina, happening to look out of the window, the blind of which had been drawn down, saw the driver of our X-ray car jabbing with a knife at the tyres of the Berliet which I had been driving. We rushed out and asked him what on earth he was doing. . . . He seemed rather taken aback and answered that he was only testing the tyres, but they were "Quite all right."

EXPLANATION

We were full of suspicion and got into the Berliet at once, determined not to leave the cars again. We started, and after a few moments discovered that one tyre was flat. We called to the convoy to stop, and told the man to put on a spare tyre. Off we went again; a mile or so and two more tyres were flat. M. de Beaumont's secretary was very commiserative, and regretted that he was unable to wait and help us as he was due in Paris by a certain time. So off they all went, taking our X-ray cars with them and leaving Nina and me to manage as best we could. We were fortunately in a village not far from Compiègne and had made friends with the officials there during the time that we had been helping Eva Wemyss's hospital. Nina remained with the car to guard it, and I went as fast as I could to the General's quarters and asked to see him at once. Luckily he remembered us and at once gave orders for us to be supplied with four new tyres and a spare one, also a driver who knew a short cut to Paris, as we said we must be there before the convoy which had taken our X-ray cars on with it. The driver went faster than I have ever been driven before, and we arrived at M. de Beaumont's house just five minutes before the convoy drove up to the entrance. Here, notwithstanding the secretary's remonstrances, we immediately resumed possession of the X-ray cars, and drove them to the garage of the American Embassy. Even then we were not quite sure of their safety, so I set to work to paint out their French military numbers and put in the old English numbers instead. Lucky I did. The garage-keeper told us the next day that an officer had come to the garage in the early morning saying that they had cars with military numbers which must at once be given up, and he quoted the numbers. The keeper showed him all round the garage, assuring him that he had no such numbers, and the officer

NEW PLANS

went away, owning that there must have been some mistake.

The promised twenty-four hours' respite over, we reported our adventures to the British Embassy and the First Secretary promised that he would see that we had no further trouble. Thus ended our efforts to help our French allies.

So far we had had no opportunity of working for Italy; but on meeting Mr. Arthur Stanley [1] in Paris, he at once asked us if we would go there saying that he thought we should be very welcome. All arrangements were made and we two radiographers soon found ourselves on our way to the Italian front, on December 7th, 1915. There we stayed until October, 1917.

It may be thought by some to whom the War brought sorrow and nothing but sorrow, that the following letters show an unfeeling light-heartedness at such a time; but it must be remembered in excuse that we were working all out, and at the highest pressure we were able to maintain. This, added to the excitement of a certain amount of danger, seems to have a tonic effect on most people which enables them to take their part in scenes which in ordinary times they could not have borne to witness. We found that if we allowed ourselves or our assistants (who joined us later on) to relax for a moment and feel and show sympathy to the patients, both would crack and both would suffer for it in the long run. Once or twice this happened; in one case, a new assistant in a burst of sympathy put her hand on a patient's shoulder. The man, who had been splendidly brave up till then, broke into tears at her touch; other patients in the room lost their self-control too, and the surgeons were unable to do anything with them. One of these scenes was enough to convince the whole section that all personal feelings must be put aside for " the duration."

[1] Now Sir Arthur Stanley, G.B.E.

The following description of our time at the War is chiefly taken from letters written home to my family.

II

DEPARTURE FOR ITALY
December 1915, Italy.

OUR start was not easy. At the last moment we discovered that the authorities had left one of the cars behind. The drivers' passports, too, had been omitted, so they stayed behind as well and we went on, rather depressed that difficulties had arisen so soon. We had been told that everything would be ready for us at the port of departure. The sea was very rough and the boat filled with troops, all lying about the decks in the throes of seasickness, not a pleasant crossing! To give us extra comfort on our journey to Italy, General Sir John Cowans, the Quartermaster-General, gave us special passes and we were recommended to the care of the principal police officials to see that we passed through with the least possible delay.

The chief detective met us on board the boat and was standing talking to us in the doorway of our cabin, when suddenly a man in the gangway outside clapped his hand on the detective's shoulder saying, " I've got you, my fine fellow, now then, no trouble." Our friend swung round to face his captor with " Don't be a damn fool," and at the same time turned the lapel of his coat back to show his badge. The other jumped back with a deep apology and the chief, after a moment's conversation with him, came back and said, " I am sorry to have to leave you but there is a spy known to be aboard and I

A PRUSSIAN SPY

must go and help find him. I will tell someone else to look after you, and see you and your luggage safely landed."

An hour later, as we were landing, we saw a tall grizzled man, holding himself very straight and upright carrying a small black bag. He was walking between two French gendarmes and was followed and preceded by English detectives, amongst them our friend the chief who, seeing us, came across and said, " We have got him, he is very well known and you will hear the result to-morrow morning if you listen." We heard the result, as he said, in an outburst of rifle firing next morning from the castle above Boulogne. I shall never forget the dignity of the tall man as he passed (evidently a Prussian officer from his carriage) and the calmness of his outlook. From that moment the word spy became to us synonymous of a brave man.

We stayed in Boulogne till our cars and drivers turned up. Both drivers were amusing characters. One, like Auguste, the clown at the circus, always running to help and falling down, generally with our most precious possessions. He took cars to pieces and then had to call us to help put them together again. It is a wonder how long we bore with him, but he was good-tempered and willing and we might easily have had a worse one. The second driver was solemn and seldom spoke, but when he did, it was generally to the point. He was a first-rate driver and never got rattled in a tight place.

Before going on to Paris, Sir Arthur Lawley, the head of the Red Cross and of St. John's Ambulance in Boulogne, gave us both the badge of the joint committee to wear in our caps, telling us that it was a great compliment, as very few people not on the committee were allowed to wear them. We had had to get khaki uniforms as the usual dark blue of the British Red Cross was much too visible and the Italians would not allow it near the Front, for fear it might draw fire.

DEPARTURE FOR ITALY

We expected to be held up in Paris for some time, but when we went to the Italian Embassy to interview the head of the Italian Military Mission, Colonel Sauteiron de St. Clement, he told us that he had had a telegram from the Minister of War in Rome with orders to do everything possible to expedite our arrival in Italy, and we actually started that same evening with drivers, baggage and cars for Udine. The Italians gave us free passes for all their railways. Arrived at Udine we were met at the station by Lord Monson, the head of the British Red Cross in Italy, who took us to be introduced to all the officials before settling us in Cormons, which we were to make our headquarters.

The Italians were working splendidly, so keen and quite prepared for the War to continue for two years or more. Of course they are a people of mountaineers, but even so their difficulties, having to take all their transport over high mountains, were tremendous. We found no red tape, the officials being willing to do all they could to help us, and not only promises, their help materialized at once. Lord Monson was excellent friends with everybody, getting all he wanted with the minimum of difficulty; of course his speaking Italian very fluently was of great help.

I shall never forget our first sight of that lovely little town of Udine by moonlight, with its miniature Doge's palace and beautiful Cinquecento houses. Long black shadows were cast across the piazza by the full moon, and we could see the big solemn campanile, with its square, red-roofed tower reaching far up into the peaceful sky. As we gazed awe-struck at so much beauty, the sudden noise of rattling and back-firing motor-bicycles rushing across the moonlit square and teams of gun-horses and mules dragging their heavy loads over the cobblestones forced itself on our consciousness and made us realize that this was indeed war.

SETTLING IN

Then a hurried skedaddle as two enemy Taubes appeared, chased by two Italian aeroplanes, and everyone ran to the colonnades for shelter as shells burst in all directions . . . the streets emptying themselves in marvellously quick time. The first day we were in Udine this happened three times, and again in the evening, when we arrived at Cormons, a small town about seven kilometres behind the front line where it had been arranged that we were to stay.

We were given four rooms and a kitchen in a large villa which had belonged to a Count Zucco, an Austrian, whose family had left hurriedly when the Italians arrived. The decorations were modern German, not beautiful from our point of view, but there was some very good china and also some manuscripts and papers, all of which we put carefully away in cupboards so that their owners should find them safe when they came back. Alas, our good intentions were useless, as the soldiers attached to our section found them and thinking that we had put them away because we didn't like them, used all the best china for their own mess. Most of it was broken and nearly all the documents were used to light the stoves with ! . . . I tremble to think what priceless papers may have been burnt.

It was fearfully cold weather when we arrived in Italy and I was thankful for my fur rug in the big empty bedrooms as we had only our camp-beds and no matresses; I used to fold it under me at night and discovered that if you are warm below you can do with very little on top. It was also lucky that we had brought our rubber baths and basins as there were no washing implements whatever. There was no furniture in our rooms and at first we had only our packing-cases to act as tables and chairs. All the rooms were fine and large but quite filthy, and we set to work immediately to get them clean, helped by Professor Thomas Ashby, the

DEPARTURE FOR ITALY

head of the British School of Rome. He was working as a volunteer at Villa Trento about ten kilometres farther back where George Trevelyan had established an English hospital. This kind friend went out into the streets and byways to try and find some women to help clean and cook and he brought back two—one Italian and one Austrian, and strife started at once between them. The Austrian, Mietzi by name, was unable to speak either Austrian or Italian, only Slovene, a dialect of which we knew no word. She was as sulky as a bear, but a very good cook.

The authorities promised us a telephone, and Lord Monson left us saying he hoped we should get on well and be quite independent and self-supporting. He asked us to arrange everything for ourselves as a completely separate unit, which we, of course, infinitely preferred. He added, " I particularly do not want you to ask for any help from the English Hospital at Villa Trento."

We had a difficulty almost at once with a *tenente* who inhabited the next room to ours (there were *contadini* in the back of the house who soon left and a group of engineers who lived on the other side of the courtyard). The *tenente* belonged to a medical section that had been moved farther back as Villa Zucco was supposed to be too exposed. He tried to seize our fourth room, saying he wanted it as his office. However, very soon he was severely rapped over the knuckles by the General and was turned out altogether. We were quite prepared to rough it, but that did not mean that we were not exceedingly thankful when it was all changed. General Capello, the General of our Army Corps, came in one day when we were at luncheon. I saw his eye wander to the food which was on the table, and he broke into his conversation to ask what orders we had about rations. When we told him that we were having the

LUXURY

same as the privates,[1] his fury was untold. He turned on one of his A.D.C.s asking who was answerable for our food; the answer was that they had been told by the English Lord that we should be quite content with anything we were given. We did not know enough Italian then to understand all the General said, but by the faces of his staff, we gathered that he was not pleased. Turning to us he said, " For the future send your orderly to my headquarters for your rations." After that he demanded to see our quarters and hearing the tale of the *tenente*, ordered an aide-de-camp to burst open all locked doors. This he did by a running kick, and lo, comfortable beds and mattresses, armchairs, tables, etc., even looking-glasses in a suite of rooms all occupied by one young man. The General ordered all his clothes and private property to be thrown out of the window immediately, and then left us, saying that he would send in orderlies to clean everything and arrange all the rooms as we wished, also that he would send in sheets and blankets, and that from that moment on we were to apply to him personally for anything we might require.

The yard at the back, inhabited by the engineers, was always filled with kicking and squealing mules which I promised myself much joy in painting; however, there proved to be very little time for that as our work began the very next day after our arrival.

[1] Two *quarti* of red wine, frozen meat with an occasional change to fresh mule or horse, beans, rice or coarse pasta, a rather nasty kind of chocolate or coffee, salt, and a sort of sour brown bread, which we liked very much at first, but soon got very tired of. Chestnuts, too, were issued, but they were quite disgusting, having been preserved in saltpetre.

12

FIRST IMPRESSIONS

December, 1915.

IN the first two days we did seventeen cases; the doctors, both English and Italian, were pleased, although we were rather tried by the English doctors of Villa Trento altering our wires when we were not looking—I suppose the English idea that women could not possibly know anything about electricity. Result, sparking and shorting in every direction, which took some time to put right.

The first night that there was a really big attack it sounded like a heavy sea beating against rocks and it burst open our shutters and windows, the sky being full of light like summer lightning. The windows looked towards the Austrian lines, about seven kilometres away, and the persistent flashing reflecting in one's room, and the incessant booming of the big guns, quite did away with all possibilities of sleep. I suppose I must have been snoozing, when I suddenly became aware that the noise of the big guns had changed to the quick rattle of rifles and machine-guns, to my unaccustomed ears suspiciously close. I lay and listened for some time, but did not like to get up, as, being new to the game, I thought it probably was always like that. At last I could bear it no longer, and getting up went into Nina's room. I found her firmly in bed, saying, " We shall have to get accustomed to this; it is perfectly

ITALIAN DOCTORS

natural, and will happen every night." We agreed that it was a little excessive, but as it undoubtedly was a most natural thing in the zone of war, we had better go to sleep and get accustomed to it as soon as possible. So I departed, and slept the sleep of the just till next morning, when our orderly came in with the news that there had been a big attack by the Austrians in the night, and that they had got through in one place, and had reached a little village not three kilometres from our house. They had been driven back to their original lines only at five that morning. So my getting out of bed had not been so very uncalled-for after all. I packed my bag with necessaries, and kept it under my bed for quite a long time after that, including sufficient for my partner, as she was proud, and refused to take any precautions for herself.

Extract from Letter, 24th December, 1915.

We like the Italians very much, and it is so satisfactory to be received with open arms of delight like this. We are much impressed by the niceness of the Italian doctors to their patients. Of course in the front-line hospitals there are no nurses, only orderlies, and the doctors do all the dressings themselves. They say it is so much more satisfactory than in a civilian hospital, I have heard more than one surgeon say that when he goes back to civilian life he shall do all his own dressings for the future.

The only radiographic automobile they had had at the front, an Italian one, ran for a month and then went home and none other has appeared since. The roads are terrific, you can never go faster than bottom speed with the engine boiling, in and out of vast holes, skidding towards deep ditches and in wet mud like a feather bed. They are crowded with soldiers tramping back from the trenches to rest, too slack to get out of the

FIRST IMPRESSIONS

way—but not looking ill or particularly tired—and mules with packs on their backs in forties and fifties each side of the narrow road, the mules in first-rate condition, as also the horses. Of course there are occasional sore shoulders, but nothing more than can be helped. The Italian soldier is very quiet with his beast, he never seems to want to pay him out like other nationalities. Several times I have seen mules kick or bite at a man and have expected to see him hit back at them in return. Not at all, they go quietly up, unfasten them, and put them in a different place, quite gently, and then with a pat leave them. We have ample opportunity of judging, as about forty are groomed in our backyard every day. They tell us that a great many of their horses are Spanish, but they look like well-bred English hunters . . . I think it is a pity to hog them when out in all weathers and doing all sorts of work, but certainly they look none the worse for it. Even with all this mud, you never see a sign of cracked heels or grease and hardly ever a lame horse.

I saw such a nice thing two days ago which I longed to stop and paint. Half a dozen mules were standing by a well, with big wooden tubs slung on each side of them, and a soldier, standing up on the edge of the well, silhouetted against the evening sky, was filling the wooden tubs with water from a big copper bucket which reflected all the colours of the sunset as it moved, and was a lovely sight.

12th January 1916.

Last night Nina and I went for a walk, just at sunset, and against the red and eau-de-nil sky were two aeroplanes fighting, with shells bursting all round them. Yellow, red and white puffs of smoke and the bluest of blue mountains below. You never saw such a com-

ALL GOING WELL

bination of colour, and in the half-light the flashes from their guns showed up brilliantly. We climbed up the mountain behind the house afterwards and could see quite plainly the front line with the shells bursting over the River Isonzo. We stayed up there until the sun had gone down, gazing at the ranges of snow mountains, scarlet with heavy purple and blue shadows. Green above the snow line, purple below, and the echo after echo of big gun after big gun, bumbling from one mountain-top to another was very impressive. We are so full of work that I haven't had a moment to paint, and I'm not sure I want to; I want to soak it all in first. Our rooms are very nice and now that we have worked through most of our difficulties, all is going well. We are sacking a third Englishman who had been sent to us by the British Red Cross, as he is incapable of obeying an order and is a liar to boot. The original two are excellent and very willing. The Italian orderly unfortunately hit Teresina, our maid, in the eye, so we had to get rid of him.

It is very interesting having what amounts to power of life and death over the men, if reported to Headquarters it needs but a small misdemeanour to bring prison, followed by punishment trenches. The punishment trenches are the most exposed and dangerous ones, so we deal with our men ourselves as much as we can.

The Italians have now given us both the rank of Majors in the Italian army and we have been attached to the 3rd Army, but at present do not change our quarters as we are serving eleven hospitals and expect to have more when the fighting begins.

We are rather harassed at this moment as the coils have got joggled up owing to the bad roads and are not working properly. Major Gabriel of the British Military Mission, who has been most helpful, is sending

FIRST IMPRESSIONS

a man from Milan to see to them, so we hope all will be well in a day or two. Meanwhile, the Austin has struck work, Hewitt, one of our drivers, having taken it down and being unable to put it together again. So we towed it into our neighbouring town, which, by the way, you none of you seem to realize is thirty kilometres away and takes a good two hours to get to, the roads being so bad.

20th January 1916.

The frontier is fearfully difficult, just honeycombed by holes from a metre to 100 metres deep, joined together into trenches. The Austrians have their big guns in these pits and one can bombard them for ever without doing much damage.

To-day I have been planning a picture of what we see on the roads round here. How appreciative the Italian mind is. It is only a scrabble on brown paper, but Teresina stood in silence before it and, with a big gulp, said, " Còm è terribile la guerra ! " so I suppose that the tiredness and dreariness of the poor mud plodders had somehow come into the sketch. Everything is drab and mud and grey green except those beautiful mountains.

The roads are one long procession of men, horses and guns, ammunition carts and mud, and mud, and mud, with occasional cattle carts with their teams of *bovi*, looking so clean and gentle among all the rest. There are three-span carts, with one in the shafts and two outrunners, and teams of six, eight and even ten horses or mules with generally very light loads, and every now and then a regiment too sleepy to get out of the way, leaving only the narrowest lane possible down the middle, for the motor to pass. Often at night the men are quite silly and are nearly run over.

FOG

28th January 1916.

If you had only heard the noise of the guns in the last few days, the house shaking from top to toe. We have got so accustomed to sleeping with our heads under the bedclothes that we only hear the very big Italian one which is close by and nearly cracks the window-panes every time it goes off. We were much interested in hearing about the attack the other night, after all the noise I told you about. The enemy seems to have tried to creep round and having been caught by the Italians was thoroughly smashed up . . . two battalions being completely wiped out. We are told that the Austrians are always advancing with white flags, and then, when the Italians stop firing, they suddenly attack; this time it did not succeed. The fog has been incessant, except for a bit of sun in the middle of the day, otherwise solid white fog. They say, never before have they had anything like it. Coming back from Udine the other evening we had rather a horrid experience. We were creeping along at about 5 m.p.h. with our handkerchiefs stretched over the headlights to diffuse the light, when we heard a car coming up behind us. It passed quite close, going much too fast for safety, evidently its occupants were feeling very cheerful, as they were singing at the tops of their voices. About half an hour later we came on to a bridge and were proceeding with infinite caution when we heard groans and cries from below. We stopped and groped our way down the bank only to find that the car which had passed us so cheerfully a short time before had hit the parapet of the bridge and had turned over, falling into one of the very deep ditches that border the road. We did our best to help, but there was only one of them left alive and he very badly injured. While we were debating what to do, as Nina and I were not capable of hauling the wounded man up the steep bank, the carabinieri arrived, much to our

FIRST IMPRESSIONS

relief. They at once sent one of their number off for an ambulance which soon appeared, and we left, there being no more we could do. Next day we were sent for to a neighbouring hospital and there was our friend of the night before. To our astonishment he was still quite cheerful and cracked jokes about his adventure, apparently not minding in the least having lost his boon companions in such a tragic way. No one can account for these fogs, they say they have never had them before and think they must be caused by the incessant gunfire.

It is still bitterly cold and the Italians have given us each officer's fur coats of light blue cloth, lovely and warm, lined with white sheepskin. They have white fox collars, or perhaps they are white cat, anyway, a great joy as the collars turn up well over one's ears. I have chilblains on every finger, and most of my toes, and dabbling with the radiographic plates in water doesn't improve them. We had rather a nasty jar about some of our plates. They had been left wrapped in cotton-wool in their boxes in a cupboard two rooms away from where we test our plant every morning, and the X-rays had actually penetrated the two thick stone walls and had photographed cotton-wool fluff and the edges of their boxes on to them! . . . this will teach us not to run risks with them again and is an example of the terrifying power of the rays.

13

METHOD OF WORKING

January, 1916.

I THINK now is the moment to tell you how we work. We have rigged up a dark room in our Villa Zucco, where Nina and I stand developing plates until two and three in the morning, so sleepy that we rock against each other, and it is only the bump that wakes us up; plates have to be developed at once, as the surgeons do their operations in the early morning and need the plates to guide them. We have a bicycle orderly whose job it is to take the developed plates round to the various field hospitals which we visited during the day. The work is getting so heavy that we have asked for a motor-cyclist to get round quicker, and the General has promised us one for next week.

We usually have breakfast at seven o'clock, then clean and test the apparatus downstairs. The men pack it into the car and we start off. Nina and I in front with the driver, and a spare man at the back to help unpack and to arrange the heavy things. I will give you one day as an example. A telegram has come in the night: "Will you come, urgent, Castello di Dobra, fifteen wounded."

We climb into the big car, Hewitt is driving, Whitehead behind. Icy cold, a bitter wind, which gets more and more bitter as we climb the mountains, so that our ears feel as if they were going to drop off, and even

METHOD OF WORKING

our beautiful sheep-skin coats with their high white fur collars feel as if they were made of thin muslin. It takes a good hour and a half to reach the *castello*. The mountains are between us and the front lines, so except for the occasional whine of a shell in the far distance followed by a muffled explosion we have no excitements. There is always the danger of tipping over the edge of the road, but so far Hewitt has always driven well, and Whitehead, too, is very careful. The entrance to the castle is very fine, a great heavy gateway with rocks either side and huge clumsy doors covered with iron bosses. The castle itself is most depressing and dingy inside. We are greeted in the courtyard by three or four surgeons, all very much pleased to see us and our apparatus. We are first given hot coffee or *zabaione* (a raw egg beaten up either in Marsala or coffee), and are then ushered up stone stair after stone stair till we get to the top of the huge square tower. On every turn of the stair there is a room, generally with the door just ajar, and we can see amused and anxious faces peering out to see us pass.

By this time Whitehead and some of the hospital orderlies have carried up the coil, interrupter, switchboard, table, Pillon tube and the heavy lead holder for the tube, followed by the flex or electric wires to connect them all one to the other. Then, down go Whitehead and another man to toil up again with the big heavy cable to connect the apparatus to the dynamo of the car. The end of this they throw out of the window for Hewitt to catch and attach to the engine. Everything is now in position and there are at least twenty interested spectators. Nina and I go steadily over each connection, testing carefully; then comes the anxious moment, the unpacking of the precious lamp, or tube as it is called, out of its box (we always take three tubes in case anything should happen to one or the other). Never once

LOCALIZATION

have we had one broken yet in transit, but occasionally, after long examinations, a tube will get too "hard" to use and then we have to give it a rest and use another one. (A too hard tube gives a grey thin shadow, a too soft one gives a blurry outline; you have therefore to adjust the tube by running the current through until it gives the required result. We have found a dodge for softening them, very risky at first, as you may ruin your tube in doing it, but it is worth risking for a bad case, and we have found the way now to do it safely and very successfully by suddenly and violently reversing the current which softens the hardest tube.)

The tube is then placed in its lead-covered holder. The lead, as you know, is supposed to protect the operator and onlookers from the dangerous rays emanating from the tube. There is a small opening in the holder which allows the rays to pass to the sensitive plate or to pass to the Barium screen—a glass plate, prepared with Barium salts, and framed in wood—which one uses to look through when making examinations, when there is no time to take plates. In war-time it is impossible to take a radiograph of each case, and we search through the Barium screen for the bullet or piece of shell. Once found, a cross is marked on the man's skin; he is turned on to his side, the bullet again found and another cross made. Where the right angle of these two crosses meet, there will be found the bullet. It is a rough and ready way of doing it, but has always so far proved successful. When we have a great many to do I draw on the glass of the screen with a fountain-pen and copy it on to a piece of paper afterwards, for the surgeon to work from. My training in anatomy at Art schools has proved invaluable.

However, in this case at the Castle of Dobra we have plenty of time. Whitehead has hung up curtains and blankets over all the openings and windows, so the

METHOD OF WORKING

room is in absolute darkness. One of us sits down at the switch-board and the other proceeds to centre the tube. This is a complicated business which has to be checked over and over again to make sure that it is absolutely correct. If there is the slightest inaccuracy the shadow of the foreign body will be cast at an angle instead of direct, the radiographer will mark the bullet in the wrong place, and the unfortunate patient will be operated on where no bullet exists. So, on this centring depends the life of the patient; no *à peu près* will do. Every time it must be exact to a millimetre. It is done by a little travelling gallows above the stretcher, with a plumb-line depending from it. This is fixed to the tube holder which runs on rails below the stretcher. (We always carry two spare stretchers for the patients . . . so that when one is in use the other is fetching the next patient.) The light from the tube is turned on, a sickly green penetrating light, the Barium screen is laid on the stretcher and a box with crossed wires and a piece of lead hanging by a thread from the centre of the cross is deposited on the screen and over the tube or lamp. The shadow cast by this piece of lead must be exactly in the middle of the box where the two wires cross; the box is removed and all is now ready for the patient, who is carried in on the spare stretcher. What the feelings of the ignorant and unhappy patient must be on being carried into a pitch-dark room full of people whom he can only hear and not see can only be imagined, and we used to try and reassure them and make them understand that no painful operation was going to be performed on them; when I tell you that an officer who had been given the highest medal for gallantry the day before started screaming before he was even touched, you can imagine what they feel like. It was only when I called him a bambino (baby), much to the horror of the bystanders, that I could get him to leave off shouting.

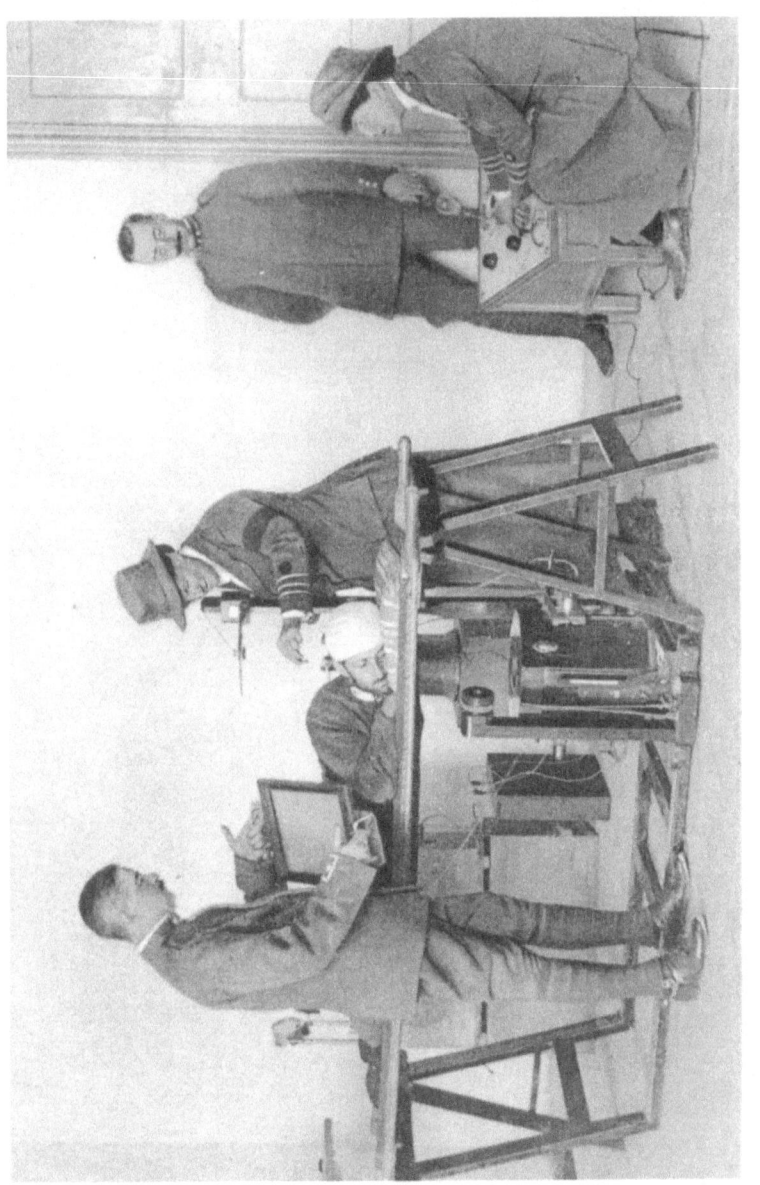

Mrs. Hollings and the author at work in hospital on the Italian Front

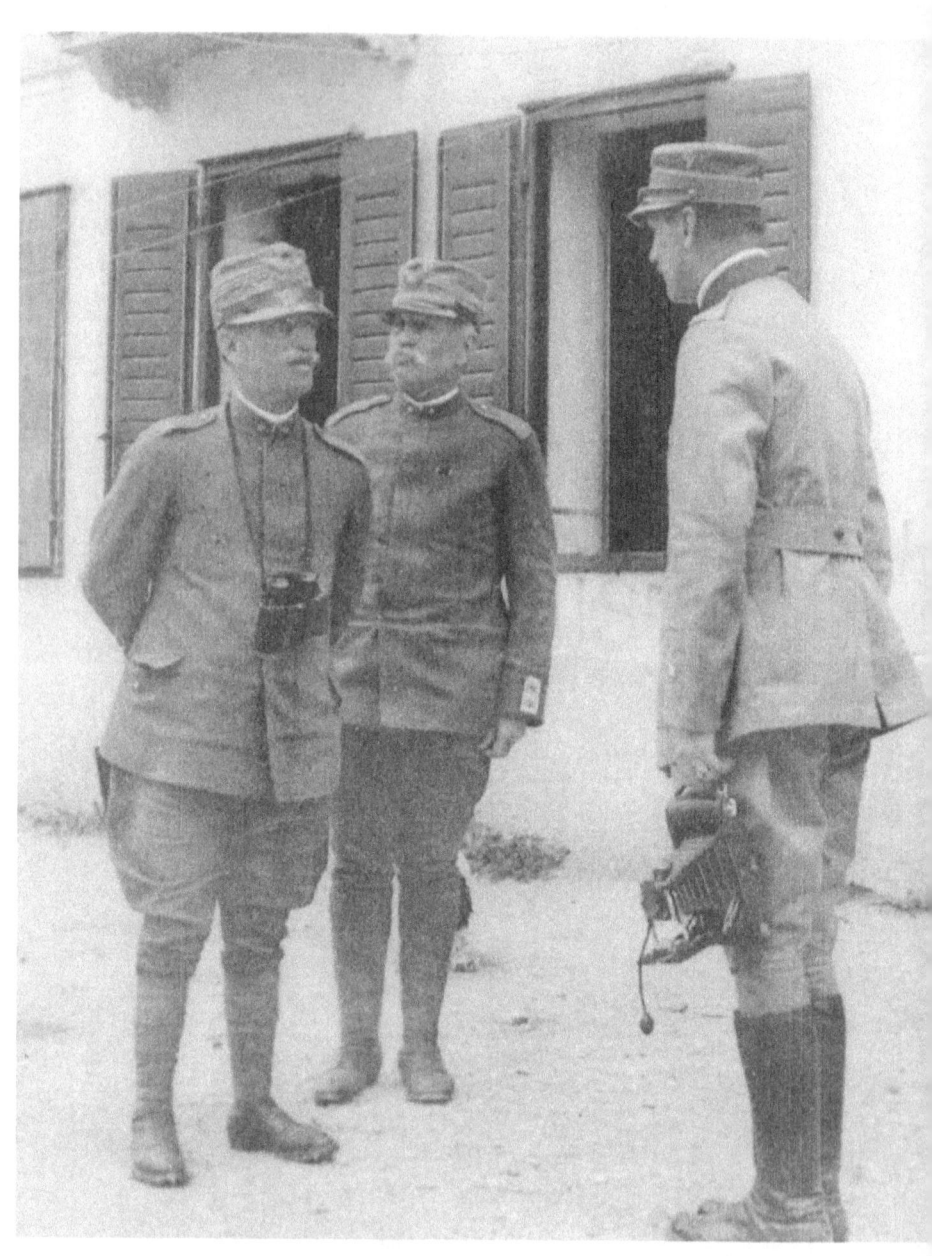

H.M. THE KING OF ITALY

X-RAY AS A PAIN-KILLER

Our fear was that he would put the wind up all the other men who were waiting to be radiographed, as they would imagine that something terrible was being done to their hero.

The foreign body once located the plumb-line from the gallows is dropped over it to mark the place, a pencil mark is made on the skin and the operation is over, the patient carried away, much relieved that nothing painful has happened to him, and the next man is brought in.

The next case we are asked to take a plate. The bullet is found by the screen and centred, as before. The plate is placed immediately under the plumb-line, sensitive side downwards, sandbags are pushed in to keep it level and to keep the patient's limb immovable, and he is told to hold his breath while the seconds are counted out. The switch is clicked over, seconds are counted aloud to take the patient's attention, click, it is finished, and the next man brought in. A curious thing we notice, if a man is restless or flinging himself about in unconsciousness, the very fact of turning on the tube will soothe him and after a second or two he will lie quiet, although up till then it may have taken several men holding him to keep him on the stretcher at all. Another interesting point, when my back is bad,[1] I have only to lie on the stretcher and get someone to turn on the tube and the pain goes off almost at once. A good deal still remains to be discovered about the powers of the X-ray and it will be found that the ray will be very useful as a pain-killer. Another thing that we notice is that a fair-skinned person takes much longer to radiograph than a dark skin, and we always have to allow a few seconds longer exposure for a fair-skinned man or woman.

[1] *Editor's note.*—H. G. had injured her back some years before out hunting.

METHOD OF WORKING

What a long letter! But you always say you want more details. To continue with the day at Dobra; we finish with excellent coffee and hurry off to get the plates home to be developed and dried ready to send off as soon as possible, some that same evening, the rest for the next morning. On arriving home we usually find that there has been an urgent call for us fifteen or twenty kilometres in the opposite direction, and off we have to go again after a hasty scrap of food, getting home this time probably about 9 p.m., when we have to start developing again, leaving the plates to dry in spirit for our bicyclist to take long before we are awake in the morning, and he greets us at breakfast-time with signed receipts from each place where he has delivered them. It is a great thing having Italians to do all these jobs with breakable material, as they are so gentle in their handling of them. We are still hoping that the Red Cross will soon send us out a developing assistant as we really need one. We have given up doing it in the car unless it is absolutely necessary, as it is too close quarters and is not really light-proof; also it will be too stuffy when the weather gets hot.

14

ADVENTURE WITH CARABINIERI

February, 1916.

AS soon as we found that some of our plates had been spoilt, we decided that one of us must go to Milan to see what Cappelli could provide. We were determined that we would be ready for a rush of work when it came, as it inevitably would come, and that fairly soon. So I settled to go in our Berliet touring-car. My idea was to go through as quickly as possible, and bring back with me in the car fresh plates, developing materials, etc. I had many adventures on that mile-long journey across Italy, mostly due to the fact that I had no proper permit with me to get petrol. It was not my fault, as the Colonel of the Headquarters Staff had assured me that his signature was sufficient to procure me petrol in any army; here, however, I learnt a lesson—that no permit belonging to one army is of the slightest use in any other, whatever the person who signed it may tell you. We got there all right, and started back as quickly as might be. I slept in Brescia, and started for Cormons at seven in the morning. We made good travelling until dark, when it became necessary to fill up the petrol tank. I had had the brilliant idea of trying a short cut home. I have now learnt that short cuts are not advisable in the zone of war.

Our first adventure happened when we tried to get the petrol. It was dark and pouring with rain, and as

ADVENTURE WITH CARABINIERI

we drove into a little town, Whitehead, my Red Cross chauffeur, a first-rate man, got down to ask the way to the military petrol-depot. Not being able to make himself understood, he returned to ask me to explain. By this time a carabiniere appeared, and on seeing our lights rushed up and ordered us to put them out immediately. I agreed politely, and gave the order to Whitehead to put out the big ones, but to leave the little ones. On my speaking English the carabiniere became convinced that we were spies. He ordered us, in a very abrupt manner, to put out even the little oil lamps, which was manifestly ridiculous, as everyone else in the street was using them. He said we were to go immediately with him to the police quarters. Whitehead turned to me and said that if the man insisted on his turning out the small lamps too, he should assuredly drive into the ditch in the darkness. The dark was solid, and you couldn't see your hand in front of your face. The carabiniere by this time was rabid with us for speaking English, and again ordered us to come with him to the headquarters of the carabinieri; this I promised to do directly I had finished filling up my tank, the military depot being two doors off. He was furious, saying he forbade it, and that I must immediately give him the number of the car. This I had completely forgotten, and as the car was thick in mud, I told him to look for himself, which enraged him still further. I, too, by this time, was getting angry, and go back I would not until the car was filled up. So I told Whitehead to drive on to the depot. Here the man in charge was charming, and had just finished filling us up when his corporal came out and whispered something in his ear. The first man, a sergeant I think, then advanced in a very shy manner and said, " I don't know how to tell you, Signora, but an order has just come through on the telephone from the head of the carabinieri to say that you are to be

AN AWKWARD MOMENT

detained here until an officer arrives. I am ashamed to incommode a lady, but orders are orders, and I daren't disobey—if you would like to come into my office I should be delighted." I chose to remain in the car, as warmer and more comfortable, and wondered if I should ever get home that night. Now that I know the game better, I should be much more worried if such a thing were to happen again, but I was new to the country then, and had not realized the many agitating things that may happen to the most respectable people in a scrap with the powerful carabinieri! So I sat calmly in the car and read a book secure in the thought of the fat case in my pocket containing innumerable permits.

After about ten minutes had passed, I heard the bell of an approaching bicycle. I did not move, and presently a large face was thrust in at the window and a gruff voice said, " The orders are that you are to accompany me at once to the headquarters of the carabinieri." I answered with much dignity, " Am I to understand that this is an arrest ? " This time he spoke more civilly, " Si, Signora." I informed him that I was an officer, and that if they wished to arrest me they must send an officer to do so. I then composed myself to read again and paid no further attention to the man, who was evidently much worried as to what to do, and retired to consult the sergeant of the depot as to the next procedure. I, meanwhile, was half scared and half amused at my own swagger, and much relieved when I heard the carabiniere depart. Then ensued another long wait, cheered by the encouraging remarks of my friend the depot sergeant, who looked at me with undisguised admiration, and murmured at intervals, " Che coraggio ! " He also murmured that English people were known to have very bad tempers, and that it was very unsafe to excite them too much. I waited another ten minutes, and was beginning to think I had had

ADVENTURE WITH CARABINIERI

enough waiting about, when a cheerful face showed itself at the window and saluted, saying, " Signora, I regret my captain cannot come himself, but if you will accept my escort we shall soon be at headquarters, and this tiresome matter will then be settled. I regret that I am only a *brigadiere*, but it cannot be helped." I at once asked him to get in, and told Whitehead to go where the *brigadiere* told him. It was not far, but he made himself most agreeable, and said I must not judge the man too hardly who had originally made all the trouble, that he was young and only a *contadino*, and new to the work, etc., and that the carabinieri are not what they were in peace-time, when they were all picked men—that they had to take anybody they could get nowadays, etc.

Cheered by my conversation with the nice *brigadiere*, on our arrival at the headquarters I walked in, feeling all would be well, and that I should in a minute or two be free to continue my journey.

Not at all—I found myself in a large room fitted up as an office. In front of me sat an officer of carabinieri surrounded by a half circle of other officers standing. It looked exactly like a court-martial, and I felt I was losing what little Italian I had, as well as my head! The officer at the table looked up as I came in, but did not move from his seat. I had some vague idea that it was better for me to attack first, so I began a complaint of his subordinate's manners. Suddenly, in the middle of one of my own sentences, I became aware I was being left to stand while he was comfortably sitting. I stopped in the middle of a word, and said very slowly, looking hard at him, "I do not think, Signor Capitano, that you have understood that I am a Dama della Croce rossa Inglese." There was a rustle of movement among the other officers present, and the bad-mannered (or absent-minded?) one slowly got to his feet, with a very red face, and bowed. Quickly changing my tone to a friendly one, I advanced on him with all my papers, and before he could ask for them, spread the whole lot on his table, saying, "No doubt you would like to see my papers—here they are; and while you study them I will look at your map, as I am quite lost, and do not in the least know where I am"— and I walked straight past him to a big map which was hanging on the wall behind his table. The cheek of this took his breath away, and he only gasped in answer. Looking at the map enabled me to recover my somewhat rattled wits, and after a short glance at my papers he rolled them up and came to help me to find my road on the map. The tense moment was over, but as he accompanied me to the car, I felt that I had been within an ace of spending my night in a cell. I was afterwards told that I had been quite right to refuse to be arrested by a private soldier, and that it probably saved me a long wait and many disagreeables, as the officer, who was young and inexperienced, might have made things very unpleasant if I had not been so cocksure.

Our adventures were not over for that day, because hardly had we left the town when our chain broke. By this time the rain had stopped, and Whitehead spent a weary three-quarters of an hour sitting in the middle of the road mending it, with me holding one of the lamps for him. By this time it was about nine o'clock, no stars and no moon, and we had had no food since twelve o'clock. Luckily I had some meat lozenges in my pocket, which had been there many months. The usual excellent taste of glue and ink was in no way impaired by their age, and we feasted on them gratefully. I had a map, but it was so dark, and all the inhabitants of the villages having gone to bed, whilst all the sentries were "strangers in those parts," that we had the greatest trouble in locating the roads we

ADVENTURE WITH CARABINIERI

were on. Then, about midnight, our chain went again—this time it meant a much longer stop, as Whitehead, in despair, found that two links had gone. Down we sat in the mud and tried to make links out of bits of wire, etc. Nothing held, and at last we stood up and sadly agreed that we had better try and make ourselves comfortable in the car till daylight came, when suddenly I had the brilliant idea of sending him back with a lamp to the place where the chain broke. He stayed away a good quarter of an hour, and I was getting sleepier and sleepier, when he appeared cheerfully with both links, which he proceeded to fix on. He really was a good man, for he never got cross or disheartened, and was always willing to try anything one suggested when in a difficulty.

The chain mended, we were continuing our road, carefully feeling our way with only the little lamps (the ditches were very big and deep in that part of the country), when suddenly we were challenged by a sentry. We stopped, and he asked for our papers; we showed them, he saluted, saying they were quite in order, but we could not pass without the password for the night. He added that he was exceedingly sorry, but his orders were final; no one could pass over the bridge after nine o'clock without the password. This was the first we had heard of a bridge, and on peering out we discovered that we were standing on a bridge over a broad river, with no parapet whatever. It was lucky we had been going so carefully. We asked the sentry's advice as to how to obtain the password, and he answered that only one person could give it to us, the General of the Army Corps, who on our enquiry proved to be quartered about six miles back along the road by which we had just come. We backed carefully off the bridge and started on our weary way back to the General's quarters.

WITHOUT THE PASSWORD

Arrived at the village, we asked the sentry at the entrance for the whereabouts of the General; he directed us to a house close to the gate. It didn't look at all like a General's quarters, but I hopefully tried a soldier who was standing at the door. His answer was that this was the Mess, and the General had left a good hour before. He did not know where he had gone to. Luckily, at this moment, I spied two officers going along on the other side of the street, with their collars turned up, evidently hurrying to get into the warmth of their own billets.

We hastily pursued them, and I begged them to tell me how to get the password to get over the bridge. The same answer, "You must go to the General—he is the only person who can give it to you, and he went to bed an hour ago." At my doleful countenance, the man who was talking burst out laughing, and asked what had happened, and why I was driving about at that time of night. I told him my sad tale, and explained that we had a lot of work to do and I was most anxious to get back to Cormons that night.

The two were at once most sympathetic, and the senior one, a major, suggested getting into the car and taking me himself to where the General lived; but he warned me that if the General had indeed gone to bed, it would be more than our lives were worth to wake him up. I gathered he was not easy, and I did not find him so.

He hadn't gone to bed, and presently appeared at the door of the motor, very testy, and wanting to know who I was and what I was doing, and what reason I had to suppose that he had any intention of providing me with any password whatever. He also asked what business I had to rout him out at that time of night, and asked if I were aware that it was close on 1 a.m. He kept on repeating "Ma chi sia" till my head whirled.

ADVENTURE WITH CARABINIERI

I answered humbly that if he would let me come in where there was a light, I could show him all my papers, telling him at the same time that I had at least fourteen different ones to prove my identity, and that I understood that he was my only hope, so I threw myself on his mercy. I caught a sign of softening in his eye, and got out of the car on the far side from where he was standing, blocking the way, and most unwillingly he led the way into the house. The kind major, who had waited on the far side of the street until he saw what luck I had, fled when he saw me go in, and not a moment too soon, as the General turned round on reaching the door to say, "Where is that pestilential major who showed you where I lived?" and turning to me, added, "Do you know his name?" I assured him I hadn't any idea as to who he was or where he had gone, and the General, grumbling to himself, followed me into a little room on the ground floor, where there was a fire, and some coffee on the table. I laid my papers on the table, and went to the fire to try and get warm, while he busied himself with them. I suppose he saw me looking longingly at the coffee, as he suddenly asked, still in a very grumpy voice, when I had last had anything to eat. I told him, not since midday, as we were hurrying to try and get back to Cormons that night, but that owing to breakdowns with the car I was sadly convinced that we should not manage it. He glanced at the clock, and said dryly, "No, I shouldn't think you would," and continued reading my papers, but looked up again in a few minutes to say I might take some coffee if I liked. I should think it was half an hour before he seemed to have finished, and then he began again, as if I hadn't told him already: "What do you want me to do for you?"

I repeated patiently, "May I, please, have the password to cross the bridge?" He at once said, quite

HOME AT LAST

simply and plainly, "No." I got wearily on to my feet, and asked him if there was an hotel in the village. He said there was one, but it was full of his officers, and there was no other possible house. So I advanced towards the door and said good night, I was sorry I had disturbed him for nothing. He looked up and asked me what I meant to do, and I said, "Sleep in the car."

I think his conscience smote him, as he suddenly became quite friendly and said, "I won't give you the password, because it will only pass you into another army, and you would have to rout up another general to get out of it again, and you might not be so successful in finding him up as you have been in finding me; so I will show you a short cut to Udine, and from there you ought to be able to find your way, as you will then be in your own army."

He then proceeded to give the most complicated directions of "Third turn to the left, first turn to the right, then turn right again, and it doesn't look like a road," etc.

I stopped him there and said, "Nothing looks like a road in this darkness. Please let me see a map."

He thereupon brought out a map, and all became clear—his excuse for not having done it before being that he thought women could not read maps!

We then parted, and Whitehead and I drove on into the night to try our luck at more short cuts. We eventually found our way, but not without great difficulty, as, added to the darkness, there was now impenetrable fog. We crawled home, arriving at 3 a.m., and very grateful to find some soup still simmering on the stove for us.

15

EARTHQUAKES, ETC.

MEANWHILE my family at home were working hard to collect money to keep our apparatus going and to buy more plant. We needed another complete plant as the Italians asked us to have one always ready in our house in Cormons for the hospitals to send patients to whenever they felt inclined. Lord Monson was very keen that we should have out more helpers as the work promised to become too heavy for only two operators. We were getting so superior by now that Nina and I could pull the whole machine to pieces and put it together again with perfect ease. We had had time to re-make entirely the small medical supply stores set which was not strong enough to take out in the cars and would not stand any jolting whatever, but we wanted duplicate parts for everything so as to be prepared for all emergencies. The head doctor at Cormons said to us, " I think that you will understand how useful you are, when I tell you that until you came, this army had not had any radiography obtainable since the War began; you see how much work you are having now, even though there is practically no fighting at present; but when the advance begins, you will cry, ' Basta, basta.' " (Enough, enough.) The Italians were so understanding, they used to turn us into a room by ourselves and say, " When you are

"NINA'S BRAIN WORKS IN AN EMERGENCY"

ready, let us know and we will bring the patients in; on no account hurry, we have plenty of time," so we had perfect peace to put the whole thing together and test wires, tube, etc., before the crowd came in. And crowd it generally was, surgeons, patients, orderlies and occasionally a general or so with his staff who came in to look on. One despairing letter says, " Yesterday for the first time our whole plant gave out. We had been sent for to find a bullet lodged in a man's spine. When we reached the dressing station, nothing doubting, we put the machine together, switched on and the only current we could get was reversing madly, so we quickly changed the poles; it reversed worse than ever. We looked at every connection, tried every wire, racked our brains to think what could be wrong. Now instead of reversing, it was short-circuiting in every direction with no current going through the tube at all, but plenty everywhere else. We tried every imaginable combination for two hours and more, and finally had to give it up and go home. Directly we got back Nina insisted on forcing open the coil, and lo the insulating wax which covered it was cracked in several places, which of course enabled the damp to get in, and made the wires short-circuit. She had the brilliant idea to go to the priests of the village church and buy two huge altar candles, boil them down and pour the wax into the coil and all over the surface of it. We tried the set and thanked the Almighty that all was well and it was working perfectly again.

Food was very important to us, as to all who were out in the War. One hospital who always gave us excellent coffee when we worked for them sent us a present of two delicious iced puddings made of chocolate and mixed fruits, and having finished them both at a sitting we talked of nothing else for many days. The hospital had a very celebrated chef from Bologna and

EARTHQUAKES, ETC.

they sent him over to teach our orderly how to make coffee properly. A great comfort.

We have two nice Italian friends who are very helpful, one the General's A.D.C., Hass by name, and one Dr. Knapp, the head staff doctor. I noticed a good many German names among the French when we were working there, but here they are far more numerous and people are quite un-noticing of them and take them as a matter of course.

2nd March, 1916.

Yesterday we went down to Cervignano to have our permits renewed and drove down behind a great part of the lines, all magnificently entrenched with wood floors to stand on. The water runs underneath and they are always in the dry. They are mostly lined with cement and some of them are really very decorative. I saw one dugout with a doorway of cement surmounted by a grenade and Greek pilasters on each side with green grass overhead, most lovely. The drive was all along the Carso front and was very interesting, for we were passing troops of all kinds on the road, barbed-wire entanglements, observation balloons and in the distance we could see flat plains and blue mountains with puffs of brown smoke, where shells were bursting, dotted all over them.

Yesterday I climbed very high so as to paint snow mountains, accompanied by Nina and Rana, a small dog who had given herself to me, and whom I named Rana (meaning Frog) because her eyes stick out. When we got there we were pursued by carabinieri who were right at the bottom of a ravine and ran to the top as fast as they could to intercept us. We sat on a crag and prayed of them in our best Italian not to hurry or they would burst, and they abased themselves when they saw our permits to paint wherever we liked.

THE SOLDIERS IN OUR YARD

Meanwhile, the snow mountains had disappeared in cloud, so I had to paint what I could see of Gorizia, which is still in the hands of the enemy of course, result, historic, but of no artistic merit whatever. What dull letters I do write, and we are having such a wonderful time, but there is so much that I may not tell you. Every day something interesting happens. Great excavations are taking place in the road outside the villa, as we made a complaint that it was always flooded when other roads were dry; also we asked for the tank in the garden and the ditch to be cleaned out before the mosquitoes arrive. We thought we should be given two men, instead of which they have turned on thirty or forty soldiers to clean all the ditches, etc., round here, they have sent four extra men to tidy up the garden and make it habitable, and four men *muratori* have come in to whitewash out the rooms which were dirty. The engineers are making such a fiendish noise outside that I can't pay attention to what I write. They scream and yell for an hour at 6.30 a.m. and another hour at midday, and we cannot make out what it is all about. They are quartered in our backyard and are now singing part-songs with some of them doing an imitation guitar accompaniment. Nina has just spread cigarettes among them, so the noise is redoubled.

Our house, being under the hill, frequently has shells over it, but they all pitch a long way to the far side and give us infinite excitement. The long-drawn whine is a high-explosive, but shrapnel sounds whump-hauch-ch-ch (pronounced German), then explosions far off. The other day we trotted down our road to watch them burst and were much thrilled at seeing a pair-horse shay coming full gallop down the road, when off came a wheel and it capsized. The occupants picked themselves up and ran like hares for shelter, leaving the

EARTHQUAKES, ETC.

unfortunate driver alone to cope with his terrified horses and collect his wheel which had gone into the ditch; then another pair of bolting horses, this time without a driver, came tearing down the road and banged into the first team, all getting thoroughly mixed up, so, as no one else went, Nina and I ran to help, followed eventually by a sergeant. By that time the shells had stopped, so we disentangled the horses and I took them, two by two, back to shelter while Nina and the sergeant stayed to help the man put his wheel on again. We went later on to see the holes and found an officer and two men very gingerly extricating an unexploded shell from under the railway line with their hands. We did not stay and look on.

The Austrians were determined to get the station, and shelled first the station of Cormons and then the little siding of Povia, which was at the end of our road. (They were firing fan-shape, which is always disagreeable if you are included in the fan.) The first few shells brought streams of peasants and townspeople carrying babies, and dragging small children by any portion of their persons or clothes that first came handy. They came running under our windows wailing and crying, all making for the dug-outs that were in the hill about half a kilometre behind our house. After them, at the bursting of more shells, came oxen lumbering along, goaded into a gallop by their terrified masters, who could not get them along fast enough. We became accustomed to all this, as they (the Austrians) took to sending a few shells every morning at about nine o'clock and we soon took very little interest in them.

It was marvellous how very little damage they did. One morning they sent seventy-three high-explosive shells into and all around the station, and the sum total of the damage was one girl killed and one mule.

The people at Cormons don't care a damn who wins.

VIOLETS

They are all either Italians married to Austrians or semi-Austrians—Teresina, when I asked her what she would do if the Austrians came, said cheerfully, "Oh, I shall be Austrian then, and if the Italians remain I shall be Italian. What does it matter, they are both a very kind people." Mietzi, our Austrian cook, says she has never had an unkind word from the Italians, and added: "Die Oesterreicher haben ein nicht so gutes Herz wie die Italiener im Krieg." ("The Austrians do not have such a good heart in war as the Italians.") Actually the Italians are paying rent to the Austrian owners for the Austrian villas that they are using as billets even though, as in our case, the owner is in the Austrian army and fighting against them.

We have had some very interesting days, as we have been taken to a lot of new places by the General's A.D.C. We went to Gradisca amongst others; I'm sending by the bag a book of chants I found in a poor blown-up church, early sixteenth century; the whole place was in ruins with all the things lying soaking in wet mud.

The same day that we found the book of chants, such a nice thing happened to us, one of the things which make us love the Italians. We had been asked to interview a certain colonel who was anxious to know if we could bring out X-ray apparatus to a dressing station which was rather difficult to get up to. We left our car outside his dug-out and were gone about an hour, having walked to the top of the hill. When we got back we found that the car had been filled with violets, so many that Nina and I could hardly get in; and behind some bushes were hiding a quantity of soldiers, who had rushed off to pick them when we arrived and were hiding to see if we were pleased. You can imagine how touched we were by their kind idea, and the Colonel explained that they hadn't seen any women for more than a year, hence their delight.

EARTHQUAKES, ETC.

Yesterday we had to do a most interesting head of an officer aged about twenty—they had trepanned him the night before directly he came in from the trenches and thought by his symptoms that they had left a splinter of bone, pressing somewhere. We did a radiograph profile and found a *proiettile* (projectile) in the centre of his head. The doctors wouldn't believe it and asked us if we were sure it was not a flaw in the plate. We swore that we were dog sure, and offered to do another, full face, to prove it. This we did, and thank the Lord there it was; we had staked our professional reputation and succeeded, so they were much impressed.

This morning there was an earthquake at 4.30 a.m., most unpleasant I thought. First my bed shook and then it swayed to and fro and tipped up and the shutters burst open. I disliked it much and so did Nina. A huge brass dish which was in her room standing on the mantelpiece had been hurled into the middle of the room. We hurriedly threw on some clothes and ran down to find all quiet and no one stirring, although the whole place is full of soldiers, so we went forlornly back to bed again feeling we had done the wrong thing. To-day, although everyone apparently had felt it, they seem to think nothing of it. We are told that when the house sways to and fro there is no danger, but when it starts to heave up and down, run for your life. They say they hardly ever have bad earthquakes here, so let us hope we shan't have another, as I don't like it. A man who came here to-day said he was in the Catania earthquake and heard the " Earth speak." It was the most terrifying thing he said, like a groan which got louder and louder till you felt it was all round you, and over, and under, and coming on top of you. We were told also about two boys who were sitting out in the garden with their tutor doing lessons

TWO CURES

at a table. Suddenly, without any warning, the ground opened at their feet. The table, the tutor and one of the boys vanished into the crack, which closed again at once, leaving one small boy alone. We saw that boy later on, a man of about thirty and, on our asking why he looked so depressed and miserable, we were told this story, and told that he had never recovered his nerve or his spirits.

We see a great deal of company. . . . Lots of doctors and also Headquarters people who trail in and take a meal often when passing; occasionally, too, some of the Villa Trento drivers or the new 3rd English Ambulance Section who are doing very well. The Italians are delighted with them and say they are untiring, fetching wounded day and night.

16th March, 1916.

It is wonderful that you have already collected £650 for us. Here are two examples taken at random from the hundreds of cases that we have been doing.

Only two days ago we were ushered in to see a man who was considered hopelessly and incurably insane; we found the piece of shell pressing on his brain. He has been operated on and now can move his arm and is learning all over again how to talk and how to walk. And a man was blind, and the other day we found the bit of shell and it was removed and now he can see. You know, all your hard work collecting money has been well worth while, has it not?

We are very worn out this evening: we have been to Chiopris, which is about eight or nine miles off and a very bumpy road. Had to go in the Austin because the Berliet was being painted. The doctor there is most tiring to cope with. He doesn't understand radiography and insists on the miserable patient being put into the most impossible positions. We were there until seven-thirty last night and he made us do three plates of a man whose thigh-bone and hip joint (!) had been removed, leaving the knee and all below intact. He insisted on our trying to photograph him sideways; of course nothing came out, as we said it wouldn't and only caused agony to the unfortunate man. Then to-day we were sent for to go there, and again he insisted on trying to screen the man's hip sideways. Knowing our apparatus wasn't strong enough for such a depth we got furious and refused to do it, saying it was giving unnecessary pain. At last he gave in and then he wanted to do his own silly localization instead of ours. After endless argument he had to give in on that point also and he let us do our own radiograph and the Mackenzie Davidson localization. We had started at 9 a.m. and got back to luncheon at 5 p.m. On arrival at the house we found another call to a hospital twelve kilometres in the opposite direction to do a man's back. After running the tube for some time to try and get it into order and failing, we had, to our despair, to send an orderly to say we could not go until next day. (This shows you how much we need more tubes.) Luckily we already know that back and know that it isn't very urgent, but it is hateful to have to refuse a call through want of sufficient tubes.

Yesterday the head of our *sanità* arrived and said, " Why do you go to Chiopris and Romans, etc." So we said, " Because we are sent for." He said, " But don't you realize it is not your Army." In a chorus we replied, " No matter, we go where we are wanted." His answer was a grunt—and he said no more. We have since been told that there is much jealousy about the possession of us.

Yesterday General Delmé Radcliffe came with Captain Baird; he has always been most kind and helpful. An English chauffeur who had been lent to us had been

AN ATTRACTIVE RUIN

insubordinate, and General Radcliffe rubbed his nose in the mud, so we are very grateful, and he has promised to deal with any more domestic troubles of the sort which may occur with Englishmen; he is very stern about discipline, which is very important so near the Front.

We came on such an attractive ruin yesterday on our way back from Vipulzano, where we had been to do heads. From a distance the house looked sound but when we got there we found a high explosive had gone through it from roof to ground floor. No glass, no doors and the inside all one mass of rubbish and *scheggie* (splinters) of bombs, with wonderful violets growing everywhere. We got armfuls of " Princess of Wales " with very long stalks, and wild dog-tooth violets with their spotted leaves clustered amongst trenches and barbed wire. While we were picking violets we saw a big bomb explode on the bridge below and all the gun-teams and convoys galloping for shelter. We ourselves were perfectly safe, for the Austrians, having blown the place to Kingdom Come a long time ago, no longer bother about it.

16

VIPULZANO

WE had many amusing episodes to cheer us up; one of them when we were crossing the River Natizone; we missed the causeway and the Berliet had to be hauled out by six Artillery horses. Whitehead, who was driving, funked at the last moment when I think a rush might have got us through, but he hesitated and we sank in the shingle well above our axles. We could see some guns crossing farther up the river; at our frantic signals they unlimbered and came down to help us; the horses were hitched on to the front of the car, I took the wheel and then the whole team pulled us out: it was so amusing steering with six horses galloping ahead. Then several times we fell into the deep ditches which bordered the roads, as it was next to impossible on very wet days to see where the road ended and the ditch began. One day we had been ordered to one of the foremost field hospitals; it had been pouring with rain, and the road was practically under water. Nina and I were behind in the Berliet, and the big Austin car with the apparatus was trundling along in front, when there was a lurch, and over she went on to her side into a deep ditch which we had not known was there. We all descended into two feet of water to consult as to what was to be done. We had a rope, and tried attaching it to our touring car. Having started up the Berliet (70 h.p.), she pulled well

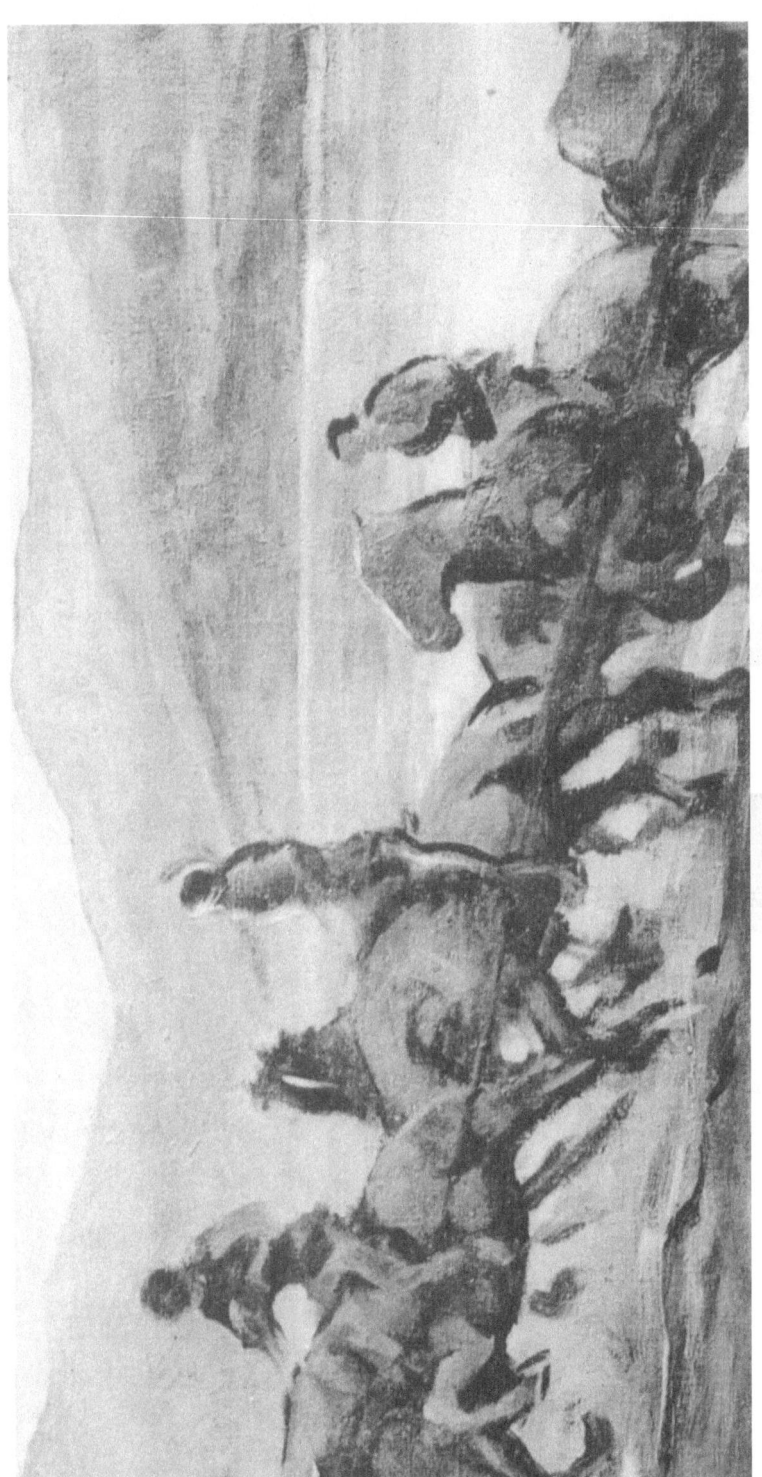

Artillery Horses come to the help of car stuck in quicksands in Natizone River

THE ITALIAN SOLDIER

enough, but the X-ray car only settled more firmly on her side into the ditch. The Austrians chose that moment to begin firing on the road; so we told Whitehead to take the Berliet on and put her under the cover of some rather battered houses, and then come back to see what could be done.

We were still standing cogitating when a shell sang over and dropped in the field just beyond the car, followed in a few minutes by another and yet another. I think they had seen us, and were taking pot-shots at us—we had a huge red cross on the top as well as on the sides of the car so they had no excuse; anyway, it had the effect of making a lot of men who were sheltering under a wall come quickly to our help. In vain we said it was not worth their risking themselves; they insisted on helping, and with about twenty of them propping the car up and a lorry pulling on the road, we soon got the Austin out again, and none the worse for the upset. The Austrians had put about six shells, all told, round the car, and we were very lucky not to have had any damage. The apparatus was so well packed and fitted that nothing had moved. The soldiers flatly refused to take any kind of reward, as they said that we were all doing the same sort of work. Whenever we got into difficulties we had the same help, and the same answer if we remonstrated. Is it a wonder that we love the Italian soldier? They are so cheerful too. I remember strings of them waiting under our window—it was 11 p.m.—in pouring rain, and they were chaffing and singing though they had been blocked there for hours. They were waiting to get into their camp a little farther down the road, where I believe there was a convoy *camion* turned over in the lane. It was pitch dark, so we could only judge by the noise.

VIPULZANO

28th March, 1916.

Two assistants, Mrs. O'Neale and Mrs. Belfield, have arrived, sent by the Red Cross. The same night Mrs. O'Neale broke out with pleurisy and congestion of the lungs and was removed to Villa Trento to be nursed, and now Nina has had a bad fall. They say it will be quite ten days before she can move, and Mrs. Belfield and I must carry on alone, rather difficult as, of course, she knows nothing whatever about X-rays. Poor Nina is very depressed at not being able to work. . . .

30th March, 1916, Vipulzano.

We have had quite an exciting day. Mrs. Belfield and I started out for Vipulzano with two cars; she went on first with the apparatus and Whitehead. Having had all the requisition papers for the section to write out, I was rather late, so followed on with the Berliet. It was a perfectly heavenly day, with a clear blue sky and fluffy white clouds. The road led through San Lorenzo di Mossa and on over some marshy, flat ground with golden poplars on either side and pale blue mountains rising straight out of the marshes. Blue irises everywhere and they and the sky reflected in the small pools of water which were all over the marsh. I did so want to get out and paint, but it was not a very healthy spot and I was already late.

We found a whole day's work waiting for us, and we stayed on at the hospital until well on in the afternoon. All the time we were at Vipulzano the Austrians had been giving desultory attention to the road we had come along in the morning. I don't know what Mrs. Belfield felt, but I know that I had a distinctly uncomfortable feeling in the region of my solar plexus (I think we all learnt the uses of a solar plexus during the War). The moment came to leave; we had no

AN EXCITING DAY

excuse for lingering any longer . . . the work was finished, the plant had been packed and Whitehead and the orderlies were standing by the cars, when the Austrians began putting shells over the hospital; the road was strewn with splinters as one, two, three, four followed each other in quick succession, our colleagues of the morning had vanished into their dugouts, so we thought we had better disappear too. We jumped into our respective cars and off we went at top speed across the marshes; my car was leading and I took her as hard as she would go along the causeway so as to reach cover under the hills as soon as possible. The first bit of cover reached, I stopped to look back to see if the other car with the apparatus in it had got across all right. Not a sign of it. . . . I waited some time asking Stagni, the corporal who was with me, if he was sure that the other car had been ready to start when we left. Yes, he was sure. I could see the splash of shells falling in the pools of water on either side of the causeway, and knew that it was only a matter of time before it would be hit. With sinking in my heart, I felt it was my duty to return over what had by now become a hateful road as I had to see what had become of the others, so back we bumped across the six kilometres. Just about two kilometres from Vipulzano we found them standing in the middle of the road looking ruefully at their car. Something, they said, had hit their petrol tank at the back and all their petrol had run out onto the road. . . . We tried to stop up the hole, but it was far too big and ragged, so we had to leave the car where it was, in an unpleasantly exposed place, and they all climbed into the Berliet to bump back at all speed to San Lorenzo di Mossa, where we hoped to find a *camion* to tow in the damaged car. We soon found one and Whitehead returned with it to help drive the car home. In about

VIPULZANO

half an hour they arrived in a great state of excitement, a shell having burst on the causeway just after they had passed, covering it with mud and stones and absolutely wrecking the road. One second later and they would have been wrecked too. They were very much pleased with themselves, especially Whitehead, who never seems to mind anything. He is worth his weight in gold. Mrs. Belfield, too, was quite calm. This adventure taught us always for the future to send our X-ray car in front and bring up the rear ourselves.

Sometimes Mrs. Belfield came with me; occasionally I went by myself with Whitehead or an orderly. One case I remember as being interesting. A *sotto-tenente* had a piece of shrapnel in his jaw. When I turned on the tube it was to be seen quite plainly, so I took a plate and sent it to the hospital for the surgeon to see (it was the big military hospital in Cormons). The next day the surgeon appeared at the house with the plate in his hand, he also carried a small object wrapped in paper. He asked if I was sure that the object marked in the plate was a piece of shell, and I said that I was sure. He then unwrapped his parcel and showed us a piece of bone, the exact size and shape of the object in the plate. "There," he said, "I took that out this morning, and you still say that object on the plate is a piece of metal?" I looked again at the plate and said I was *sure*. Amid much laughter and chaff he asked me to come to the hospital next morning and take another plate which would prove that I was mistaken and that he had taken out the object which I said was a piece of shrapnel. So next morning, still quite positive, but rather nervous, I went to the hospital and took another radiograph of the boy's jaw which I developed there and then under their eyes in the dark room in the car. . . . Lo and behold! the same object again appeared on the plate with the sharp outline always to

ANOTHER INTERESTING CASE

be seen when it is metal. The surgeons were greatly impressed and the poor boy had to undergo a further operation, when exactly below the " X " that I had marked on his jaw, and exactly at the depth I had originally stated, the surgeon found the piece of shrapnel. The two pieces, bone and metal, must have been lying immediately over each other, and having cut one piece out, the surgeon never dreamed that there was another piece identically the same, only of a different material, lying directly behind it.

Another curious case when I was working without Nina was that of a man in a hospital some way behind the line. He was supposed to have a bullet in his arm and had had several operations to look for it. As they couldn't find it they sent for us. The hole was in his arm right enough and I found two pieces of shell and marked their position. That done, they said " Thank you " and expected me to pack and leave ; but an idea had struck me. I had made the examination through the screen with the man on his back, his arm lying close to his side ; I now wanted to look again with his arm stretched out at right angles to his body. The doctors were much bored by my persistence, as it was supper-time and they said that they had seen all they wanted ; but I insisted and found what I was looking for, namely, that one of the pieces which we had all thought were both in the arm was really embedded in the muscle at the back of the shoulder. This had been crossed by the shadow of the upper part of the arm, both pieces thus seeming to be in the arm itself. When working with Sir James Mackenzie Davidson he had told us of a similar incident. . . . A young Belgian officer had been sent to him in London who had had operation after operation to his arm and no bullet found, although it was clearly to be seen with the X-rays. Sir James had the brilliant idea of making

VIPULZANO

him put his arm out at right angles to his body, and there was the bullet lying in the shoulder muscle which bulges out behind the upper arm, and not in the arm at all. Luckily I hadn't forgotten this story and managed to adapt it to my patient's case. Great applause and admiration from all present. . . . They little knew—and I didn't tell them—that I should never have thought of it if it hadn't been for Sir James Mackenzie Davidson's story.

1st May, 1916.

One day the General sent his A.D.C. and his motor to fetch Nina and me, and we were taken right up into the second line to see all the batteries. Firstly to see the big 305s, gigantic things that shoot twenty or more kilometres, and then the huge naval guns (*marina prolongata*) that shoot twelve kilometres; we were then taken to see the fat howitzers called *Mortieri* or *mortaio* that shoot straight up into the air and drop things into the enemy lines nearly two kilometres away. We went clean through the mountain by underground passages cut through the rock, and peeped out through a hole on the other side at the enemy trenches. We weren't allowed to stay long as the Austrians had not discovered the peep-hole yet and the Italians were afraid they might see us.

One pleasant fact I have to relate and that is that when in the beginning of our stay here a hospital did not believe our radiograph, they sent for a man working at Nogaro to prove whether we were right. Now they send for us to check *his* work. That has happened twice in the last week, so we are rather cock-a-hoop.

We have had some busy days lately mending and adapting an X-ray set which has been sent up from Palermo and arrived all broken and rusty, having taken ages to get here. We feel quite lonely because the nights have been so quiet lately, hardly a bump to be heard. I have, I think, done three brown-paper sketches only since I have been here, but perhaps now that I have a room upstairs as a studio I may do more. I have papered the walls of the attic with large sheets of brown paper, so that I can do hurried sketches when I come in of whatever has been most impressive. We sprawl in the garden and quarrel for something to do, and our volunteer assistant prints diligently the four hundred odd plates we have done at different times.

The rats positively swarm here; five, two white and three grey, galumph all night through the rooms regardless of light or dogs. They are rather nice, but bumptious. We came out on to the landing rather suddenly the other night and all five tight-roped along and down the banisters, the big white one first, then a grey, then white, then two grey. Very pretty it was. Nina the other evening left the sitting-room door open, and when I remonstrated said, "I left it for the rats," and as she spoke in they trooped and hurried behind the cupboard. There is a charming white one here with ruby eyes that comes into the sitting-room every night to drink the water out of the flowers; Nina pins biscuits on to the table for him.

7th May, 1916.

I have changed my room now. Nina, feeling the need of something to do, insisted on "General Post," and I have now the biggest room in the house looking into the garden. I miss the noise, but no doubt shall appreciate it soon; I think there is a ghost in the room, which rather gives me the jumps, and Rana (the little little Dachshund) has treated me to fits of hysterical barking at the corners which upsets my nerves in the middle of the night . . . also, the night before

VIPULZANO

last the telephone suddenly burst into flames and we had to pour water on it and disconnect all the wires in a great hurry. It is an old type without a safety fuse, and the lightning must have hit it as a storm was going on at the moment.

Our *genio* friends are unceasingly useful : they lend us their electricians whenever we are in difficulties and they inundate us with presents of Austrian shells. We rashly showed them to the King of Italy and the Prince of Wales, who came the other day. And the King asked us to give two of our most treasured pieces to the Prince of Wales, one a square bullet out of a new kind of shell and the other an Austrian hand-grenade of a rare pattern like a Greek discobulus. Nina nobly gave hers and our *genio* have already found her another, so all is well. We had only half an hour to get tidy before their arrival as it was the day Nina had insisted on " General Post," and all the cupboards were in the passage and all the beds in the sitting-room.

We are very lucky as no one else is housed like us and the Italians have taken endless pains to clean not only the house and garden but the surroundings, even the ditches on the roads round having been dug out and cleaned and all stagnant ponds filled up. Nothing has been too much trouble.

I was so pleased to get your letter from the cottage, which sounds very pleasant. The plant you mentioned must have been from some seeds which we sent back from the rocky gorges the other side of Fontainebleau, when we were there in the beginning of the War. The little wild delphiniums swarm here, also a tall pink-red vetch and a brilliant blue salvia alternating with a purple one; huge red-purple thistles and tiny purple sultans, scarlet poppies, and close-growing, pale lilac-pink saxifrage; a wonderful effect of pale grey, red-purple and heavy purple passing through every shade, but it is

THE NEW ASSISTANT

slightly spoilt by the swarms of daisies of a very crude yellow.

Do send some more pressed beef as our last lot was stolen. We have someone in the house who takes food whenever it is not locked up. And someone also who looks over all our papers and letters when we are out and puts them back in different places. I should write much oftener if you sent me another pen. Our new assistant is not at all suitable. She arrived having lost her luggage, giggles with her head on one side when introduced to anyone, and makes *gaffes* at meals when we have people here. We sent her to Milan in the car to buy tubes. She bought the exact contrary to what we had told her and never even took the trouble to ask the price, so heaven knows what bills will come in. She brought a wolf-puppy back with her which Rosales had given us, and when he said, " I hope you saw my dogs, aren't they beautiful ? " she answered, " I thought them hideous and mangy and didn't like them at all." We didn't know where to look and he saved the situation after a gasp of surprise by turning to me and starting a long dissertation on country life in Italian. . . .

My Italian is awful and even hurts my own ears, so it must be very painful to theirs. It is fluent, without grammar, and frequent literal translation from French and English—French words put in when I know no Italian. Everyone, however, is very kind and helpful, and marvellously quick at grasping what we want. Nina talks French mixed with bad Italian to them, and they turn helplessly to me to translate it, which I can't always do, but we are all very cheerful over it. Last week we thought it rather warm, but being prepared for much hotter weather made no complaint. We now find that the Italians call it very hot and they tell us that we shall not have it any worse all the summer. This place has a week or so of hot sun and then two

VIPULZANO

or three days grey, with rain, so that you always have relief. It has now been pouring steadily for the last forty-eight hours. We had a very dreary luncheon party yesterday. We went to one of our most advanced hospitals and having a lot of cases to do stayed to luncheon with sixteen doctors, none of whom spoke English and only one a little French. It was very hard work and their manners were too good to talk amongst themselves, which some of the others do. At another hospital, where we have to feed sometimes, they ignore us and talk of the War and argue violently among themselves, but these addressed all their remarks to us. Nina played up splendidly, but it wasn't easy.

We now have a charming little man, Roversi [1] by

---

[1] Roversi was a little old man with a snub nose, a wide face and a broad anxious smile. He was handed over to me as my special orderly—spotlessly clean himself, his one idea in life was to wash, brush and keep my uniform clean and presentable. No holes or tears were allowed to remain for one moment. Indeed, so anxious was he to make my appearance a credit to the section that he unashamedly stole ties, handkerchiefs, etc., from the other members of the section to put into my chest of drawers. It became rather painful as whenever anything was missing the first place searched was the Joint-Commandant's (that is my own) room. In fact, many times the other Commandant would seize a blue hunting tie (worn by Commandants only) when it was round my neck, turn it round and say, " There, I thought so, an ' N. H. ' on the back of your tie, Roversi, and you are perfectly shameless, I haven't one clean tie left in my box." His loyalty, too, was most touching. He felt that he had to defend us in every way, and later when we were in Gorizia, although green with fear at the sound of every shell, he insisted on sleeping upstairs at my door instead of with the rest of the men down in the cellar. The first night we slept in Gorizia I heard a noise outside my door and thinking it might be a lost dog got out of bed and opened it—there was Roversi lying on the bare boards in the doorway wrapped in his heavy *grigio-verde* cape. When I remonstrated and told him to go down to the cellar where the other men were sleeping, he nearly burst into tears, saying, " Fancy if

MORE CARS REQUIRED

name, as our orderly and he cleans our apparatus and keeps it in order.

1st June, 1916.

Wild Siberian irises all over the marshes on the way to Vipulzano yesterday were too lovely, looking just like a violet haze high above the green grass of the marshes. This is the same place where I wanted to sketch yesterday, but as it is within sight of the enemy trenches and they seem to take notice of every passer-by, I could only do a hasty pencil note.

We are full of woe, the chassis of the Berliet has got cracked somehow, and it will be gone for ages. The Austin coil that works the X-rays has burnt out and the Daimler axle is bent. We must have two more cars; can you manage to get any given to us?

I am afraid of losing the photographs and sketches I have done, so shall send home everything I do, for you to keep. I met a painter pupil of Sartorio's yesterday who told me that they are all very anxious about him, as after having been taken prisoner by the Austrians he seems to have cheeked a high official, was tried by court-martial and since then nothing has been heard of him.[1]

Quite suddenly all the people round, generals, etc., have awakened to the fact that we have been working

the Signore were hit and there were no one here to help them." A heavy bombardment was going on at the time and at the sound of each shell passing over our house he cringed *malgré lui* and could hardly stand for the shaking of his poor legs. But leave us he would not. Once when I went up to the attics in the middle of the night armed with a revolver to search for burglars or ghosts who were apparently moving furniture up there, he insisted on coming too, but stood shaking with agitation at the door murmuring, " Che coraggio—che coraggio," while I searched behind the bits of furniture for the noise-makers. Needless to say I found no one.

[1] Sartorio, a well-known painter, was safe.

VIPULZANO

here for six months, and have waxed enthusiastic. We swallow it all with unction. They have demanded that some of our best plates should be sent to Rome for the chief radiographer to see. Lord Monson has been here again, and this time, thanks to many kind Italian helpers, our additions are correct and our bills quite presentable. Mr. Hubert Beaumont came with him and was most helpful as he has a vast sense of humour, and he saved the situation several times for us. To-day is grilling. Last night we dined with the Headquarters Staff and I gently remarked to my neighbour that I wanted to go and see my family soon. The General heard what I said and leant across, saying, " Not just now please, I want you to be patient for a bit." . . . That remark may sound uninteresting to you but it is desperately thrilling to us.[1] I am sending you a copy of a wonderful letter of appreciation we have received from General Ponzio who is head of the *sanità* of the Second Army. Please order two new Pillon tubes for General Delmé Radcliffe to bring out to us; he has been extraordinarily kind and no trouble is too much for him to take to help on our work; yesterday, knowing how fussed Nina is about Dick[2] who is in a destroyer in the North Sea, he motored here to Cormons to bring her the news of the latest naval battle. What a battle it appears to have been! We have had no details yet.

We have not had enormously much work lately because of the fighting being on another section of the Front, and I am rather glad as I have been having sciatica. It is the only day I have had to lie up since I have been here. We came round a corner and found the road completely blocked by a civilian and his donkey-

---

[1] This, of course, meant that a big attack was being planned.
[2] Nina's son, Lieutenant-Commander R. E. Hollings, who died later from tuberculosis caused by the War.

OUR COOK

cart on the wrong side of the road and a soldier and a mule-cart on the other, and I had all I could do to stop the Daimler, both foot and hand-brakes full on, and I expect I wrenched the muscles of my leg. I wish we could get some news, it is most worrying only getting it once a week. The Austrian attack is apparently quelled; there were some anxious moments but I gather all is now well. Cadorna is a wonderful man and absolutely calm in emergency. Our nice friend, the Surgeon De Cigna, has been moved, but we can still work for him in his new hospital when we have time to go thirty miles. We did thirty-seven cases for him the other afternoon after an enormous luncheon of *polenta*, starlings, beefsteak, beer, Bordeaux and Asti. Why we did not die I cannot think. There are thunderstorms nearly every night, which is a bore as they keep one awake.

We have been having a grand upset in the house lately, we have swept everyone out and started again with Roversi and a bicyclist and chauffeur, and they do all the work. Mietzi, the cook, was odious; we have done lots to make her comfortable and she had high strikes, and shrieked and shrieked and shrieked and bit and scratched the day the orderly went, yelling on him and the Almighty alternately to defend her, as she was being kept as a slave by us. ("Eine sklave, Eine sklave!") The *genio* officers had rushed to see who was being murdered and we found them all in the room assisting. Mietzi was tearing all her clothes off and pulling her hair down. I got there first and threw water in her face and then Nina took charge, helped by Roversi, and we turned all the officers and peasants out. Mietzi was given morphia that night as we had telephoned to the General's doctor to come and help, and it was the only way to make her relax her muscles. Then next day we removed her back to her own rela-

VIPULZANO

tions and were given an Italian soldier cook in exchange. So there is now peace.

Yesterday I had a most pleasant time in the afternoon sketching big white *bovi* or *bue* as they are called here. One hundred and eighty arrived at Cervignano while we were there, some for killing and some for work. To-day is the first day since we have been here that I have had the time or the zeal to go far to paint. We only sleep as a rule when not working. One of our most beautiful drives is now impossible as the hospital which we used to visit has had to be removed to serener climes. Very lovely country but beastly for heavy motors. I particularly hated the other day, as I was driving the Daimler and the brakes would not hold. I had to make our Italian orderly, Bianchi by name, run alongside to help jam on the side-brake, and other soldiers who luckily were on the path jumped up to help me, one of them incidentally stamping full on my foot in his efforts to put the foot-brake on harder. Others caught hold of the wheels, and we at last managed to stop the brute, but only at the very last moment, just as we had got to the edge of the precipice. Now the car has gone to have its brakes seen to and will, I hope, return more amenable, but it was not pleasant as there was a sheer drop of some hundred feet straight in front of me where the road ended.

17

THE REAL THING

2nd July, 1916, Cormons.

THE fighting has come at last and there are great doings here and lots of successes; it is interesting to note that the Italians have acquired in a single night the detestation of their enemies. There had never been that feeling here until the other night, when nearly a whole division was gassed. The poor lambs had never realized what it meant, had had no gas drill, had read about it, but, I think, thought the Western Front had made a fuss about nothing; and then it came. . . . They had their masks in their pockets and never thought of putting them on, and the result was quite awful. The hospitals have been crammed with gassed men. Please write the exact quantity of atropine you told me that the English doctors had found so useful when injected. De Cigna is anxious to try it. They are cupping them, but nothing seems to be much good and they say there is prussic acid in it as well. The Italians have asked us to find out if it is the same gas that was used in Flanders. The soldiers behaved very well, for once the fumes had passed, those who were able, attacked, and took back all the trenches and lots more besides. Luckily for us we did not come in for very much of it, although we always carried gas-masks as a precaution.

One day Nina and I were called to a dressing-station which had been established in a school near Sdraussina, not very far from the Carso, where a lot of fighting was going on. Arrived there we found the courtyard blocked with men just down from the trenches, some sitting, some lying against the walls, all more or less gassed. They were a terrible sight, some struggling for breath, some already dead. We could hardly get into the hall, it was so crowded with gassed men. We were unpacking our X-ray apparatus when a sergeant staggered up the steps carrying his colonel over his shoulder. As he reached the top he stumbled and fell. Everyone present rushed to him, but he was beyond help, the effort of carrying such a weight so far had done away with any chance he might have had of recovering from the gas. The Colonel, who was at once removed for treatment, I believe recovered. Then we were asked to X-ray a man who had just been brought in badly gassed and evidently at the last gasp. The surgeons were very anxious to see for themselves what effect the gas was having on the lungs. On looking through the screen we found that the lungs had shrivelled and looked like a piece of coke about two inches in diameter. They asked us to take a plate, but just as we were preparing to do so, the surgeon hastily signed to the orderlies to carry away the stretcher and turning to us said, " It is too late, the man is dying." Another time as we were on our way up to the Carso we passed a mule-cart with a man standing up in the front of the cart holding the reins in one hand and a stick in the other. The immobility of the man and mules attracted our notice and we stopped to see if anything was the matter. On approaching close we found that both the man and mules were dead. The gas must have passed that way some time before and instantaneous death had been the result. The mules were leaning against the pole and looked absolutely alive until you touched them and found they were quite stiff.

Later we were shown some photographs of the result

DIFFERENT NATIONALITIES

of that gas by Colonel Badoglio, the Chief of the Staff.[1] The photographs showed men standing in the trenches with rifles and bayonets at the ready, but stone dead; in one case a man had been drinking out of a glass, his arm still raised, and the glass still at his lips; in another an officer stood with his field-glasses to his eyes. He also was quite dead.

In the beginning a gas was used by the enemy which burnt up and killed all the trees and vegetation. We used to drive through miles and miles of sulphur-coloured tree-trunks, the leaves all gone, the grass all gone, and the ground looking as if it had been scarified; even the blue mountains lost their colour and looked grey and reddish where the gas had passed.

There is such an odd state of affairs here. I have been talking to an Italian woman about her husband. . . . He is an Austrian and in the Austrian Army, but can only talk Friulani and not one word of German or Italian. Yesterday we had six Austrian prisoners to radiograph and only one could speak a few words of German. There are Hungarians, Croats, Slavs, etc., and they all seem very glad to be in hospital making friends with the Italian orderlies. The Italians took heaps of prisoners yesterday; we ourselves passed nearly 2,000 of them on our way back from work in the evening. If it was not for the poor men themselves this gassing would be a good thing, as it really has roused the Italians as nothing else would have done, and threats of vengeance are pouring out from everyone.

Much as we like visitors we get a little overdone with society. People coming into the garden after dinner and sitting smoking for hours when we want to go to bed; also we are asked out to dinner when we would rather sit and laze in the garden during our few minutes of

[1] Now Field-Marshal and Chief of the General Staff (Army, Navy, and Air Force).

THE REAL THING

peace; but it cannot be helped and we are flattered that they find our garden a rest and a change from their work. We are much amused as we are to be given an entertainment allowance by Lord Monson. He is going to give us three francs a day each and says that he expects us on this to return all the dinners we are asked to! We dine to-night at the Headquarters Mess to meet the Inspecting Artillery Expert, a tearing swell, and I trust that I shall have more Italian than I had last night, as what I had left me altogether, and our company rose up, saying, "We think the ladies are asleep so we will go." Unfortunate but true; besides, we had both been seeing gassed people all day, which was not calculated to make one cheerful. . . .

We passed our thousandth case yesterday and were sent a bottle of champagne to celebrate it. We go to twenty-seven different hospitals now besides the dressing-stations.

We were sent for yesterday to a dressing-station which was difficult to find as it was hidden in a narrow valley which the Italians fondly hoped would not be discovered by the enemy. . . . . But an Austrian aeroplane had come soaring over in the morning and although it dropped no bombs the surgeons had become very nervous, as it came down quite low, obviously to see what the little wooden huts were being used for and whether they were inhabited.

As we drove down the narrow lane leading to it, a shell fell on the grass at the side of the road, luckily a very marshy place, so it went in deep before exploding, and covered our car and us with mud and stones. Another fell immediately behind us, knocking a carabiniere off his bicycle but not hurting him. We at once started a heated argument, as Nina, who happened to be sitting at the back of the car over the dynamo, declared that we had been hit and in a spirit of contra-

OUR MACHINE STRIKES WORK

diction I swore we had not. Stagni, our corporal, who happened to be driving, put on all the speed possible and we got out of the line of fire as quickly as we could, arriving at the dressing-station to find the surgeons much alarmed as to whether we had been hit or not, as they had been watching the road with glasses and had seen where the shells had pitched. We waited a bit to see if there was going to be any more shooting, but as there appeared to be no more we proceeded with our job of unpacking the apparatus-car which had been driven by Whitehead and which had arrived before us. No one could think why the enemy should choose to waste time by shelling a little empty valley so far behind the lines, where there were no troops, and never had been any. While we were talking and the men were unloading, the Austrians sent three or four more over, all of them falling in a radius of about 500 yards. We had a bad head case to X-ray for an immediate operation, and luckily determined to take a plate at once without screening. We turned on the light, which was much stronger than usual. Our customary time exposure for a head was fifty seconds; it ran perfectly for about twenty seconds, and suddenly the machine struck work altogether. We hurried out to see what could be the matter, and found Whitehead already under the motor. He called to us to come and see. I crawled under, and lo! a piece of shell *had* hit the car. It had cut the wires of the dynamo clean through—they were wound round and round the axle; and a piece of shell had stuck between the axle and the floor of the car just under where Nina had been sitting. No wonder she had been so positive about the car having been hit! Apparently when we first turned on the current it had connected all the wires up for a second or two and then everything fusible had fused. We were in despair, as nothing could be done on the spot to remedy it and the man we had come to X-ray was a very urgent case. However, when we got home and developed the exposed plate, to our surprise we found it to be one of the best head-plates we had ever done. The flash must have been so powerful that it did in less than half a minute what we usually take fifty to sixty seconds to do, and it enabled the surgeon to save the man's life.

Our adventures for the day were not quite ended, as on our way back (I was driving) a distant gun began firing again and dropped a big shell just behind us in the road, blowing a great crater where we had just passed. The curious part was that we both heard the gun-fire and the whine of the shell coming, but it was no good hurrying as we might have hurried into it, and no good stopping or it might have caught us, so we went on at the same pace not looking at each other or daring to speak, and the road behind us had vanished when we recovered enough to look round.

We used to take all the Italian orderlies and drivers out in turn to learn the work of loading and unloading, fetching plates out of the car, helping to carry the wounded, etc., and they had all become very useful. We hardly ever had to tell them a thing twice, for when once they understood the whys and wherefores they never forgot it.

Another thing which is so excellent about the Italians is that they never break anything, you can trust them even with X-ray tubes and have no qualms. They were always willing and never thought about their own comforts. Food, rest, nothing counted as long as the jobs for the day were satisfactorily finished.

Our work used to be very uneven; sometimes two or three days would pass without any calls coming and the section would relapse into despair and feel that the work was bad and that we had better retire to England, a miserable failure wanted by no one; then would come

PLENTY TO DO

an attack and the other extreme of despair would seize us. Telephone messages and telegrams would pour in night and day. Motor-bicycles blocked the doors, orderlies waited at the bottom of the stairs to catch us as we went out, with demands for the car to be sent immediately in at least six different directions at the same time, and the heap of calls on the engagement table grew higher and higher till we despaired of ever reducing it. Nina Hollings and I were still appealing to the Red Cross to send us out someone to develop plates for us. We found that often we only got home at twelve o'clock at night when there was a push on, and that however late we were the plates had to be developed the same night or they were not dry enough to send off the following morning.[1]

12th July, 1916.

They have issued us an Italian type of gas-mask; please send us out five of the newest pattern [2] when you can. I am told that a bag you clap over your head with talc and a pipe for breathing *out* of is the best.

I wish they did not have to use dogs to experiment on in the hope of finding a cure for gas poisoning. I got into a vivisection argument at luncheon the other day with a lot of doctors, and they say there is nothing else to be done. They use cats as much as possible, but rabbits and guinea-pigs are too small to be of any use and are impossible to procure here. Horses and cattle are, of course, too valuable, both for work and food, and there remain but the hundreds of lost dogs from all

---

[1] The record day, when the section was at its full complement, was 121 examinations in seven different hospitals, the hospitals averaging six to twelve kilometres apart, three of them being in Gorizia.

[2] When the English guns came to the Italian front the English General issued us modern gas-masks and English helmets.

the deserted villages. I suppose there is no reason that dogs should be exempt when everyone else is having such a bad time and, as they say, it is not vivisection. They are made to stay in the gas, and only when dead are tested and examined. If it helps people I suppose it must be.

You would be amused at the primitive, but very effective, watering of the roads, men with pails and cans attached to poles ladling the water out of the ditches on to the roads, but they keep the dust down most successfully. How wonderful their road-making is. No road one day, and you pass not a week later and a big military road is there with convoys of heavy *camions* toiling six abreast along it.

19th July, 1916.

We frequently have men sent to pick our brains, both Italian and English, as everyone is anxious to copy our X-ray plant. We met the Duke of Aosta the other day at a hospital and he said he had heard that ours was better than any other in Italy, and asked if all the English army ones were as good. We assured him that there were no others like ours, which was unique, the parts having been collected by ourselves, the first in France and England and the second in Italy. He was much interested, particularly when I told him that Eddie [1] had written saying he wished to goodness the English authorities would allow us to come to his division as they have only one apparatus and that a rotten one, but that being women he supposed we should never be allowed. The Duke of Aosta laughed and said, " We are cleverer than the English then, because we employ who and what we can for our wounded, regardless whether they wear trousers or petticoats."

[1] My brother who was in command of the 37th Division in France.

ADAPTING A SEARCHLIGHT

You know we are so useful that it is a pity not to be working for the English, but if they had accepted our offer they would only have put us at a base hospital, while here our whole point is the going from hospital to hospital close up to the Front and also going to the dressing-stations. You see, they can then judge whom they keep and operate on, and who can be sent farther back.

I told you, didn't I? that once we caught a big search-light and made their dynamo work for us, as ours had struck work. The electrician belonging to the searchlight was very much fussed as he said his dynamo was far too powerful for our apparatus and would smash it all up, but Nina had the brilliant idea to pass the current through many buckets of water—this made a resistance which reduced it to suit our machine and it was a great success.

26th July, 1916.

Tell Roger [1] that we have found caterpillars, huge fat green ones with turquoises set in bunches of three hairs each, like precious stones, also a marvellous butterfly, rich golden yellow with a heavy tip to his wings and brown stripes, but not a swallow-tail. We think we are going to collect butterflies amongst our other jobs.

Yesterday we went to a new hospital in a most lovely *castello* on a peak overlooking all the Austrian Front. It has already suffered a good deal, but they go on using it. The date, I should think, about fifteenth century, with great iron bars to the windows and a very fine door. I crawled up on all fours by the remnants of a staircase to the top windows to look out. The roof had mostly disappeared as well. I was very cautious and refused to leave the undignified position of all fours, though two doctors who had gone up with me urged

[1] My small nephew, Roger Machell, aged eight.

me to rise. Nina wisely had refused to come up at all as she detests heights.

I think I shall give myself a day in bed to-morrow, the second in seven and a half months. I am rather weary and want to be fresh for the next day.

18

THE ATTACK ON GORIZIA

6th August, 1916, Cormons.

THERE is unceasing noise in the distance, and we purpose to go up to our observation post [1] to-day to see what we can. Our work always begins the day after an attack, so I expect we shall not have much to do to-day. We are much agitated as one of our two interrupters has chosen to get out of order, having broken something inside and refuses to turn. The trouble is, I am afraid, impossible for us to cope with, and I don't know what will happen. I suppose we shall try and adapt an old broken cone that we have. It is really bad luck and the English ones are quite useless for our plant; we must have a French one from Malaquin, or it will not work. This last one has all the screws rusted in.

The noise is earth-shaking to-day and I suppose will be much worse to-morrow. We shan't be going such long distances between our hospitals now as we are reserved for our own army from this moment on and most of our work will be much nearer home.

7th August.

They have been at it with big guns now for twenty-four hours and they say that we have taken the two

[1] Langoris, afterwards taken by General Cadorna and Staff, so we had to find another one.

THE ATTACK ON GORIZIA

most strategic points already. I suppose I had better not mention names, besides, you get them in the newspapers much quicker than you will get this. Nina and I had to take our interrupter to Palma Nova yesterday to try and get it mended and on the way went to our own little observatory at Langoris. You never saw anything like it. All the things that look like trees are explosions, the tall ones high explosives and the little ones shrapnel. On our way back the fog and smoke was so thick that you could see nothing but the actual bursting of each shell. Of course, no lights whatever allowed on the cars, but it does not worry me as I can see like a cat in the dark. Last night was thrilling; firstly, the quantity of prisoners marching by and all the soldiers cheering, and then the crowds and crowds of troops waiting at the end of our road, for their turn to go up. There was a moon which just dimly showed them, and as we went by a motor arrived with a staff officer to give directions where they were to go. The motor then swished on through all the waiting soldiers to pass on orders to the next lot, it was like a glorified field-day all day long, with despatch-riders tearing past us, men on sweating horses galloping with messages, cars full of generals hurrying up for the attack, and one thing not a field-day, twenty or thirty or forty ambulances waiting under the hedges and coming past very slowly in the evening with wounded, mostly slightly wounded, looking very pleased with themselves for getting off so lightly.

This is a diary letter and will go when I have opportunity and be written when I have a minute. Yesterday we fetched our interrupter and found it done, I am glad to say. On the way back we met about three hundred prisoners, escorted by cavalry, and saw one try to run out, pursued by a man on horseback with a lance (*Cavalleria Leggiera*), who rounded him up like a whip with hounds, finally jumping his horse up a wall on to the road, just in front of our car. This morning *granate* at the station as usual, but obviously from very much farther off. It used to be bung . . . whump, now it is bung-whump, which means that the sound taking longer to come arrives at the same time as the projectile. It is fearfully exciting, as every time a new village is taken, round comes a delighted message from the *genio* to tell us.

Then, this morning an urgent telegram from the head of the *sanità* to go up to Medana to do a general who had been wounded. We were rather pleased with ourselves as we were packed and up there within thirty minutes of receiving the telegram. The General, a most cheerful soul, is the most successful of the lot, having been the one to take the mountain of Sabotino yesterday. Then, while we were radiographing, in came the King and stayed while we did it. Our little *piantone* (orderly) was highly excited, saying he had never seen his King so close before. Four thousand prisoners taken and everyone screaming with excitement. We are lucky to be right in the thick of it like this.

9th August.

Yesterday good news after good news. Firstly Sabotino, secondly Podgòra, then Oslavia, Gorizia itself, and now this morning we hear some villages beyond Gorizia were taken during the night. It is all going almost frighteningly well, 8,000 prisoners taken in Gorizia alone. Some severe street fighting which appears to have been very unpleasant, but no gas on either side, I wonder why? Sabotino was an absolutely frontal straight attack; they say that after having not a soul moving on those hills for twelve months, people are now dawdling about on the top of them as at a garden-party. We ourselves these last two days have had very little to do, as the first-line hospitals are choc-a-bloc and have no

THE ATTACK ON GORIZIA

time to do anything but bandage and send on at once. No hunting for bullets possible except in the case of one or two senior officers like we had yesterday. This afternoon we shall probably toil round with bandages; hospitals keep asking us for beds and we have none. One of the Italian Red Cross hospitals yesterday had prepared for eighty and received 350; they were tearing their hair. Another had room for fifty and had just heard they were to take in 200. It is despairing that we can't help in that way. We are making a storehouse here for the Villa Trento people who are carrying wounded day and night, so we keep cold food, coffee and petrol ready for them always. We are told to be patient and the moment this rush has ceased then our rush will begin.

The same evening.

Just come back from a most interesting afternoon, having been up as far as Lucinico with bandages, cotton-wool, etc. Arrived at Lucinico we found that the dressing-station at the other end of the village, that we had been making for, had had to come back as the village was all on fire and was being pretty heavily shelled, mostly by shrapnel, which was bursting in every direction. Batteries and batteries of guns all under the lee of gutted houses were waiting to make their dash over the bridge which was still being shelled. Our own guns just behind us cracking every two minutes, and the high explosives with their rustling iron petticoats whizzing overhead. A few enemy shells were coming, but they mostly fell some way behind us.

Meaning to go on farther, we had offered only half our bandages, etc., but the moment the doctors of the dressing-station at Lucinico saw us and our large box of surgical necessaries, they all fell upon them and,

THE OBSERVATION POST

although we remonstrated feebly saying they were meant to go on to other stations as well, they took the whole lot. They didn't hide their joy at the unexpected contribution, and we were very much pleased at the success of our expedition. Our car being now empty there was no further excuse for our staying, and we were turning homewards when one of the officers asked if we would care to go up to the observation post on the hill above, as the guns were just going into Gorizia and we should be able to see them cross the bridges from there. And away we toiled along endless trenches and under covered passages hearing all sorts of exciting things going on and unable to see out. The trenches are maddening for that. Then up and up, the officer who was leading us going horribly fast, excusing himself for hurrying us by saying that his gun was to be one of the first to lead over the bridge and he had very little time in which to get back.

Half-way up we came upon hundreds of soldiers sitting on the side of the hill in their gas-masks. They looked like rows and rows of Spanish Inquisitors, and were all sitting in dead silence. Then we met the colonel of the batteries on that hill and he naturally wanted to know where we were going and who we were. We were very much blown and purple in the face, and began pulling out our permits, explaining between gasps who we were. Before we could finish he burst out, " Oh, yes, I know all about you ; you are most welcome to go up." And turning to our guide said, " Make haste, you have only ten minutes to get to the top and down to your battery." We ran the rest of the way, and arrived speechless at the observation post.

Luckily our guide was not as blown as we were ; he explained hastily who we were to the observer, and then with a polite wave and salute was gone. We had our

THE ATTACK ON GORIZIA

field-glasses and we settled down to watch the most wonderful sight imaginable.

The whole landscape was one mass of flame and smoke. The village just beneath us was red with smouldering fire, and shells were bursting every two minutes over it. The bridge over the Isonzo was broken in many places and great holes and gaps showed the water through them. As we watched we saw the first gun appear down the road towards the bridge going at a good smart trot. As it came fully into sight, it broke into a hand-gallop. A big high explosive burst at the other end of the bridge, but the gun kept steadily on, swung round the bend and off up into the town. It was followed closely by another and yet another. Shells were by this time bursting all round them and we were breathless for fear one should be hit. Then, just as two guns were on the bridge at the same time, came a big shell, bang in the middle of the bridge; a huge smoke went up, and nothing could be seen of the bridge or of the guns. As the smoke lifted, we saw that one gun was down, the other making a détour to avoid it: it seemed as if all must be killed—a mass of struggling men and beasts—and a groan went up from the officers standing near us. But no, they picked themselves up, hauled the horses to their feet and, as at the Military Tournament in London, quickly put on another wheel, and were up and off before you could count five. There was a roar of cheering from all the men who had been standing just below us; the officers turned, quickly made us a bow, saying, "It is our turn now," and ran off down the hill, leaving us in sole possession of the post. We stayed there another full half-hour watching the crossing of the cavalry, a most impressive sight.[1]

[1] We heard afterwards that the cavalry were being used to draw the enemy fire away from the infantry who were trying to cross the river near Podgòra.

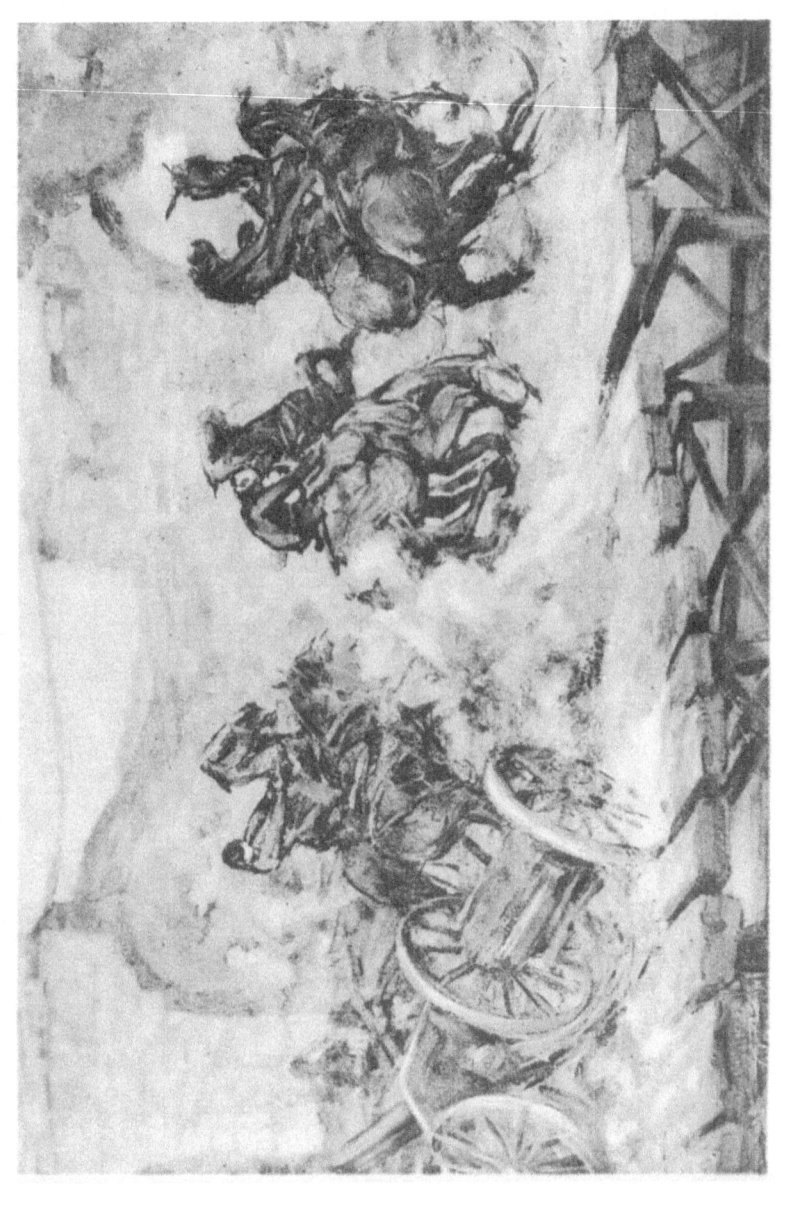

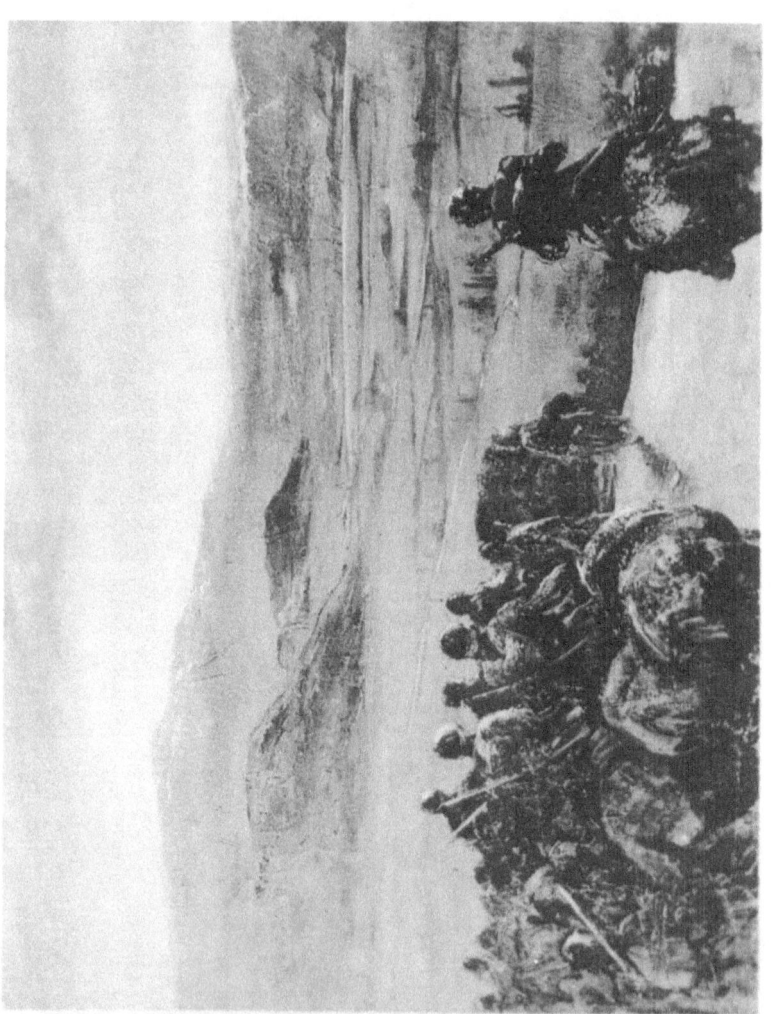

ENTRY OF TROOPS INTO GORIZIA, AUGUST 9TH, 1916

LEFT BEHIND

They took the bridge at a gallop singly, lying flat on their horses' necks, the shells falling steadily on the road and on the bridge, but we didn't see any of them hit, why, I can't think, as there was scarcely a square inch, at least so it seemed to us, that was not covered with explosives. It was getting too dark to see by this time, so we descended to find our car, which we had left under the shelter of the church tower, in a little hamlet at the foot of the hill. We were rather agitated at not finding it at once, but Whitehead soon appeared saying that as the tower had twice been hit while he was there, he had thought it as well to move away from its vicinity.

10th August, 1916.

To-day more work and already orders pouring in for to-morrow.

We feel much left behind. The observation balloons are in front of us now instead of miles back and the Italians have taken possession of the 305. guns that used to bombard Cormons, ammunition and all. The Austrians had underground passages under the river Isonzo to bring up their ammunition, and their dug-outs had sofas and pictures and arm-chairs and piano-fortes. We have seen lots of the clubs which the enemy use as weapons. These clubs sometimes have two iron rings, sometimes three with spikes all round. What do you think of that for modern civilization? I believe Lord Northcliffe is coming here for the night to-morrow. I wonder if you know him. We are looked upon as the curiosity section, I can't think why, except for the profusion of cases we get through and the miles we travel.

13th August, 1916.

I haven't had one minute to write. We have toiled and moiled from morn till night, yesterday doing sixty-

THE ATTACK ON GORIZIA

seven cases in the day. Nina did the morning alone as I was out hunting for a chassis, as we have broken our Austin one. It was our biggest day and we got in to dinner at 10.45 p.m. To-night we were back at nine-thirty, quite respectably early; I had started out at 8.15 a.m. to again try and borrow a chassis. However, as Lord Northcliffe, when he came to see us, said he would get us one immediately, we are not fussing. People are so nice that I can't help thinking it must be a mistake and be meant for someone else.

What has been so horrid since this advance is that we have been called to nearly every hospital to decide about fractured spines. Of course, if metal is lying on the spine an operation may help, but if, as we find nine times out of ten, it has passed through the spine and lodged the other side of the body, it means that no operation will help and the wounded man just has to wait a fortnight, three weeks, or even three months to die. And they always ask us if their backs are broken, nearly always. It is so hard to answer, but I have become such a hardened actor, and so has Nina, that we invent whatever we think will give them confidence. We had five at Dobrà yesterday all the same and all going to die, and three at Crauglio and three more to-day.

Fancy, to-day we had a man with fifteen shrapnel balls in him. Eleven they had taken out, the remaining four we found: one in his shoulder, one in his head, one in his elbow, and one in his thorax. He was so plucky helping us all he could, but kept holding on to me (I was doing the looking to-day) and whispering, "I am so tired"; then he quite suddenly fainted and we quickly finished our hunt for the bullets, while he was unconscious, very much better for him.

Now I will tell you a tale. On our way to St. Vito del Torre to-day from Medina we passed over a bridge.

TIRED OF WAR

On the far side was a carabiniere and a soldier, who both waved to us to stop. We stopped, very cross, because we were on our way to a case, and they hurried up saying, " Come quickly, there are two dead men and we daren't go down." There was a deep sand-pit with a huge *camion* standing on its bonnet in it, and underneath were two men lying on their backs apparently dead. Nina started to scramble down the branches of a tree on one side of the pit and I on the other, by the wheels of the *camion*. I shook one whom I saw move, and he opened a sleepy eye and smiled, so I said, " Dove sei ferito ? " which means " Where are you wounded ? " and his answer was " Grazie, Sto molto bene " (" Quite well, thank you "). I said anxiously, " Not bruised ? "— " Not at all, thank you." Then Nina withdrew the handkerchief from the face of the other. He, having red wine taken, was less coherent than his friend but equally smiling. They said they had had three days and nights in Gorizia and were sleepy ; that is all we could get out of them. By that time, and urged by us with forcible language, the carabiniere had descended, so we handed the responsibility over to him and departed. Evidently the two drivers had had enough of war and had just tipped their car over, then followed it down and gone to sleep under it. I felt quite sorry for the car, as it was completely smashed. But I believe they often do it when bored or frightened. We thought it very funny. However, when we told the story a few days later at Mess, the General and staff did not seem to see the humour of it. The heat is terrific and we are getting quite accustomed to streaming and mop like everyone else. The trouble is when we and the doctors drip together over the screen we are looking through, we all three withdraw hurriedly saying, " Scusi," not knowing who the drop came from. The house is quite fairly cool and the car always makes its own breeze,

THE ATTACK ON GORIZIA

so we freshen up between the hospitals, always getting either cold lemonade or hot coffee everywhere.

To-day, 17th August, we did ten officers at Quisca, one of whom was most interesting. He had a small mark under his left ear and we searched everywhere for the exit hole of the bullet which must have entered there. Nowhere could we find it. We asked him if he had felt no discomfort anywhere, had he felt sick perhaps? This question seemed to awake a memory. "Yes," he said, "I remember I did spit some blood, but very little." We moved the screen down to his lungs and there on the ribs lay the bullet just under the skin. It had just touched his lungs in passing. The nick of a scalpel and it was out. I never saw a man more relieved.

Yesterday we did a poor man who had no visible wound but was unaccountably paralysed in both legs, and when we radiographed him we found a rifle bullet on his spine. The odd part is that no wound has yet been found, so no one knows how it got there. We never get home to dinner until ten or ten-thirty and very seldom do less than thirty or forty cases a day. It is not so tiring as it sounds, as we don't have to start out till 9 a.m., getting back for some food usually about twelve-thirty, snoring on our beds till two-thirty, then out again till ten or eleven. This afternoon we struck—we were sent for to a place forty kilometres back behind the lines where they have plenty of other radiographers. We said we were too busy for such long distances as the drives there and back waste too much time.

23rd August, 1916.

It has been bitterly cold these last few days and is now, I hope, boiling up for heat again. I really thought that I didn't like dripping and pouring in rivers, but

A JOY-RIDE!

it is better than not being able to sleep for the cold. Bomba, our foundling dog, is as cold as me, and we hug each other all night to keep warm. I had two agonizing moments yesterday: I took him out for a run and he got under a motor-bicycle, lost his head, dashed under a staff car and then under a mule-cart. Why he wasn't killed three times over I can't think. He then fled howling down the road pursued by me. Luckily he had sufficient sense to turn up our lane, which was quieter, and I caught him before the next lorry came along. He was much agitated with a bloody leg, which may teach him to be more careful in future, but it's no good, dogs can't go loose here even for one moment, even the private soldiers all lead their dogs.

The day before yesterday we were taken a joy-ride by Knapp. Our coil had struck work, and while it was being mended we took the Berliet and started by Capriva and Mossa to Vipulzano via the Lenzuolo Bianco, up over the mountains to Valerisce, very steep and zigzaggy, with hair-pin bends, but Whitehead drove very well. Knapp had been in the battle and showed us just where everything had happened. We came across a huge gun hanging over the cliff, saw all the Austrian trenches and the caves dug under the hill, then Grafenberg, and Podgòra villages (none of them left of course), and under a railway, where we paused to look at the Lucinico bridge over the river. There we were rushed at by an elderly person who said, "You can't stand there, the bridge is being shelled this very moment." So rather than turn and back, we rushed on over the Lucinico bridge itself, which incidentally we had promised the General we would not cross. Unfortunate, but there was nothing else to be done, as we should have been caught turning if we had not rushed on at once. Anyway, we got across all

THE ATTACK ON GORIZIA

right and in to Gorizia. Such a pretty old town running down to the river. (I must go.)

Continuation of same letter, 24th August, 1916.

Knapp took us straight through to his ambulance section the other side. They have a big mother-section, and during a battle all the little ones are thrown out and after the battle come in to recuperate. The head of his section was a Captain Landreani, whom we liked very much. It had been formerly a huge monastery or clerical college and we were taken to the windows to look at the Austrian lines only one and a half kilometres away. Knapp was rather silly as he opened the shutters of his own room, much to Landreani's annoyance, as the enemy can see the house and snipe through the windows whenever one is open. Landreani told us that he was very anxious to prevent the enemy finding out that it was used as a dressing-station. Then we were given coffee and departed by the other bridge this time, which is out of sight of the Austrians, but—we joined the road leading to Lucinico bridge later and an awful thing happened. We were in a short bit of road where we had to hurry and suddenly the Berliet said she could no more! Something wrong with the clutch or the gears jammed; we stopped dead, blocking the narrow road completely. *Camion* after *camion* got blocked behind us, until they were actually stretching on to the bridge itself, which was under fire, and we knew the Austrians would see the traffic jam and would put shells into the middle of it. Knapp grew white with agitation, and a friendly *camion* in front backed down to us with a rope and thirty men to push, and we got on, luckily without a shell having burst on the hindmost *camion*, but everyone was most agitated. The Berliet was placed behind a wall and left there until it could be towed back; we went home ourselves in the friendly *camion*.

Yesterday we were along the same road and met Captain Landreani, who jumped out of his car and said, "I must tell you what happened last night after you had left. We were at dinner when the whole of one end of the house was blown away, all Knapp's fault for opening that window." Landreani's bedroom was included, where he had put some bits of shell which he was going to engrave for us with the date of our visit. It was only about two hours after we left so we were lucky not to have been there.

31st August, 1916.

At last they have given us a chauffeur. I am delighted as I personally hate driving up in the mountains. The Daimler car is far too heavy and too unwieldy and wears me out trying to keep her under control. Whitehead has been ill these last two weeks, so Hewitt and I have had to do all the driving.

Do spread General Capello's name about as having taken Gorizia and carried out the whole attack. There are wheels within wheels and his enemies are trying to take the credit from him, whereas he planned and carried out the whole thing from start to finish. It was his Army Corps (the VI) which was increased for the occasion to thirteen divisions instead of four. He and his Chief of Staff, Badoglio, did the whole thing, and I have never even seen his name mentioned in the English newspapers. His Army Corps behaved splendidly. They attacked and took Sabotino in an hour and ten minutes, and it usually takes an hour in peace-time even to walk up. The great conductor, Toscanini, ran ahead with his bandsmen playing to encourage the men.

Coming back yesterday from Gorizia, poor ruined

THE ATTACK ON GORIZIA

Lucinico was looking so beautiful that I am going to try and find half an hour to do a sketch there. It was wonderful as a mass of golden-coloured ruins standing out against the blue mountains.

I never write and tell you of the horrors or of the sadnesses we see because it helps no one. You, so far away, can do nothing to help, and we here mustn't let ourselves realize the suffering and pain or we shouldn't be able to do our work. To-day we were working in a big building where they bring the worst cases before sending them on to hospital, and many quick operations have to be performed before they can be moved. The bustle and noise, the groaning, the cries for " Mamma mia," the smell of disinfectants and the smell of blood all help to make the place a nightmare, never to be forgotten, but the work has to be got through in double-quick time, as more and more men are being carried in and more are expected. I found one boy, not more than fifteen years of age, lying on his stretcher under the window, quite quietly watching with big eyes all that was going on, knowing that his turn was coming soon. I asked him about his wound and with pride he showed me a hole in his thigh, big enough to put both your fists into. " It doesn't hurt," he said, " and I'm not a bit frightened, only very much interested," and when the stretcher-bearers came for him, and he was carried into the next room, where I counted eleven operating tables with operations going on at each, he held out his hand as he passed me with a smile and a reassurance that he was not frightened and knew quite well that they wouldn't hurt him more than they could help. I wonder what happened to him, it was a very nasty wound. An officer, a *sotto-tenente*, came to our rooms one day to ask us to X-ray his leg which had a bullet in it. He said, if we could find it, he would dig it out with his knife, as he particularly did not want to

A GOOD BOY

go into hospital; there was an attack coming on next day which he would not miss for anything, and he knew that once in hospital, they would never let him go. We were so sorry to have to refuse to help, but it would never have done to have let him dig it out himself, he might have died of blood-poisoning. So we drove a very disappointed boy to hospital, and he went in very sadly, and we heard no more of him. I think we are lucky having this kind of work to do instead of working in hospitals. The wounded, when we see them, have only just been hurt and are quite well men, suffering from shock or loss of blood, and generally are not in much pain as the shock seems to numb the pain. It is only later, when they have been in hospital some time, that they become ill, sick men. We saw that in Paris and they were a very sad sight there. Here most of the men we deal with have not had time to become ill. You ask what the hospitals are like. Up here at the Front the hospitals are kept beautifully clean, the ones farther back we haven't seen.

7th September.

The head of the *sanità* of the VI Army Corps, a blunt old person with bottle-brush grey hair, came to-day and said the Third Army had asked for us and also the XI Army Corps, also that the Italian Force going to France had asked for us, but that he had begged the General not to let us go, as we were doing such useful work and could not be spared. We wriggled coyly and said, "A great pleasure, I'm sure," but it was much nicer than butter. I have written a report (in Italian! with a wet towel round my head) of the work done during our time here. It is for the authorities in Rome and full of statistics (of course that is why I have got a headache, I could not think why). We have been

THE ATTACK ON GORIZIA

asked to choose out of 2,220 plates about forty good ones and send prints up to Rome. Nina has been doing the hospitals and I have been sitting at home toiling at the report.

19

GORIZIA

9th September, 1916.

THE report is finished and sent in, and now we are all agog for another outburst of work which ought to be here before you get this. The Red Cross has given us £500 to buy a Fiat chassis and the Italian Army has given us one as a present. So our broken Austin had its body shifted on to one of them and the Daimler's body on to the other and now at last we are really fit to climb mountains. The Daimler has been just hateful on hills and no one except Whitehead and me could drive it, as its brakes never worked till five minutes later than you thought they were going to; result, when the Italian chauffeurs drove it we always ran into walls, etc.; also, being six-cylinder, it's miles too long to turn on hairpin bends and frightens me into fits having to back right to the edge of the cliff at each turn. We caused great joy the other day in one of the villages. I was driving the Daimler and wished to make a swagger arrival at the front door of the General's quarters, where there was a sentry standing on duty in a sentry-box, looking very smart. To my rage, on putting on the brakes they didn't act, and we slid on to the sentry-box, gently overturning it and its inhabitant. I shall never forget his face of terror. The people in the piazza howled with delight and picked him and his box upright again, brushing him down and assuring him that he wasn't hurt, which providentially he was not. I have been chaffed about it ever since.

It is beastly cold and the guns have begun again like mad, never ceasing, but of course much farther off. Everyone is talking of moving on, and we should be glad, for nice as this house is, the rules and orders in this town now are most tiresome. All the officials are new and we are always being stopped and asked what business we have here and when we go up to the Front line we find all our old friends; even the carabinieri, there beam upon us.

Our first business visit to Gorizia (we had been there with Knapp once before to see the lie of the land in case we were sent for in a hurry) was an interesting one. Nina happened to be late that morning and we started a good ten minutes after we meant to. As we got down to the bridge of Lucinico it was being shelled, so the carabiniere on duty signed to us to wait under cover of a bit of wall, and to be ready to go directly he made a sign, and then to go fast, so as to get over before another shell came. We kept our engine running, and I kept her in gear with the clutch ready to slip in the second we got the signal. When it came, we went as hard as we could at the bridge and got across nicely as the next shell burst behind us. The going was not easy, as the holes in the bridge were many and large, and lots of them had been stuffed with mattresses! We buzzed up the hill past the station at Gorizia and along the main street, the Corso, a fine wide street with large trees on either side—plane-trees, I think they were.

The houses were knocked about a certain amount, but not nearly as much as we had expected, and not nearly as much as they were afterwards by the Austrians.

HOSPITAL OF THE FATE BENE FRATELLI

As we got opposite to the Opera House, we stopped and asked a sentry to tell us where the hospital of the Fate Bene Fratelli was. He pointed up the next street saying, "It is up there, but you cannot go there, it is being shelled and no one may go down the street." We told him that it was orders and that we had been sent for, so he stood back. When we got to the hospital we found it in a fine mess. A 305· shell had burst in the top storey ten minutes before, had blown off most of the roof and smashed the greater part of the staircase, which had since collapsed. The doorways had all gone crooked and were slipping sideways, while worst of all was the white lime dust knee-deep everywhere and the smell of formalin. The chemicals were kept on the top storey and every bottle had been broken. Tears were streaming from everyone's eyes as the fumes filled the space where the staircase had been.

The surgeons were delighted to see us and at once sent for the wounded who were to be X-rayed. They proposed that we should work in the cellar, whither they had taken all the wounded; but that was impossible, as it was too damp, and our wires would have short-circuited all the time, so we went on a voyage of discovery and found a small room which suited our purpose. It was only just big enough for our trestles and stretcher, and the explosions had done something odd to the doorway which had gone all crooked. There was also a big split in the wall which became considerably wider while we worked. After we had finished we were asked to go down to the cellar to cheer up the wounded who had been taken there for safety when the hospital was shelled. As we came down the dark stone stairs we were met by a strange Rembrandt-like effect. The only illumination in the great cellar, crowded with half-seen figures standing and lying about, came from a few lanterns with candles in them; one old woman sitting up, and silhouetted against a light, called to us to come and hear how wonderful had been her escape. She had been on the top storey and all the people near her had been killed when the shell burst, but the surgeon-in-chief, Fadda by name, had himself carried her down, just as the stairs fell. She was eighty, she said, and he had risked his life to save her, and she an enemy! What splendid enemies they were, to risk their own lives to save useless old women like her, etc., etc. The surgeon, a big tall Sardinian, was very shy and tried in vain to stop her praises, but it was a fine thing to have done and it is not surprising that she was grateful. In every hospital that we went to, we found the same good-fellowship between the Italians and Austrians.

This letter has just arrived from another hospital: " Grazie al suo prezioso ausilio ho potuto salvare un' altra vita avendo operato felicemente quel tenente di Bersaglieri, di cui ella ha esseguito ultimamente le radiografie." (Thanks to your precious help I have been able to save another life, having operated successfully on the lieutenant of Bersaglieri whom you radiographed the other day.) Quite satisfactory. It was one of those backs again as usual; they are generally so hopeless to cope with, besides hurting the people so much while doing them, as they have to be moved about.

12th September, 1916.

Yesterday we heard of rather a curious case. A bullet went in between a man's legs and stuck in his sacrum. He was radiographed and it was clearly seen. Too ill to be operated upon they waited and radiographed him eight days later and the bullet had disappeared; they hunted everywhere with the screen and finally found it at the entrance to his heart: it was in a vein and had got pumped up with the blood, and as they watched it, it made a wavy motion and a rotary one at the same time. They have left it where it is as the man feels no effect from it, but I should think if it blocks the valve he will die suddenly.

At last the promised attack has begun and is going on night and day. We can see the hill from our windows with the shells bursting all over it, and yesterday saw a most thrilling fight between four Italian and three Austrian aeroplanes over the Isonzo. We were in Sagrado working at the moment.

I wish the English wasps could be educated like Italian wasps. Firstly, there are very few here, and secondly, if you flap at them they leave by the window immediately.

18th September, 1916.

Yesterday a little lieutenant turned up, most fussy and said, "I wish to know by what right you are here in this house." I told him the General had put us here a year ago, but he said that that was not a sufficient answer, and we must show papers to prove it or leave at once. So, livid with rage, I showed him the very grateful acceptance of our services by the Minister of War and incidentally one from the head of the *Intendenza*, General Lombardi, who is as big as Cadorna himself, giving us, as a present from the Italian Army, a motor chassis "in recognition of our most valuable work." He didn't want to read them, but I made him, and his whole manner changed to that of an obsequious worm. He asked when he might return for our answer about the house, and we said when he had seen his colonel and reported what had passed. The result was a visit from his colonel to apologize and say it was all a mistake. I then wrote to the head of the *sanità*, Colonel Santucci, and he came down and has had papers made out which regularize everything and make it impossible for anyone to bother us. We had always wanted

GORIZIA

official documents before, but both Lord Monson and Capello said they were quite unnecessary, so we couldn't press the point. If I had already come home on leave, how would Nina have coped with that, having so little Italian, for French isn't always sufficient? It is all right with most of the heads of departments, but with underlings Italian is a necessity. She talks very fluent pidgin-Italian, but that doesn't take you very far in a heated discussion. My own isn't very good at nuances as I frequently miss the point and have to ask for it to be repeated, but it does for all practical purposes and for letters. Everyone says that I shall never be able to talk Italian really well because I always translate literally from French, and as everyone understands me I never find the necessity of learning anything different. It is quite true, if I don't know a word I just coin one and they always understand, and never laugh. It is only when I ask an Italian to correct one of my letters or reports that I find every word is wrong. Rather a shock, but as they all say that my lingo is absolutely clear, what does it matter?

No more now, I must go to bed. The attack is getting more and more violent, the hill far away straight in front of the house has been shelled five days and nights, now with great columns of smoke towering up into the sky.

21st September, 1916.

We have had a very worrying time with our material, seven hospitals calling and everything suddenly out of order.

> Fiat given by Italian Army not ready.
> Fiat bought by the Red Cross not ready.
> Berliet broken, not ready.
> Daimler broken down, burnt out.
> Lady Johnstone's motor seized up.

WORRIES

Isn't it despairing. Just as we had been so patted on the back for always being ready. We have spent two agitating days trying to find out why, and why, and why, and have sadly come to the conclusion that it's all Hewitt's carelessness. He was so excellent in the beginning but has now become the laziest little pig in existence, and so as to save himself trouble has repeatedly wired the dynamo of the Daimler in a certain position and then gone to sleep on the seat. The result being that the dynamo generated more and more force, he didn't notice it, and the current being unable to get on, short-circuited and burnt out the dynamo. This is not a scientific explanation, but it is what we gathered from our friend Captain Borsari, who came over yesterday and spent all the afternoon with us testing our material to find out what was wrong; he also found that the dynamo of Lady Johnstone's motor was not damaged, as stated by Hewitt, but seized up because he jolly well hadn't taken the trouble to oil it. If it hadn't been impossible to get another Englishman we should have got rid of him long ago, but at least one can depend on his coming on in a tight place, which is something to be grateful for.

You don't know what it has been these last few days, being called repeatedly and urgently by hospitals and having to say we can't come, knowing that probably many have died because the surgeons dare not operate without X-ray or because they have operated unnecessarily. I can't understand why their own radiographic cars don't work better. I said the other day at Sagrado, " Why do you send for us when you have two X-ray cars within reach ? " And the director said, " Firstly, because you always come when sent for " (that he can't say now), " and secondly, because they are either out of order, or say they can't do what we ask them, or won't radioscope and will only take radiographs. Anyway, we would rather send for you." You see, we attempt anything as we have no reputation to keep up, and these professors won't risk doing bad radiographs because they have their good name to think of. Also, they say their tube is getting tired and shut it off, whereas we work till it bursts; and they dictate to the surgeons and we let the surgeons dictate for themselves (sometimes).

Lord Northcliffe's article in *The Times* made the Red Cross give us the money for one car, but the other, which has been given us by the Italian Army, is the pride of our lives. Long before Lord Northcliffe's visit and the publication of his article, we had talked to Capello about our car being unfit for high mountains and he had talked to General Lombardi, head of the *Intendenza*, who wired to General Delmé Radcliffe to say we had done such good work that it was with the greatest pleasure, etc., that the Italian Army gave us one, and that we were not to think of paying it back. It was just as we got that message that we heard that the Red Cross in England had put £500 at our disposal to buy a Fiat, so we jumped at having a second car instead of our lengthy Daimler which, as somebody rudely said, looks like a bathing-machine behind and an outrigger in front and can't climb hills.

We are starting work again to-day with a list of eight clamorous hospitals with probably about fifteen cases in each.

27th September.

We did our 2,697th plate this morning and had a very exciting day. Just as we were crossing the bridge of boats out of Gorizia, they began to shell it and the whole line was held up by jibbing mules. There was much shouting and confusion till General Lombardi,[1]

[1] Quarter-Master General.

GENERAL LOMBARDI

who was in one of the cars on the bridge behind us, ran up, and had a rope fixed on to the pole of the offending wagon and ordered the lorry in front of it to pull it and the mules out of the way. You can't think how amusing it was to see the mules, with their obstinate faces and their feet stuck out in front of them, being dragged up the bank. General Lombardi then came to our car and told us that he had long wanted to see section four at work and he was delighted to meet us in such a tight place, etc. After which he got into his car and drove off, and we continued our journey to Sagrado. To get to Sagrado we had to cross another bridge of boats, which they began to shell also just as we came to it, and we are the proud possessors of a shrapnel bullet which stuck in the car which we were driving. Both it and our other car which was following us were spattered by earth and stones.

28th September, 1916.

Now that it is settled that Nina's sister, Ethel Smyth,[1] comes to take my place, I hope to start home 17th or 18th October. I hear officers' leave begins on the 1st November or, with persuasion, a week before. They count us absolutely as officers, and Headquarters sent word officially yesterday that leave would be granted then. I hear it takes two nights and a day to Paris; everyone has to stay twenty-four hours in Paris these days and then it takes twenty-four hours or more home. What a journey; roughly four days to get back.

Just been to Vipulzano where we used to go all the winter amid shot and shell. So funny to go peacefully along a beautiful wide road with never a shell hole, and other new roads all running into it.

[1] **Dame Ethel Smyth,** the well-known composer.

GORIZIA

2nd October, 1916.

I expect we are going to change position considerably and heaven knows when I shall get away. In this devilish war one's family can't count at all. I was so sorry for a nice doctor near here, director of one of the hospitals we go to. His little girl is fearfully ill and he (only through the personal favour of his general) got three days off, and I saw him the day he came back. She will either die or be a permanent invalid with a spinal complaint, and he had to leave her to another doctor and come back here. He was saying how hopeless it is to be fond of anyone at this moment.

I had rather a lucky escape yesterday. I was being introduced to a charming bulldog and he suddenly flew quite straight at my nose. I don't think he meant anything, but his master was terrified, and thumped him hard and would not let me speak to him afterwards without holding him at the same time. I was talking afterwards to Nina and saying that I thought it was only a rough form of kiss, and she said quite gently, " He bit my leg, but I didn't mention it because he had already been thumped once." They were both butts more than bites, but it would have been a pity if I had returned minus a nose and Nina minus a leg. The young man's friend told us afterwards that the dog had bitten a child very badly in the face only two days before.

An excellent letter from Eddie to-day, which I read out to two doctors who were here. I didn't find Eddie's colloquialisms easy to translate into Italian, but they seemed to understand. Luckily there was a description of the new armoured cars (tanks), and they were thrilled, having thought the rumours of them were, as they said, American.

THE BIG X-RAY PLANT IN GORIZIA

12th October, 1916, 6.30 a.m.

Thank heaven our dynamo went like a dream yesterday. We were out from 7.30 a.m. to 9.30 p.m. This big advance has given us masses to do and we cover a tremendous lot of ground, also I have lost three stone. They want us to make our headquarters in Gorizia and the VI Army Corps will not have it at any price. I personally think we shall do more work from outside, as once established there we should be so busy with the hospitals in the town that we should not have any time for those outside.

The Italians are doing very well indeed. We met the King yesterday, who stopped his car to present us to the Queen who was with him, and he told us that they had got 5,000 prisoners here and 3,000 at Monfalcone in one day. They were beaming.

16th October, 1916.

We have been asked by the General in Gorizia to take complete charge of a plant, a big Austrian one, in the hospital there. Nina has undertaken the arranging of it and is setting it up. They are altering a big room by her orders and building a dark-room, putting in running water, etc. They wanted her to run it, but we have refused to alter our original habits and have telegraphed for a first-rate radiographic woman from England [1] to work it under her, and we shall continue our old ways of going from hospital to hospital for the untransportable cases.

This magnificent apparatus had been rather badly smashed, but Nina, helped by a little Italian corporal, who had been lent to her, put it into working order

---

[1] The English radiographer never came. Eventually they put in an Italian, but not for some time, Nina continuing to run it for them, and having masses of work.

GORIZIA

in a very short time. The Italians are delighted as they had not a single X-ray plant in Gorizia excepting ours, and all the worst wounded are there. They say they will be satisfied with whoever we put in to work it.

20

THE ITALIAN ARMY AS WE SAW IT

IN all the time we were in Italy I only once knew a man show insubordination, and he, I think, was rather odd in the head. He could not understand that he might not go out whenever it pleased him.

If it ever became necessary, we asked the Captain of the Engineers, to whom our men were attached for rations and pay, to deal with them. The punishment usually consisted of their pay being docked for a week, or perhaps a couple of days' cells—this last they rather liked, as they seized the opportunity to sleep all the time. They used to be put in a tent in the middle of the courtyard with a sentry over them, and all their friends made excuses to stand near and talk so that they could hear, only hurrying away when an officer or an N.C.O. appeared.

Rules were very strict about the time the soldiers reported themselves at night. Any soldier found out and about after 9 p.m. was instantly locked up by the carabinieri unless he had a special permit from his chief, which stated that he was out on duty. Soldiers going on leave had to go to the baths and be thoroughly washed and disinfected before leaving, and the same rules were observed on their return, the junior officers being shut in with the men on their return from leave and often spending the night in a room strewn with straw, all waiting together for their bath and disinfec-

THE ITALIAN ARMY AS WE SAW IT

tion. Several of them told us that the first night back from leave is one of the most unpleasant in a campaign, and they mostly spend it walking up and down the room.

Looting of any kind is looked upon very sternly, and any man caught looting, or merely souvenir-hunting, is very severely punished. In the two years we spent in Italy we never saw a single Italian soldier the worse for drink. In the matter of cruelty to animals the Italian army is very severe, the slightest hint of any soldier being cruel to his beast and he is punished, men being sent to the punishment trenches on the second report; the reason for this being not only humanity but expediency, as every man is taught the importance of keeping his beast fit and well for the work he has to do.

The Italian soldier is very well turned out and generally looks exceedingly smart; even close up to the Front he usually wears a small white choker inside his collar, which gives the appearance of cleanliness. How they always manage to have them clean I do not know, but somehow they always did. Their breeches were very well cut, and they certainly were the smartest-looking of the Allies.

Another thing that struck us very favourably was the absolute want of red tape. We never saw any of it, and I heard English officials say the same thing. Instead of the usual insurmountable rules and regulations to be found in other armies, whatever we asked for was given with the best of goodwill, and in consequence we were careful to ask for as little as possible.

We were impressed, too, by the cleanliness of the hospitals. Of course we knew nothing of the Base as we were at the Front all the time, and so saw only the field hospitals and dressing-stations, but the cleanliness everywhere struck us very forcibly. We had every opportunity of judging, because we were in and out

ORGANIZATION AND CLEANLINESS

of them at all times and in all places. We saw them when they were so busy with fresh cases pouring in after an action that the surgeons and orderlies did not know where to turn. We saw them at all hours of the day and also at all hours of the night. Often when the work was heavy we stayed on all night to screen the cases as they came in, and always the same good organization and cleanliness. One hospital I remember, which had been prepared for 150 patients, received 380 after a big action; the staff, of course, was worried, but by no means lost its head and very soon tents had been erected in the courtyard and gardens, straw mattresses or straw-stuffed sacks borrowed or made, all the men housed till they could have their wounds attended to, and the least badly wounded sent on to other hospitals.

After an action, such as the taking of Podgòra and Gorizia the labour battalions were turned on immediately to tidy up; and although we were generally on the roads within a couple of days, all was tidy and clean, all the horrors taken away, the roads cleared of débris and the shell-holes filled.

19th October, 1916.

They have given us an electrician and a mechanic, so we are much better off than we were, but we had a mutiny yesterday at Cormons among the men, caused by a beastly English Red Cross chauffeur who has been sent out to us. He is of the type that preaches on tubs; whenever frightened says he is ill and that the Italians insult him and that he intends to go home. I told him not to be an idiot, that he had signed on for six months and had to bide by his contract; he was then excessively insolent and said he would not be ordered about; he also said that he had not been sent out here to be taken to nasty dangerous places by ladies. If there is no

THE ITALIAN ARMY AS WE SAW IT

improvement he will have to be given two days' cells, but we are giving him a chance, as cells in a carabiniere prison are not comfortable, and we do not want to have to put him there if we can help it, although the brute deserves it thoroughly. He had managed to set all our Italians by the ears, too, for the first and only time, but as Carlo Calabrini (Master of the King's Horse) happened to be here at the moment, he gave them all a talking to and all is now well with them, bless them.

We were asked out to dinner by the King and Queen the other day, miles away, and they sent Marchese Elia (Master of Ceremonies) in a car to fetch us. I happened to remark at dinner how good the chicken was, as no chickens were obtainable at Cormons, and ever since, on every Saturday, there arrive four clucking chickens which the dogs chase round the garden until all their fat leaves them. You cannot think how kind the Queen has been. She has sent us ham and tongue and all sorts of stores, also a huge box of chocolates which, I regret to say, Nina and I ate at a sitting, and best of all she, who loves mechanics, etc., and knows all the ins and outs of X-rays, has sent us a new dynamo to replace the one that we broke the other day.

How you would have laughed if you had seen me coping with six angry soldiers yesterday evening. "I quite agree with you," I said; "the new Englishman is impossible, and he will be punished; but if ever one of you complains to me or Mrs. Hollings again, or makes any disturbance in the house, not one but *all* shall be sent back to their *reparto* (regiment) with the worst report we can give, and you know that means the trenches for all of you." I also said that if anyone had anything to say they were to tell the *caporale maggiore*, who would report to Nina or me if necessary. They all said in a loud chorus, "Si, si, Signora," and all is

GOLD MEDAL FOR VALORE MILITARE

now beaming. It is only the Englishmen who are impossible. Whitehead is excellent, but the other two quite hopeless.

The Principe Ereditario has just been, such a nice boy of about twelve, with beautiful manners, and absolutely un-shy. Rhodina Bellegarde is here, learning how to interpret for Nina when I go, very clever and good-natured and so helpful with our letters, etc. We have nine hospitals calling for us this minute, and our cars won't be ready till Monday. Calabrini trots to and fro trying to hurry them.

On 22nd October the General sent a colonel of the staff to tell us that we were to be given the *Medaglia al Valore Militare*. A man gained the gold one the other day at the taking of Gorizia, a little *sotto-tenente*, Baruzzi by name. He rushed a tunnel under Podgòra with only four soldiers with him; two of these he left at the mouth, and inside the tunnel were 300 Austrians with a lot of officers. When he appeared they tried to show fight, but he shouted, " No use, surrender, I have the whole regiment just outside, and you are surrounded; I have been sent to take you prisoners." This thing of eighteen then proceeded calmly to introduce himself and shake hands with the officers and take all their arms; the two soldiers with him made all the others pile arms, while one of those he had left at the entrance was sent off post-haste to bring up more men. This took three-quarters of an hour as Baruzzi had gone right ahead of his regiment. He held the Austrians talking all that time so that they had no suspicion he was alone. Then, once his regiment had come up, and others had taken charge, he was the first to swim the Isonzo and the first to get to the *castello* and put up the Italian flag, so he has been given the gold medal.

Prince Gonzaga, who is over seventy, was in com-

THE ITALIAN ARMY AS WE SAW IT

mand of the troops attacking the heights on the far side of the Isonzo. Again and again the Italians were driven back by the Austrian guns hidden in caves. At last the splendid old Gonzaga said he would lead the troops himself. He ordered three of the strongest of his young officers to push and pull him up the mountain; one behind and one on each side heaved him up the rocks, followed enthusiastically by all the rest of his men, and the caves and guns were taken at a rush and the Austrians swept off the first heights of the Bainsizza Plateau. Needless to say Prince Gonzaga was given the Gold Medal *al valore* for this. It was a wonderful performance for a man of his age. There are three grades of this medal, the gold, the silver and the bronze. We are being given the bronze and very proud we are of it.

23rd October, 1916.

Yesterday Dr. Sbrozzi, the well-known brain surgeon for whom we do a lot of work, came to see us, bringing his wife, who had been allowed to come up to the Front on permit for two days. A nice, gentle little woman, rather shy and very quiet. When we had had tea I offered to drive them back to the hospital as she was rather tired; having walked into Cormons several miles, she was very grateful and agreed at once. We had gone about two miles when we met an officer of carabinieri on horseback with his orderly riding behind him. On seeing us approach he pulled his horse across the road and ordered us to stop. I remonstrated, saying that our cars were allowed to go anywhere in that sector of the Front, and I started to pull out my permits and passes, etc. Without even looking in my direction he said, " I know you, Contessa, and you can go anywhere you wish, in your car or out of it, but I know nothing of these people in your car, and insist

A BAD TEMPER

on seeing their papers." This was reasonable, although his manner was very offensive, so they produced their papers and handed them over. The carabinieri examined them, turned to Dr. Sbrozzi and said sharply, "Yours are all right, but this woman must return immediately to Headquarters to be examined; her papers say she may go by train, or on foot, or in a cart or carriage, but do not mention a motor-car. She will therefore walk behind my horse," and turning to her said, "Get out of that car." Madame Sbrozzi was humbly obeying, when I thought the moment had come to interfere. . . . I put my arm across the door to prevent her getting out and said that if there was a question of her having to return I should take her back myself and report to the General what had happened, and that she was my guest and I considered myself responsible for her. I also explained that she was far too delicate to be able to walk back two miles at the pace of a horse; at this the officer lost his temper suddenly and quite completely; he stood up in his stirrups swearing and shouting at her, ordering her to obey him instantly. I, too, became somewhat ruffled, and swinging my car round went off to Cormons as hard as I could, with the poor little lady in tears of terror and her husband very white-faced and frightened, as the carabinieri inspire much fear in Italy. The surgeon kept saying over and over again, "You English do not know what it is to come up against the carabinieri in this country, they always win." I was determined to do my best that this one should not win this time, so went as fast as the car would travel to the General's Headquarters. Alas, the General himself was out, but his Chief of Staff came down at once to see what I wanted. I told my story and asked his advice. He listened, with an amused face, said, "I think I can arrange it for you," and went to the telephone to call up the Colonel commanding the carabinieri. Back he came to say, "It will be all right, go quickly to the carabinieri Headquarters and see the Colonel before that man gets back with his story, but be quick." Luckily I knew where they were, and we got there in two minutes. I went in, saw the Colonel, introduced my poor shivering guest, who showed her papers, and the Colonel inserted the word "motor-car" on her permit, and we went out to our car feeling somewhat elated, although they were both still very pale.

We resumed our drive, back along the same road. Lo, our friend, trotting fast down the middle of the street towards us! With a dramatic gesture, he pulled his horse hard on to his haunches, his arm thrown up with a most commanding air . . . "Halt." We halted. "Get out of that car." I explained mildly that the lady now had a special permit from the Colonel of carabinieri to proceed to her destination in a motor-car, and I held out her pass. He bent from his horse and snatched it from my hand, looked at it, grunted and put it in his pocket, signing to me to go on . . . not so, we were not going to move until we got that hard-earned pass back. I asked politely for it, he said "No" . . . so I heaved a heavy sigh and said very well, I supposed that I must return to his colonel and tell him that his signature counted for nothing with his subordinates. I never saw anyone lose his temper more completely; he stared furiously at me, spat on the ground—he would have liked to have spat at us—snatched the permit from his pocket, rolled it into a ball and hurled it full into the poor lady's face, hitting her on the nose. He then galloped away down the street towards Headquarters, digging his spurs into his unfortunate horse. Very soon we were to find out why he had been so annoyed at having to give up the permit. He had told every carabiniere in the town and out of

THE MILITARY POLICE

it to stop us and to arrest the lady if she tried to pass again. We were stopped thirteen times in all, but the permit signed by their own colonel did the trick directly they saw it and each guard saluted and let us pass.

We were dining that night at the Headquarters' Mess and were much chaffed by the General who had heard all about our adventure.

The Carabiniere Force is a wonderful one. During the War they were invariably in the most dangerous places and could always be trusted to keep their heads in a tight place, calmly keeping order wherever most wanted, but unlike the English police, who are usually so ready to help in a difficulty, the carabinieri had no wish to help, although now and again we were able to help them.

The approaches to the bridges were generally crammed with incident, and often, especially at night, were very difficult driving. The road was generally crowded with troops, lorries and mules going both ways, usually in dead silence and pitch darkness, as no light was allowed of any kind. The high screens on each side of the road blocked out even the flashes from the guns which lit the sky, and except for the noise of the distant enemy batteries, broken occasionally by the roar of one of ours stationed alongside the road, the only noise was the shuffling of many feet and an occasional muttered curse when someone bumped into someone else.

One night about 11 p.m., I had left Nina in Gorizia, and was on my way back to Cormons, with Whitehead driving. It was pitchy dark, and when we got down to the banks of the river we found ourselves in an unholy jam. It was impossible to move one way or the other: there were kicking mules, backing horses, and huge lorries or *camions*, while the usual carabiniere seemed to be absent for once. I descended from the front of the car into the crowd, and found there was barely room to get between the various carts and motors, so tightly jammed were they. At last I wriggled my way through, and discovered an agitated carabiniere with a small lantern, carefully shaded, in his hand. On my appeal to him to make way for us, he said it was impossible, that the jam had been there two hours already, and that he was quite helpless alone. I suggested that if I went to one end of the block with my electric torch, and if he stayed at this end, perhaps we might get them on the move. He agreed hopefully, and back I toiled through the crowd, telling them as I passed to be ready to follow directly the one in front moved, even if it was only an inch. I forget how it was eventually done, but between us we soon got them on the move, and we managed to get our motor through and down to the bridge. There it was so dark that we could not see where the bridge, a pontoon, ended or began. Out I had to get again and walk over just in front of the car with my electric torch lit inside my hand, so that only a little red glow showed Whitehead where I was and where the centre of the bridge was. I was in a blue funk, because it was so slippery from wet that I nearly fell at every step, and if I had gone down the car would have been sure to run over me, as Whitehead owned he could not see an inch in front of his face, and my light was very small.

We always had adventures on that bridge: once a shell caught a cart immediately behind us, and at the same time another landed in the road immediately before us. It must be remembered that the nearest Austrian trenches were barely a mile beyond the town.

One day we had been into Udine to buy comestibles, and coming out of the town were accosted by a polite young man in Italian uniform who saluted and asked if we were returning to Gorizia that day; if so, might

SPIES

he and his companion follow us, as they did not know the way?

The companion, likewise in uniform, was driving a closed car, which made him rather difficult to see.

We apologized, and said we were not allowed to take anyone with us. The officer continued, however, to press his point, saying they had to be with their regiment at a certain time and it was very important they should not be late. But we were quite firm, and recommending them to go to the officials, who would help them, we drove away.

When we came to the first guard post on a long bridge over the river the carabinieri passed us with kind smiles of recognition, but stopping a little farther on to put on coats we looked back and saw the car behind us, with the same officers, speaking to the carabinieri at the head of the bridge, gesticulating and pointing to us, evidently saying they belonged to us. So we drove on as quickly as possible to the guard post the other end of the bridge, where we reported to the officer in charge that we knew nothing of the car following us, and that if they announced that they belonged to our section, or knew us, or had our permission to follow us, it was not true, and that they must be questioned. We looked back, and saw that the carabinieri had stopped the car, and while we watched we saw the two hapless young men placed under arrest and marched into the guard-room.

Afterwards we heard that they were spies trying to get into the Italian lines behind Gorizia, and that they had met the usual fate of spies.

24th October, 1916.

Here is a tale which will make me blush for the rest of my existence. We received a message calling for us to go to a certain big hospital in Gorizia, marked

"Very Urgent," and asking us both to be sure and come and to be there at twelve. The time ought to have made us smell a rat, as we knew quite well that the hospital fed at twelve and were not likely to begin work at that moment. We were completely trapped and arrived punctually with our apparatus all ready for use. We were greeted on the steps of the hospital by the head surgeon and all his officers with shouts of amusement that we had been taken in. They had wanted to congratulate us on having been given the *Valore* Medal and had arranged a huge feast in our honour! They knew quite well that had we known, we should have excused ourselves and said we had too much to do, so they had planned this trap for us and we had fallen headlong into it, much to their joy. The other hospitals in and near Gorizia had joined with them, and there must have been thirty or forty other guests besides ourselves. There was nothing to be done, we were caught, and although much flattered were speechless with terror, but had to play up.

We were ushered into an enormous hall with long tables spread with every kind of food collected from everywhere, a very difficult feat in those days. Nearly as many orderlies as there were guests were standing round the room, and also some of the slightly wounded. The banquet began with speeches . . . first by the head surgeon, Inspector Saggini, and then by the head of the hospital that was entertaining us. Both these speeches were addressed directly to us, and I murmured to Nina, "We shall have to answer, you do it." She whispered back, "For nothing on earth, you must."

The man sitting opposite to me rose up and was received with a tremendous ovation. He bowed, and after a moment's silence began quite quietly, talking of the War and of the causes of the War. Gradually he worked himself up, becoming more and more excited

A WELL-KNOWN ORATOR

as he told of the time that Italy had joined in . . . he thundered out abuse of the enemy, calling the fire of heaven down on the heads of those responsible for having started this holocaust of the youth of the world. His voice dropped to a whisper as he spoke of the pain and suffering we were all forced to witness every day and every hour, pain and suffering that we were unable to help, no matter how hard we tried; he called to us to imagine the misery it was causing in all the homes of the civilized world, and wound up finally with an outburst of praise for the soldiers of the Allies, especially the English, including us and all we were doing in the name of friendship and pity for the wounded, who could never be grateful enough for all our sympathy and help, etc., etc. There was an outburst of cheering as he sat down, and I jumped to my feet to answer him (imagine how rash, in a language I know as slightly as I know Italian), three or four words and I choked and collapsed with tears pouring down my cheeks. Of course we were all overstrained with what we had seen and gone through, and all our emotions, hitherto so carefully crushed, had been openly expressed by the wonderful oratory of the speaker, but my shame was great! I was saved by the man next to me, to whom I shall always be eternally grateful; as I collapsed, he leapt up and started an amusing speech which in two minutes had the whole table in roars of laughter and we were forgotten. Afterwards I was somewhat comforted by hearing that the man who had moved the whole company so much by his wonderful peroration was a very well-known orator, able to twist his audience round his little finger in any way he pleased. In fact the head surgeon was indignant with him for having turned on all his powers when we were all so strained, and said it was iniquitous of him as he must have known quite well what effect it would have. All the more annoying for me to have done so exactly what he expected! Never again do I try and make a speech in public, it was a lesson I shan't forget.

26th October, 1916, Gorizia.

Ethel Smyth has arrived, full of charm and energy, and we are now established in Gorizia, having left her in Cormons.

Our house here is getting very comfortable. It is most strange being able to walk into any garden and pick other people's roses, and whereas Cormons is now winter, this is a return to a mild September.

Last night there was an attack and the noise was very insistent and deafening, it has continued all to-day as well. The house on the opposite side of the street to us had been hit twice, but that is why we are here as our quarters are supposed to be covered by it, it is very high, and any shot going over it ought to clear us. I'm not going to send this letter until I am on the way home, so you won't be able to fuss. The batteries near our house have hysterics about every hour, and when they are not having hysterics the aeroplanes are having pitched battles overhead; our big shells are whining over and shells from the Austrians are plumping into houses near by and bringing them rattling down. It was rather impressive last night. Nina and I were walking home from the hospital about seven-thirty, pitch dark, no glimmer of light of course allowed anywhere, and there suddenly burst out behind us a torrent of noise—rifles, *mitragliatrici* (machine-guns) and field guns—more rifles than anything else, just one vast rattle, rattle, rattle—the searchlight kept sweeping down the street, absolutely blinding you, and just as you thought you could see, it would vanish, leaving you to stumble among the telephone and telegraph wires which wind themselves hopelessly round your legs.

I HATE IT, NINA LIKES IT

We are learning to walk in Indian file along the walls of the houses—only fools walk in the middle of the road here—and to-day we succumbed to wearing our tin hats as there were so many missiles about.

Strangely enough I am not frightened, only tired after so much noise, and shall be thankful for a little silence. I think one is too stupid to realize danger and the noise only makes one feel dogged and rather supine. It is interesting to study the different effect on Nina, who becomes much more alert instead of supine. I went and slept on my bed the whole afternoon, notwithstanding that the town was being shelled. I much prefer living at Cormons and having the excitement of coming in and out over the bridges and then returning to a peaceful house for the night, but we must stay here until the big apparatus is fixed up and a radiographer established to work it. Nina, who does not object to the noise, is planning to stay permanently in Gorizia, which will allow me to go to Cormons at night occasionally to get some sleep.

27th October, 1916.

To-day an interesting thing happened. Mr. Geoffrey Young, the head of the British Ambulance here, came round to ask if we would go and see a very old Englishwoman who refused to go into the underground shelters when the town was being shelled. We took the car and went to where she was living in the remains of a villa just outside the town.

She was dressed in a flannel petticoat and a chemise and was cooking her meagre rations in a tumbledown outhouse. Her kitchen had been knocked down the night before; she told us that her name was Miss Whitnell and she had been governess to some Austrians, whom she had evidently been very fond of. When the Italians approached Gorizia the Austrians had left her with two gardeners, two dogs and a Shetland pony, to keep house for them in their villa near Peuma. She used to walk into the town of Gorizia every day to get the rations dealt out to the poor of the town, and she told us that one day when the Italian shelling was coming very close and they were expecting the Italian troops at any minute, she had gone up into the town to interview the Austrian General in command to ask him to give one of the gardeners a place as his valet. The General refused to help at all—she supposed because she was English—and she went back rather sadly to tell the man that she had failed to get him the situation. On arrival at the villa she found that it had been hit by a shell and the two men, the two dogs and the pony had all been killed. She told this to us with no sign of emotion or horror and added, " It didn't matter that the General wouldn't take poor Hans as his valet, I need not have worried so much."

We tried to persuade her to come away with us, or at least to go underground when an attack was threatened, but she was quite obstinate, saying, " I am English, and I couldn't show the Italians that I was afraid." Poor old thing, she jumped out of her skin every time the guns fired or a shell burst with a loud detonation at the end of her garden, but she continued her story in the same gentle voice, till the next explosion caused her to shoot into the air off her chair. At last we persuaded her to agree to come next day if we fetched her in our car. She was rather difficult to arrange for as she took every opportunity to declare loudly how much she preferred the Austrians to the Italians (hardly tactful in time of war !) . . . but we managed to persuade the carabinieri that she was quite harmless besides being slightly mad after her experiences, and we sent her to Florence, where some kind English people took charge of her, until arrangements could be made for her to

DAME ETHEL SMYTH, MUS.DOC.

go to a governesses' home in England. There the poor old soul went quite off her head and died before we got back. Her one cry had been to be sent back to Austria.

28th October.

We have just been radiographing a woman with five pieces in her, all of which we have found and are now localizing. A woman is very difficult, as the quality of the flesh is so much more dense than a man's, in the same way the flesh of a very fair man is much denser than that of a dark one.

I did thirty cases on my lone yesterday as Nina was in Gorizia; I wonder how many she did. I shall shoot Ethel soon, so kind, so persistent and so damnably energetic. She gave us the most wonderful performance the other evening. She sat down at the pianoforte and played the whole of the Brahms *Requiem* by heart, picking out the various instruments, wind and string, until it sounded like one vast orchestra. What a wonderful artist she is!

1st November, 1916, Gorizia.

I wrote you a nice mild letter from Cormons yesterday. Now it is over I will tell you how thrilling the last few days have been. Nina and I have been in the very thick of it here and the noise has been simply stupendous and unceasing. At last the long-promised attack has come off. They are advancing now, as we know by the noise being a little less, but for thirty-six hours every battery, far and near, has been firing. The noise of passing shells in the air is most terrifying and one is only thankful to be cowering on the earth, as the metal must be in sheets up there. I can only describe the sound as being just like the overture to Tannhäuser

THE ITALIAN ARMY AS WE SAW IT

with the tune of the big guns going through the whistling of shells overhead. All night it has gone on, and of course sleep is out of the question. This morning came an outburst of machine-guns and rifles, but now chiefly distant sounds, except for our batteries in the garden, which are head-cracking always. A new sound passed me yesterday twice when I was walking down to meet Nina, who had been to the Unione Militare; it was a sharp miaow, quite short; I have not yet found what it was.[1]

Yesterday there was the most wonderful sight that I have seen yet. I was coming in here, having been working up in the mountains, to join Nina, who had been here all day, and as I got to the highest point above the town it looked like taking a header into the Inferno, or rather into an oasis in the Inferno. Three-quarters of the circle of the horizon was fire and smoke, columns and pillars of smoke, black, white or red, from right to left.

Here a natural history fact forced itself on my notice. I was feeling like a horse who wants to refuse a fence and was funking horribly going down into the said Inferno, when I happened to look down at my knees and found that the knee-caps of both knees were jumping up and down of their own volition—then one of the Italian guns suddenly started firing from a hidden position behind a bush close to the road; it made me jump out of my skin. The sudden and different kind of noise so near to me must have pulled my nerves together, and from this moment on I was not frightened

[1] Rifle bullet. It is strange how angry the sound of a rifle bullet used to make one. I remember my rage one day when one hit a telephone wire, close over our heads as we were walking down a road; it cut the wire, which curled away up the road like an angry snake, and my language was quite unfit for publication. Rage and fear seem to be very close kin.

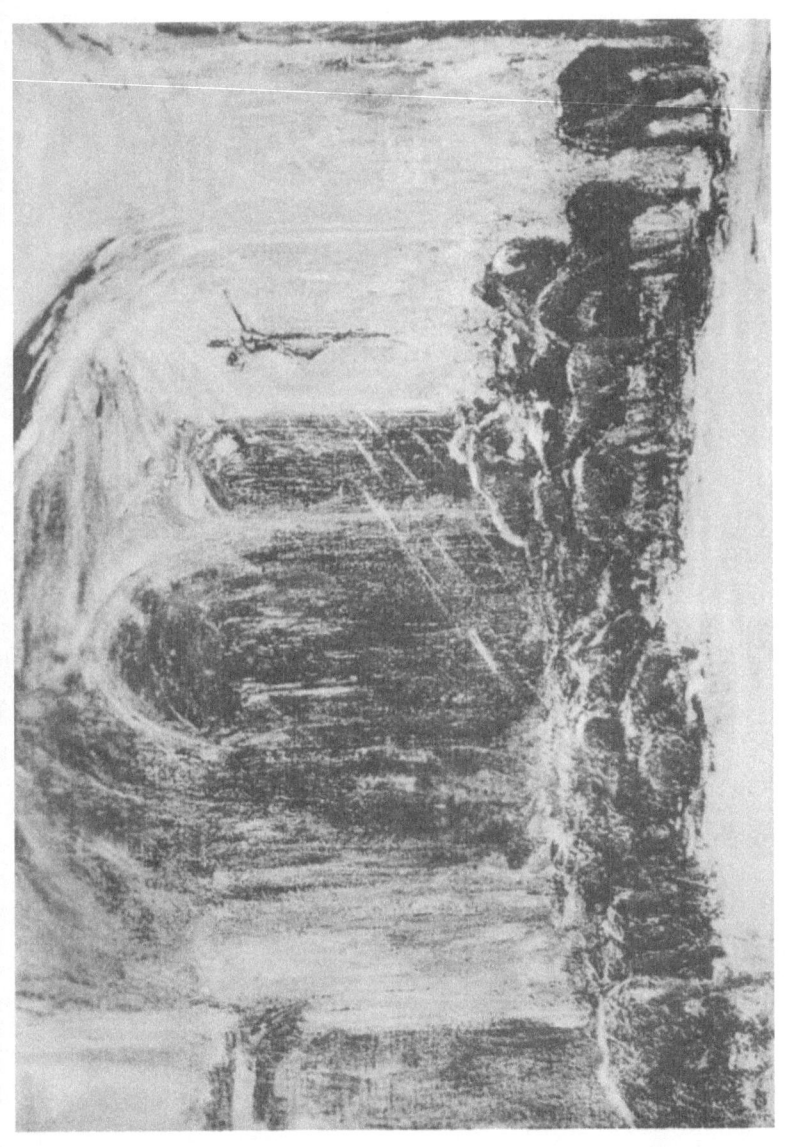

Horses stabled in the church the night before the night before the battle

AUSTRIAN ATTACK REPULSED BY FIELD GUNS
[*War Museum, Rome*]

TEAR-GAS

and went comfortably down into the town where incendiary shells were falling in every direction.

I never can get out of the way of looking up in hopes of seeing shells pass—the big ones sound so heavy that one feels instinctively they must be visible—but I am told you only see them when they are coming direct for you and then, ten to one, do not remember the fact. Don't fuss about us, we have been given a house which ought to be very safe as it is in the side of a hill and the cellars are half underground. We sleep in the cellars.

Luckily for us we have come in for very little gas since that first day, although we always carry gas-masks as a precaution.

One day we happened to go to see General Cattaneo, the Governor of Gorizia, on business, and while standing talking to him and some of his staff on the steps of his Headquarters a tear-gas shell fell in the yard quite close to us. Result, purple noses, streaming eyes, everyone crying and blowing their noses; we all treated it as a great joke, there being much laughter at the miserable appearance of everyone. They picked up the remains of the shell and gave it to us as a souvenir—a most lovely piece of workmanship, the steel of the outer cover being thinner than an eggshell.

The Italians have done very well in these last attacks, one general who was advancing on the Carso had the Austrians on the run in front of him, and instead of pursuing straight on, which was open to him, turned left and surrounded and cut off an enormous number, taking guns and prisoners in quantities. Fifteen thousand prisoners taken three days ago, and yesterday another 3,000, so we heard on good authority. The days when the pontoon bridge into Gorizia is being shelled we have to cross the river at Peuma. This I hate as there is no parapet and the bridge is only just

THE ITALIAN ARMY AS WE SAW IT

the width of the car. It crosses the Isonzo river high up from the top of one cliff to the top of another. I never dare look down when crossing. Luckily we can hardly ever cross by daylight as it is in full sight of the enemy's batteries, and at night I cannot see the river far below, but have to keep my eyes fixed on Nina who, carrying a tiny electric torch in the palm of her hand, walks very carefully right in the centre of the track. This little red gleam is our only safety and is so small it is very difficult to see.

21

THE ROSEN ALLEE

NINA and I were going out to work one morning from Gorizia and when we came to the pontoon bridge over the Isonzo we were stopped by the carabinieri on duty who said that the bridge was being shelled, so we tucked ourselves and car in under the bank of the river to wait until we could cross in safety. There were many others doing the same, amongst them an Italian Red Cross ambulance carrying *sgombrati* (wounded evacuated) across the river to one of the rear hospitals. The driver, by name Gotland, left his ambulance and dawdled over to talk to us . . . a staff car hurried up and a fat little colonel hastened into a dugout which was at the side of the road, and only big enough to hold one person. Mules and transport edged themselves as close as possible under the bank, and their drivers sat down to rest and smoke while they had the opportunity. Suddenly came an orderly running through the crowd: " Badly wounded men at the head of the bridge, is there an ambulance ? " We looked at Gotland, it was his business; he shook his head, his ambulance was full of wounded already and there was nothing else to use for carrying wounded except our X-ray car. So out went all our apparatus on to the side of the road, we put a soldier to guard it from being touched, and hastened up to the bridge-head. Shells were plopping into the river, sending

THE ROSEN ALLEE

columns of water sky-high, which caught the light of the setting sun, making them all colours of the rainbow [1] ... however, we had but little time to look, as the shooting at the bridge was increasing, and even as we hurried up to it more men were hit who had been waiting to cross. Nina went on to see if she could help with the wounded and I busied myself in trying to turn what I knew to be an obstinate car, the steering jammed as I turned but luckily freed itself with a jerk and came round just as eight wounded were shoved into the back; two were stretcher cases, the others slightly wounded, but all terribly anxious to get away quickly and urging me on to hurry. As we fled up the twisty road back into the town we passed some men on mules and horses galloping for all they were worth down to the protection of the river bank, and their shout of " You can't pass this way, the road is being shelled," did not improve our nerves. We could not turn, being between the devil and the deep sea, besides which one of the men was bleeding so badly that he would die if not seen to at once. The poor old car showed a turn of speed which I did not know it possessed, and thank goodness we got up to the hospital all right. When the wounded had been taken out I started to go back to the bridge to fetch Nina who had gone on to it to stay with a man too badly hit to be moved, and then the car did its worst, and absolutely refused to budge. I think the front wheels had jammed under the body, because, try as I might, nothing would make it turn. About ten hospital orderlies hastened to my help, lifted the car bodily round, straightened out the wheels, and off it went. Lucky it hadn't happened before, but it finished the Vauxhall's career as an X-ray car and it became the

[1] A picture of this by Helena Gleichen was bought later by the Italian Government.

TWO WOUNDED BY THE SIDE OF THE ROAD

section's coal-cart from then on, only taken to nice safe places.

By the time I got back to the bridge the shooting had stopped and I found Nina waiting by the apparatus for me to return. The man she had stayed with had died, so she was not needed any more, and she was ready for me to pick her up and get on over the bridge.

Coming back that evening through Podgòra we found two badly hit men in the road. One had been hit in the head, so we could do nothing for him. Nina had her crucifix with her and did her best to help him, but I think he was too far gone to see it; the other had been hit by a splinter of shell between the fingers and was bleeding profusely. He was like a hurt baby and kept on crying, saying, " You don't see how badly hurt I am. The other is dying, why don't you help me?" As Nina was busy I did his fingers up as best I could and comforted him by saying he would now be able to go home. Finger wounds sound so slight, but I believe they are the most painful of all excepting knee wounds, so he wasn't making too much fuss, though he might have expressed it more gracefully. We stayed with them until an ambulance came along, and having handed them over went home ourselves, feeling that we had seen quite enough for one day. However, we were not to be let off as we were sent for in the night to go to a dressing-station to X-ray a lot of men who had just been brought in from the trenches and had either to be sent on or kept for operation, according to the seriousness of their cases as shown by the X-rays.

Letter from Nina Hollings to Feo Gleichen,
16th November, 1916.

One day an officer came to me in Gorizia: " The General wishes you and the Contessa to be at home

THE ROSEN ALLEE

to-morrow morning. You are required for an important event, and he will send an officer to fetch you. Have you got an English flag which you can lend me?" I gave him one and he departed. I instantly sent an orderly to find Helena who was working somewhere else and tell her to come in to Gorizia that night.

About 10 a.m. next day, a Staff Officer arrived to fetch us, and we walked with him to the Opera House, an enormous and beautiful building with huge gaps made by shells in its roof. When we got to the entrance a wonderful sight greeted us. They had removed all the seats and the floor of the house was packed with soldiers standing shoulder to shoulder with the light gleaming on their steel helmets, accoutrements and rifles. Tier after tier, the boxes were decorated by wreaths of different-coloured roses. These had been picked by the soldiers at the risk of their lives, during the night before, from the Rosen Allee (the principal rose garden in Austria, which lay the far side of the Italian trenches and barbed-wire entanglements). Each box held officers representative of the different regiments which had taken part in the Battle of Gorizia.

As we were escorted down the centre of the house to our box all the men turned towards us, standing at attention, and the officers in all the boxes round the house rose to their feet and saluted. All this time aeroplanes which had been ordered to guard the Opera House against the Austrian planes were humming to and fro across the sky, which was visible through the open roof.

The General and staff were on the stage, backed and surrounded by banks of roses . . . a bugle sounded . . . and the General stepped forward to address the troops. He said, " We are here to do honour to those who have not only gained Italy's greatest prize, the Medal for Military Valour, but have given their lives in so doing. I do not ask if they are present, I know they are." He then called a name in a loud voice which echoed through the house. The answer came: "Presente." Again the General spoke. "Colonel —— you who were fighting so bravely in the trenches when you were shot through the spine; although mortally wounded you refused to be moved, and by your example inspired your men to hold on to an almost impossible position. We give to you and to your family the Gold Medal of Valour." Then the General handed the medal to an officer of the dead man's regiment, who stepped forward, saluted and received it.

The other gold medal was given in the same way, the name being called by the General and being answered by a voice that echoed through the silence of the hall: "Presente." Other medals were given to officers and men who came up to receive them. The General then turned to our box which had been decorated with the Italian and British flags. He spoke in a loud voice, "Soldiers here present, we greet these two English women whom we look upon, not only as two of our most gallant officers, but as beloved members of our families, and we offer them, and ask them always to wear the medal we have had struck for all the officers who took part in the Victory of Gorizia." He then stepped forward and reached up to our box and handed us each a silver medal with a replica of the seal of the town of Gorizia on the one side and a figure of Victory on the other.

7th December, 1916.

Such a heavenly drive the other day, we went to the top of a high mountain with rows and rows of snow peaks and could see the Front line almost from behind, anyway from endwise on. We went into an artillery post and watched them potting at a mountain battery hiding on a far hill, and although they didn't hit it, it was quite interesting to watch and we had a very exciting drive down a new road with hairpin bends which Whitehead drove most beautifully. We had an episode as usual on the way down as we found two horses jibbing on the steepest part of the hill; they had managed to get their cart nearly over the precipice. The driver was in great difficulties, so Nina and I got out of the car and tugged at the horses while all the men pushed the cart, but it took half an hour's patience and persuasion to get the horses to move. I may add that we firmly removed all sticks wherewith to beat them.

I saw such a subject for a picture, and have done a sketch for it, all the men waiting to come up for an attack the other night as we were coming home. The moon was just coming over the mountains, throwing a glint on their helmets and casting black shadows across the road. You and Norah said you hoped my colour would have become gayer by being in Italy; on the contrary it has now become pitch black, because we are nearly always out at night. I hope so much that the kaleidoscope I see every day and all day may, with a little peace, resolve itself into some form of pictures. I want to paint so much and yet never have a moment.

12th December, 1916, the Campo Santo.[1]

We were on our way back to Cormons from Gorizia one evening, after our day's work, and the Austrians were shelling the bridges over the River Isonzo. The approaches, too, were being shelled and we got involved in a long string of cars all trying to get away from the shelling. Behind us was the General's car (General Piacentini), in front a string of lorries; a shell burst immediately over the lorry ahead of our car, blowing it to smithereens, nothing whatever remained of it.

[1] This was written on the same day that it happened.

THE CAMPO SANTO

The men on board all killed, the lorry blown to bits.

There was a little *campo santo* close to us on the right, and my first feeling was of pity for the simple little old cemetery being disturbed by the noise and clatter, and secondly, horror at the soft touches of horsehair on one's face, so light, and softly floating down from the sky, whither it had been blown from the cushions of the lorry. We had to wait on the road for some time while they made room for the cars to pass, and the soft falling of hair from the sky continued all the time we were there.

There was a sound of murmuring, which gradually grew louder and more complaining, the sound of someone disturbed in their sleep. As we came up to the little *campo santo*, a shell burst not far from it. The hour for the dead to come up and breathe had just arrived, and they dared not come up. They were hiding down below, as those still possessing life hide . . . and the sound I heard was the sound of their complaining voices. Why were they disturbed like this? All day they had been shaken in their beds, which they had thought so safe and quiet, and now when the sun had gone, leaving only a lemon splash in a cold sky and everything on the earth was covered with a mauve veil, was the moment to come out and stretch their stiff bones, and they dared not. Actually to-day, a hole had been made amongst them . . . not a sensible oblong hole in which to comfortably fit a man, but a great crater-shaped hole, and into it had fallen planks, seats, bits of machinery and bits of men. Not one man, which would have been suitable in a *campo santo*, but unrecognizable bits. It was neither fair, nor was it good form to be buried in this off-hand manner, disturbing all your neighbours with the noise and violence. "Ah, there is another! Push,

THE ROSEN ALLEE

brothers, push. Let us get closer into the corner and perhaps we shall be left alone if we do not take too much room." And the sound of complaining changed into the sound of bones knocking softly together as they pushed and pushed. . . .

I am sorry for the dead in that little *campo santo*, they have so many strange objects thrust among them, and their privacy has quite gone. . . . This time a horse joined them, but the kindly earth buried him very deep and in such small pieces, that perhaps they did not recognize him.

In January, 1917, we went away for the first time since we had gone to Italy. General Capello wrote and asked us to come to Schio, where he had his headquarters, so as to see if it were possible to establish an X-ray section there. We went up to one of the highest points on that front. I never saw anything like the difficulties they had to overcome before they could get their troops up. The road engineering was quite wonderful and the gun emplacements were blasted out of the solid rock, chiefly granite, with occasional marble showing in places. Even the trenches were cut out of slab rock. Twelve feet of snow everywhere, and fifteen degrees below zero (centigrade), the strange part was that we were not as cold as in the valley. It was explained to us that before you can start boring, you have to cut through the twelve feet of snow which was frozen brick-hard, and then through an equal amount of frozen earth. We were shown the boring machinery, weighing tons, which had all to be brought up by hand, because even mules could not get up to the top by such narrow paths. A colonel of *alpini* offered to take us up to their highest gun; I accepted with enthusiasm, but Nina was quite decided when she saw the rocky ridge not three feet wide along which they proposed to take us,

ITALIAN ENGINEERING

and she sat firmly down in a wide place, saying she would wait for us there, adding, much to the delight of the Italians, that she knew she was a coward and gloried in it.

To my surprise, I found myself not in the least giddy, although there was a sheer drop of many hundreds of feet on one side of the path, and as you looked down you could see ravens circling round a rocky peak far below. The *alpini* colonel walked in front of me giving me one end of his alpenstock to hold on to, and I held the stick of the man behind me in my other hand, so I felt nice and safe. Once the Colonel slipped, his leg went over the edge of the precipice and he pitched forward on to his hands on the path, but I have a suspicion it was done to frighten me, his idea of a joke. After a short scramble we reached the emplacement, the Italians had cut a hole right through the very top of the mountain and had placed their gun in it. They had made a large entrance this side for the men who were serving it and a tiny hole on the opposite side for the muzzle of the gun, which commanded one of the principal lines of the enemy communications. We could see the Austrians and their transport, looking like tiny insects, moving on the opposite side of the valley below us. The cave in which we were standing was hollowed out of a marble which looked like alabaster but, on scraping it with my knife, I found it was much too hard, and must have been some kind of marble I had never seen before. None of the engineers there seemed to have even noticed that it was so beautiful and had no idea what it was. . . . There was a sad sequel to this for, having taken a piece back to Cormons with me, to send home to my sister Feo, the sculptor, a young man who came to see us on business took the opportunity, when I had left the room for one moment, to put the sample in his pocket, and I never saw it again. He was a civilian engineer and probably saw a

THE ROSEN ALLEE

chance of making a good thing out of it once the War was ended. . . .

We enjoyed much staying with General Capello who gave us rooms in an ice-cold house, most beautifully arranged, with lovely fine sheets, old wedgwood plates and old silver coffee-pots, and an excellent servant to look after us. We had luncheon and dinner at his Mess for the three days that we were there. Just Nina and me and twelve of his staff, who were all very nice to us. But except in the Mess itself it was frightfully cold. Washing took up very little of our time, it was too chilly a pursuit, and I personally slept in my leather coat, plus my night things, and dressed under the bed-clothes in the morning as everything in the room was frozen hard.

From Schio we went to sample a new Army Corps who were anxious to have a radiographic section nearer to them than Cormons. They wanted us to try and rig up another plant and lend them some assistants to run it. It was a wonderful drive up an awesomely deep valley, the mountains on either side coming sheer down to the road casting heavy black shadows, the valley itself red with dogwood and the snow peaks at the end of the valley a pale pink.

Several of the villages which we went through were Russian—so unexpected, the names on the few shops being written in Russian characters. It was explained to us that hundreds of years ago there was a *Völkerwanderung* and some of the people from Southern Russia found their way into these mountains, where they settled. They have never intermarried with the natives, nor even made friends, but keep themselves entirely apart. They still speak an old form of Russian, not to be confused with Slovak or Slovene that one finds round Cormons and the borders of Austria.

We slept in one of these villages for one night, return-

OUR ASSISTANTS

ing next day, and were made very comfortable in rooms reserved for visiting generals who come there periodically to inspect the defences in the mountains. We had taken our priceless orderly, Roversi, so as to be sure of being thoroughly well looked after; Whitehead was driving I am glad to say, as we were much warmer inside; we were very sorry for the men on the front seat as they were blue with cold. Coming home, however, we noticed that they did not seem to feel the cold at all and they were much more cheerful, although to us the wind was still bitter. Little did we imagine the sequel there would be to this expedition.

On the way home we made up our minds that it was too far from our headquarters to put a section there as we should not be able to supervise the work or the apparatus and at the same time run our own job satisfactorily. The assistants were always so pathetically helpless with machinery, if anything went wrong. Miss Gretton, a newcomer, seemed to know about developing, but at that time none of them could be trusted to use the screen as they had not the smallest knowledge of anatomy. Their actual radiographic plates were pretty good. I was never much good at teaching, Nina being the best at making them understand. Later we had Miss Woodroffe, who had a real talent for learning and became very useful. They were all so nice in their different ways, but, as Nina put it, were all inclined to go mental joy-riding at times.

There was much excitement in the section when General Piacentini, our new Army Commander, gave us his second-best cook. We used to count the time from one meal to another. His name was Tito Raimondo, and he was the best cook I have ever come across, making up dishes from mules that had died by the wayside or anything he could get hold of. He looked after us beautifully, appearing whenever we came in at any moment of the day or night, magnificently attired in white, carrying steaming hot soup or coffee *zabaione*, or, in the hot weather, ice-cold drinks which he had kept down the well for us. He was cook at the Ritz before the War and now was a grenadier, and a most splendid person to look at. He helped with the machinery, bicycled with our radiographic plates to dressing-stations, in fact helped in every way as well as doing his own work.

It was just about this time that we were appointed Army radiographers instead of Army Corps radiographers. A great step!

While in Gorizia Nina used to attend Mass with the troops in an underground chapel below the ruined cathedral. She and the Colonel sat side by side and went up to Communion together. Also, when we went to dine at the General's and at the Governor's Mess, we took our seniority in the procession into the room as majors, the junior officers trooping in behind us. Once in the dining-room, however, we became guests and sat one on each side of the General. We dined fairly often at Mess in Cormons, but in Gorizia were made honorary members, and very proud we were of the honour, and very careful not to tire our kind friends by taking advantage of it too often.

The first time we dined at Mess in Cormons we surprised the company present by getting to our feet when "God Save the King" was played at the end of dinner. All present slowly rose up, as we had done so, and when all had sat down again the General asked us why we had got up. We explained that it is a gesture of respect to the King which is the custom in England—and he said that from that day on they would do the same in his Mess whenever their National Anthem was played.

Another English custom that was a surprise to them:

"TURNING OUT THE GUARD"

when the King of Italy came to see us in our quarters in Cormons we turned out our men to receive him as the guard do at St. James's Palace when the King comes. He seemed much surprised and asked why the men belonging to our section lined the archway and yard which he had to cross to get to our rooms. We explained and asked him to inspect them; they were looking very smart and clean, and he did so. This inspection pleased them very much and they spoke of it for weeks after. I have often wondered whether that custom, too, has been instituted since.

22

RETURN FROM LEAVE

March, 1917.

I HAD been to England for three weeks on leave, and on my way back to Italy an amusing incident happened. Directly the passengers arrived on board the Calais boat we had all to pass through a cabin and show our passports and papers to the inspecting officials who were sitting close together at a long table. The inspector who looked at mine examined them with great care and without looking up asked, "How many wives has your brother got?" Luckily I had my wits about me and answered, "Only one now, isn't it a pity?" He looked up, laughed and handed me my papers, saying, "No doubt as to who you are—you can go on," and I passed out chuckling, wondering how it was that he knew the Gleichen legend.[1]

I found the weather just as cold in Italy as in London and arrived with a streaming cold. We had to turn out of the train between Modane and Turin as there had been

---

[1] The story we had always been told by my father was that during one of the Crusades the Count Gleichen of that day was taken prisoner by the Saracens and was used as a slave by the Sultan. The Sultan's beautiful daughter fell in love with him and helped him to escape. To the young man's dismay the lady insisted on accompanying him, for she said that her father would surely murder her if she remained behind. In vain he explained that he had a wife in Germany; she assured him that she did

NINA SETTLES IN GORIZIA

a landslide and the rails were covered with rocks and tons of earth. We must have looked like the people of Israel with their luggage, streaming in a long procession down the valley. I was much agitated about the X-ray tubes that I had bought in Paris, but they survived the adventure and were not broken. General Delmé Radcliffe was, luckily for me, on the train, and he managed to get me a sleeping-car, all the arrangements made in Paris having fallen through. Also he somehow obtained a good dinner, which we shared, there being no food on the emergency train which had been sent to pick us up.

I was rather depressed when I found on arrival at Udine that Nina had gone into Gorizia to stay for good, and do the work there. She had taken two of the assistants as she thought they would learn the work more quickly alone with her.

Our apparatus at Cormons gave a good deal of trouble after I got back and one morning, just when we had a lot of important cases to do, my best interrupter bust up, and when that was mended the dynamo went wrong; that settled, I had to go down and sit by a new chauffeur and show him how to keep the machine running evenly. By the time I had done that, I went up to see how the assistants were getting on and found them and the surgeons wildly excited. They had discovered the most enormous piece of shell just over a man's heart. They were engaged on centring it, preparatory to marking it for immediate operation and had

not mind that at all, so they made their way to Rome where they told their romantic story to the Pope. He was so touched by it that he issued a dispensation which allowed all Counts Gleichen for the future to have two wives. There are three hills in Württemberg called the "Drei Gleichen," and in the Castle of Weikersheim there is shown to this day the huge bed, big enough to hold three people in comfort.

RETURN FROM LEAVE

turned up the light to send the patient away into the operating-room, when I came in. Some instinct told me that all was not well and I asked to have a look through the screen. All said that it was quite unnecessary to have his bandages off as the piece of metal was quite clear. However, I insisted, and we discovered that they had been busy radioscoping three medals and two crucifixes attached to a chain, which were under his bandages! You see, that might have happened to any of us, but we should have recognized that they were not the shape of a piece of bone or steel and should have insisted on taking off the patient's bandages to make sure. I think that the assistants had a slight feeling of prude-shrink and did not like to order a man's clothes to be taken off. We had none of those feelings; but our hair turned grey with the responsibility of allowing other people to do the work. Every bit had to be checked again and again so that no possible mistake could creep in. That is why we were so stern in our orders that no localizations were to be sent in before either Nina or I had proved them, and that no operations were to be done from screening, done by the assistants, unless one of us two had seen it also.

One of our best assistants, one day, made a terrible mistake, marking down a bullet as being on the left side of a man's head when it was really on the right. We got a message from the surgeon of the hospital asking us to come and verify a localization and asking Nina or me to be sure and come ourselves. I explained to the miserable assistant that she might come along and listen but was not to speak. I also explained, when she said that it was her fault, that the colonel of a regiment always took the blame when his men did wrong, and that I took the blame, as Commandant, if the assistants did wrong. So, when the surgeon met us at the door of the hospital, I wiped the floor with myself, with the

LOOTING

unhappy assistant standing by. I noticed a twinkle in the eye of the surgeon as he graciously accepted my crawling apologies and we never had to complain of carelessness from that particular assistant again. She said after that she had never felt such a worm in her life before.

The laws against looting were, of course, very strict, and we had two painful incidents which required very tactful handling. For instance, a few days after Nina had settled into quarters in Gorizia the Colonel of carabinieri sent in a message asking her to see him. He came into the room looking very grim, and informed her that her men were stealing the valuable furniture from the upper story of her house, adding that this was a serious military crime, and punishable accordingly.

Nina, of course, said that there must be some mistake, that our men would never do such a thing and, with a sudden inspiration, added, " Will you come and inspect all the rooms to-morrow afternoon ? " The Colonel's expression relaxed, and, with a slight smile, he agreed to do so. Nina then sent for her sergeant, and told him, with a shocked countenance, of the terrible thing of which he and his men were accused, but said that she had invited the Colonel of carabinieri to come and inspect the rooms the next afternoon, and that she was sure he would find everything in perfect order. The Sergeant saluted, and with a grateful " Thank you " hastily departed. Nina then shut herself in her room and ignored all the noises of furniture being carried upstairs, which resounded throughout the house for some hours.

The next morning she said to the Sergeant, " Will all be well when the Colonel comes ? " and had a reassuring " Ma si, signora, sicuro." At 4 p.m. punctually the Colonel with another officer duly appeared, inspected all the rooms and then returned to Nina with the re-

RETURN FROM LEAVE

port: "All correct, my best congratulations, Signora Maggiore!"

Now came the sad sequel of our journey up to the new army corps who had wanted us to fix an X-ray section there. Our personal, most capable orderly, Roversi, was reported as having stolen a quilt from the General's house at Ravna and was arrested. A very worried private came and appealed to Nina to help Roversi by saying a good word for him, as he was to be tried by court-martial. Nina started off immediately by car for Codroipo, about fifty miles away, where the court-martial was to take place, and when she arrived managed to secure an interview with the Colonel who was to hold it. She then spread herself in assurances of our *confidenza* in the unhappy Roversi. The Colonel looked very much amused and murmured, "I think you mean *fiducia*" (for in Italian *confidenza* has a very different meaning to the English word "confidence" that she was trying to express!). But Nina, quite unperturbed by her own Italian, declared that she had the highest opinion of him and was sure that he would never have taken the quilt had he not thought it was lost property, etc., etc.

The court-martial took place, and Nina waited outside in her car. Suddenly Roversi rushed out, fell upon his knees, kissing her hand in gratitude and announced that he was not going to be shot, but was to rejoin his regiment at the Front, and meanwhile could he not help her with the stores that she wanted to buy? . . . Nina had already ordered things, for which the shopkeeper had given her a bill for 700 lire, and she meant to go back and pay for them after the court-martial was over. Roversi hurried into the shop with the bill, and the next moment the shopkeeper appeared, exclaiming with tears of emotion that out of gratitude, he was reducing his bill to 70 lire instead of the 700 aforesaid, as he had

"TROP DE ZÈLE"

only now learned that this kind lady, who had so nobly testified in favour of his dear friend Roversi, was one of the ladies who did such marvels in aid of their beloved Italian wounded, etc., etc. It was really quite a mistake that he had made out the bill as if for a mere *forestiere*!

And so we sadly parted with Roversi. He was not sent to the Front to join his regiment, as he was too old, but alas, he never returned to us and we missed his cheerful and willing services very much. Whitehead, too, had to be sent home, as he also had looted quilts from the General's house and we could not let an Italian soldier be punished alone, for a fault committed by both of them, so two of our best men left us, much to our sorrow.

On off days we used to take our machines to pieces to make sure that they were all in order for any sudden call. One day nothing would make our apparatus function, so down came every part to be examined. When we got to the coil, we found that the damp had got in; this had to be stopped at once as damp meant short-circuiting, which would soon destroy it and necessitate rewinding it, a slow business for which we couldn't spare the time. So Nina planned to fill the coil-container with melted wax as once before she had successfully done. No damp could possibly get into it if completely and thickly surrounded with wax. We took a newly arrived assistant into Gorizia with us to help; the candles were duly melted down in a large bath placed over the fire which we were allowed during the daytime (we were never allowed to light one at night as it could be seen by the enemy and invariably brought a strafe over). The wicks were removed, a jug was brought and two of us held up the heavy box containing the coil, while the third filled the jug with boiling wax and carefully poured it in. Jugful after jugful was poured in by the assistant; then to our sorrow we

RETURN FROM LEAVE

perceived that the wax was not sufficient, quite, to fill the box to the brim and we were discussing what we should do to get some more when our bright assistant shouted " I know," and rushed from the room, returning in one moment with a jug which she emptied into the coil-box before we could stop her. She had had the splendid idea of mixing hot water with the wax. Water! the one thing we were trying to keep out. . . . We were in despair, but hoped against hope that when the wax got cold and hardened, it would drive out the water and we should be able to pour it off the top. Not a bit of it, the water, to our surprise, amalgamated with the wax and it solidified with bubbles of water mixed in it. The end of the whole thing was that we had to scoop it all out and send the coil to be rewound. . . . How strange is the human brain!

I feel I don't say half enough about the assistants or about the splendid way they all of them put their backs into their work . . . especially Miss Hanbury-Williams, Miss Woodroffe and Miss Chapman. Nothing was ever too much trouble for them, and Miss Chapman and Miss Woodroffe were born radiographers, Miss Hanbury-Williams was well drilled, always well-turned out and exceedingly useful as " tabs " as she was always called by the others. One of them was rather inclined to powder-puffs and a flowing veil in uniform . . . this had to be crushed with a stern hand; another was a typical artist with a good deal of difficulty with her hair, but she improved greatly in smartness on parade. Those three were distinctly the most useful that we had and the most to be trusted in a tight hole. Miss Gretton was also very trustworthy in a difficult place and worked like a black; and there was a very nice Miss Grant from South Africa. What a number we had at different times, and I regret to say we were so busy that the moment one left and another took her place we forgot

PROFESSOR SBROZZI, BRAIN SPECIALIST

all about her. How ungrateful that sounds, but *c'est la guerre*.

On one occasion Nina and I were sent for to go to a certain villa near Gorizia which had been turned into a hospital and was constantly shelled by the Austrians. They wanted us to radiograph various cases for the great brain specialist, Sbrozzi. We arrived with the apparatus, including, as usual, a skeleton. This was frequently set up in order to help the doctors to verify positions of fractures, etc. Dark curtains were hung in front of the windows and the patient brought in.

It was a very serious case, and Sbrozzi was beginning to operate under the screen when a shell crashed into the garden of the villa, smashing what remained of the windows and blowing the dark curtains down. These little difficulties were to be expected, the curtains were quickly replaced, and work began again. Then came a second shell and the same disaster; poor Sbrozzi, dropping his tools, ran in desperation up the room and, holding out his hands in an attitude of prayer before the skeleton, wailed, "Oh, Madonna mia, what has thy servant done that his best work should be ruined by these ridiculous noises!" The little, round, white-coated figure appealing with clasped hands to the skeleton was an extremely funny sight which we have never forgotten.

30th March, 1917.

To-day I hit the head surgeon at one of the dressing-stations. . . . This is the history of that scandalous episode. . . . We were called up about 2 a.m. to go at once to a certain dressing-station not far from the trenches. Would we please be there as soon as possible, as there was a great deal of work. Nina and I tumbled out of bed, sent our orderly flying to call the men and in literally ten minutes from the time of call,

RETURN FROM LEAVE

left our front door. It took about an hour to reach our objective, our apparatus having been standing ready since the night before in case of an urgent call. There had been fighting all through the night, and by the time we got to the dressing-station in an old building, which had been rather badly knocked about in some earlier fighting, the courtyard and passages were crammed with stretchers as well as with the wounded men sitting and standing propped against the walls. Hardly room to step over or between them. There must have been at least ten surgeons at work in all the different rooms which had hastily been turned into operating-theatres. The head surgeon seized on us and established us with our X-ray plant in a little room next to where he was operating. Every case was brought to us first. Their clothes were stripped off in the hall, they were put on stretchers covered with a sheet and then brought in and the stretcher placed on our Mackenzie Davidson trestle-table.

On this occasion I was managing the screen and Nina the switchboard. We had to be very quick, no time for plates or developing, all was screening. Man after man was brought in, the tube adjusted, the screen laid over him, the bullet found and its place marked on the skin, the man turned over, the bullet again located and another mark made . . . at the angle where those two marks joined there was the bullet. Occasionally I had to make a tracing and copy it off on to a piece of paper as quickly as possible and send it in to the surgeon with the patient. This all sounds very rough and ready, I grant you, but marvellously accurate, as it turned out. We did sixty cases before leaving off for a short breathing space, and those sixty men all passed through the surgeon's hands immediately. Then there came a difficult one . . . a boy with a bullet or bit of shrapnel in his shoulder. I wanted the surgeon to see this for him-

NERVE-STRAIN

self as it was impossible to mark it in the usual manner. In he came at once, looking completely exhausted. We could not get the patient to lie in the right position for us to see properly . . . he was very slow-witted and could not understand, poor soul, what we were driving at. Suddenly the surgeon lost his much-tried temper, seized the man and thumped him down on the stretcher in the right position, followed by a yowl of pain from the man. The surgeon had inadvertently touched his wounded shoulder. Before I knew what I was doing I had hit the surgeon as hard as I could in the chest, sending him staggering back against the wall, to the horror of all the assistants and orderlies who were in the room, also to my own horror, as I had had no idea that I was going to do it . . . ! I suppose we were all overstrained and the noise the boy had made was just like a hurt puppy. The surgeon, who was enormously tall and wore pince-nez, recovered his balance and, before I could apologize, smiled gently down at me saying, " Scusi, Signora Contessa, mia colpa." (" I beg your pardon, I was to blame.") He then went calmly on with his work, as if nothing had happened. At the first opportunity I naturally apologized profusely ; we embraced, and it was not referred to again.

This was not the only embrace between us and the surgeons we were working with. One day I arrived at the tunnel in which we had fitted an X-ray room, and, to my amazement, found Nina and a dear, fat old surgeon with their arms round each other's necks, embracing warmly ! I couldn't get out of either of them what had caused this apparent access of affection, my partner merely remarking, " We had fallen out about something, but we have fallen in again now," went calmly on with her work of fitting in the wires for the X-ray apparatus. The fact was, we were all on edge at that time. I remember one surgeon, the cleverest of

RETURN FROM LEAVE

all, bursting into tears one day in the tunnel and sobbing with his head in his hands, "It is no use, I cannot save them, I am doing all I can, and ninety per cent. of the men passing through my hands die." It was true, he only had the men with the worst abdominal or head wounds, and they were all practically hopeless before he got them. It was terribly disheartening. Those that could be moved were, of course, at once sent on to hospital, and he only kept the very worst cases in his tunnel dressing-station, or rather field hospital.

The tunnel (Zagora) had been used by the Austrians for troops and mules and was deep in filth when the Italians first took it. They asked us to come and look at it and see if we could establish an X-ray plant there. It was on the bank of the Isonzo, and was an old railway tunnel that went deep through the mountain and therefore was exceptionally safe from shells. It was below Canaletto and opposite the celebrated Bainsizza plateau. In less than a week the tunnel was cleaned, purified and lime-washed so that you would not have known it was the same place, and Nina had fixed up the X-ray apparatus with two assistants to run it. (We changed them every other day so that they should not get too tired.) The surgeons then asked us to provide them with electric light as well. My partner had a brilliant idea; we telephoned to Headquarters to say that our work was hampered for want of light, could they supply it? They were sorry, no dynamo was to be had; but if we could get a dynamo they would send men at once to fix wires, lamps, etc. Somehow, somewhere, I forget how, we got one lent us and in twenty-four hours electric light streamed through that nightmare of a tunnel for the use of everyone.

This was not the only time we were used as light producers; for once, in Gorizia, the head of one of the hospitals complained that no one paid attention to his

LIGHT

demands for electricity and he did not know what to do. We suggested that we would see what we could do, if he would allow us to try. He smiled kindly, thanked us, and said he was afraid that as his demands had failed ours would not fare any better, so we said no more, but on leaving the hospital went straight to Headquarters and asked to speak to the Governor, General Cattaneo. We explained the difficulty and the absolute necessity for light. He quietly said that it should be seen to, and we departed; that very evening we had occasion to return to the same hospital and were met by the head surgeon with "How did you manage it? Not half an hour after you left, twenty men arrived with wires, lamps, switchboards, etc., and we now have electricity all over the building." This is a little example of how marvellously prompt the Italians are. Whatever we asked them for, they said, "It shall be seen to," and it was done, when possible, within the hour.

Nina and I were returning to Gorizia from the tunnel, having deposited Miss Chapman and Miss Hanbury-Williams there, and we thought we would try a new road home. The lower road to Gorizia had been in the hands of the Austrians until the day before, but the rumour had gone round that the Italians had cleared all that bit of country in their last advance that very morning; so, we thought, as the low road was much shorter than our usual zigzag one over the mountains, that we would try it. We crossed the river over the temporary bridge some way above the tunnel and slowly picked our way through the immense throng of mules, guns and troops of all sorts, who were going up to reinforce the tired men who had just rushed Monte Kuk with such wonderful *élan*. We drove quietly down the far side of the valley, passing several small dressing-stations filled with wounded. As we passed some bushes on the right-hand side of the road an Italian mortar suddenly crashed out . . . we had not even seen it, and it made us both leap into the air, besides blowing off my hat . . . but we continued down the valley, with the river on our right and great rocks on each side of us towering narrowly up to the sky. As we crept cautiously on we came to a major of artillery, standing behind a rock, staring down the road through his field-glasses. We pulled up and asked him if the road was open. Without taking his glasses down he answered absently, " I think so," so we went on. The next people we met were some stretcher-bearers with their loads of wounded, staggering with the weight of their burdens. The silence was rather eerie until we reached a turn where the protective screens on each side of the road ceased and we were on a road without any cover. A great rock jutted out, and as we advanced into the open beyond, a stutter of guns burst out, apparently from all sides (although I dare say echo had a good deal to do with the noise, which was terrific). The few men visible ran for their lives, and for the first time we experienced machine-gun fire at close quarters. The bullets were literally bespattering the road like hailstones, jumping and ricochetting off rocks and ground all round us. No time to turn, we luckily had only been crawling, so it took only a second to stop and throw the gears into reverse; never have I reversed at such a pace before, and we got back behind the big rock without being hit, I cannot think how.

Once in comparative safety, we turned the car round and hastened back to our usual road the other side of the river, passing the same artillery officer as before, who was still looking down the road through his glasses. There was no need to explain, and we smiled sweetly at each other, and continued our way. It was a pity we could not get through, the road was much shorter.

A VICTIM OF THE WAR

We were marvellously lucky that day, for hardly had we gone half a mile on our usual way home when our back axle broke and we had to leave the car and go home in a passing lorry. If the axle had broken five minutes sooner, when we were on the valley road, we should have been no more.

19th April, 1917, Gorizia.

A beautiful funk-hole has been made by General Cattaneo's order in our garden down below the house. Electric light, telephone, stove, etc., most lovely if we ever have to use it, but we never have yet. I do think that diplomatically we have been of use; I feel shy about saying it, but we are both rather pleased that that self-imposed part of our job has been a success as we always hoped to make the English liked abroad. We have had that at the back of our minds from the very beginning.

A curious thing happened the other night. I was in Gorizia and had left my indiarubber bath full of water in the middle of my room when I went to bed. I was awakened by a strange soft noise, splish splosh, splish splosh; I sat up in bed and turned on my torch. There, walking round and round in my bath was a large tabby cat, emaciated to the last degree, with great hollows for eyes. He paid no attention to me but continued to wade round and round in the water, so I called Nina and we held a consultation, finally deciding to put him out of his misery. We got a huge bath towel and threw it over him; he was too weak to fight much, poor beast, and Nina rolled him up in it while I put chloroform on cotton-wool into a tumbler and pressed it over his nose. It didn't take long to do, and we felt we had done a good work; for a cat to walk round and round in water proves he must have been in great pain.

RETURN FROM LEAVE

Last week we had to ask the Captain of Engineers to give one of the men two days cells for insolence. This was the first time it had occurred in our section and I hope it will be the last. He was one of the new men, so had to be quelled at once; I think the reason was nerves. On my way back from Gorizia I had to come round by a way that he considered dangerous, and he tried to disobey orders. An Austrian aeroplane had seen us and thought that we were a staff car with an important general, so started to drop bombs, hoping to get us; as the plane swooped down the man's driving became very erratic and I was afraid he would upset the car, so I made him drive close in under a ruined wall, and to steady his nerves, made him get out and clean the plugs; a lucky move as it turned out, for the aeroplane lost us and, after circling round once or twice, gave us up as a bad job and went off. I am not surprised that he disliked me and became rude; I am always cross myself when frightened. Eventually we had to get rid of him, as another time, when Gorizia was being shelled, he bolted, leaving my car in the road, where, after a long search, I found it, and had to drive myself back to Cormons alone. (We hardly ever went out quite alone in case anything happened, there always having to be a second person who could drive if necessary.)

Coming back late one night on the front seat of the lorry with Tordella driving, I noticed that the traffic was being turned off the road on to a small by-road. If we had followed it we should not have got home for hours, so I told Tordella to drive on along the empty main road. We spun on in the dark till we got to a cross-road, where we could faintly see some figures standing. As we drew alongside of them a loud voice shouted "Halt there," and before we could pull up, a man jumped up on to the car and, pushing something

AN ANXIOUS MOMENT

hard against my forehead, turned a flashlight full into my face. Though I had never before had a revolver pressed against my head it was marvellous how quickly I grasped what it was, and how quiet I sat. The holder of the revolver burst out laughing when he saw who it was, and with a hasty " Scusi, Contessa, avanti, ma presto " (" I beg your pardon, Contessa, go on, but be quick "), jumped off into the darkness and we hastened on. It is funny how I can still feel the cold of that small steel circle. The road seemed very silent after the crowded roads we are accustomed to, and just before we got into Cormons we found out the reason; thousands of men were packed on the roads beyond waiting to move up to a surprise night attack; no wonder they were suspicious of our lorry, as orders had been given that no car of any kind was to be allowed along the road that night. We were just able to get home to our house before the word was given for the troops to move on.

Next day, 25th April, Nina and I were driving down a mountain road when we came upon a cart in great difficulties. It had two mules, and their driver could not induce them to move forward, they had dug their toes in, in the way that mules have, and no endearments or otherwise would make them budge. The arrival of our car started them, but unfortunately backwards and, before we could do anything to help, their cart had gone over the edge of the cliff, dragging both mules with it.

The ubiquitous carabinieri had, by that time, arrived on the scene, and we all peered over the edge of the road to see what was happening to the mules. They had crashed through the tops of the trees, growing immediately below the road, leaving bits of harness and bits of cart amongst the topmost branches, and had continued their way, rolling and crashing through

RETURN FROM LEAVE

bushes and over rocks until they reached a ledge just above the River Isonzo. One mule was standing in a dejected attitude on the ledge with the other, still tied to him, lying on his side . . . no cart, or even part of a cart, visible, all had been left in the trees and bushes as they crashed through. The carabinieri and the driver let themselves gingerly down over the edge of the road by their hands, and slipping, jumping, sitting and rolling, got down to the ledge. They were so far down that, to our eyes, they looked like specks only. We saw them kick up the couchant mule and, with encouraging signs, start up the cliff again, followed by the two beasts. The mules were not led or attached in any way, but followed up the steep crags like dogs. When the men had reached the edge of the road they hung and pulled themselves up on to it by their hands. We looked anxiously to see what the mules would do, and behold, first one and then the other squatted back on his haunches, hooked his forelegs over the edge, well above his head, and with a heave and a kick got himself up on to the road. The neatest thing ever seen. We all examined them with care; one was not so very bad, some skin and hair gone but nothing broken, the other, nothing actually broken either, but practically no fur or skin left; poor beast, he was a sad sight; the driver and carabinieri said that he would probably die of shock. Number One was so gay that he was able to be removed at once, but Number Two had to be left with the carabinieri until someone could come with a van to fetch him.

23

GORIZIA

2nd May, 1917.

THE assistant, whom I think so far the best radiographer, is Miss Chapman; I suppose because of her artist's training. She knows what to look for, has an eye for difference in tone and material, and knows anatomy.

I am discovering many trite things, like Pascal (who I am told made himself forget everything he had ever learnt and discovered everything afresh for himself). One thing I have found out is that the more you sink yourself (after having perpetrated an action) and credit other people with having done a noble and fine piece of work which they have not done, the better they work for you, both English and Italian. When the machine goes wrong and I have discovered the cause, I pat Carrara, our new electrician, on the head, tell him how to put it right and then give him many compliments on his cleverness. When first we had him, we ignored him and mended things ourselves, so he was bored, sulked and did no work; now that I say to him that he, and he only, is our saviour he has bucked up and does heaps of work, including lots of technical things that we could not do—we suggest and he carries out, an excellent plan. Then with the assistants, they know quite well that I often give them the credit although they have not really deserved it, but they try harder next time, besides sewing up holes in my garments and putting flowers in my room, which I thoroughly appreciate.

At last the weather is getting better. Fancy, the 2nd May in Italy, and only just getting slightly warm.

I am so glad to hear that some of the English ambulance drivers are being given the Medal of Valour; they deserve it thoroughly. We had an air-raid this morning at 5 a.m., it was so pretty, all the shrapnel bursting in the half-light sky.

12th May, 1917, Gorizia.

We have been asked to put an apparatus at one of the field dressing-stations, for abdominal cases mostly, and have dumped Miss Gretton and Miss Chapman there with an English A.S.C. man (who has been lent to us) and a corporal to run the car, cook for them and look after them generally. Nina and I are doing the running-about work in the town and we have left the other two assistants to work Cormons. As a matter of fact, I do not suppose these latter will have very much to do for a few days as attacks generally mean masses of work near the Front but not so much back in what have now become the second-line hospitals.

The new attack began the middle of the night before last and has continued steadily ever since. I now know what "coal-boxes" mean; it is as if everybody had thrown down all the possible coal-boxes and fire-irons in a heap; I hadn't heard the noise before.

We have been given gas screens to our windows and bonfire stuff to light, to blow away the gas clouds, also new gas-masks and sandbags innumerable in expectation of a possible, and even probable, return bombardment by the Austrians. But so far only fifteen shells came near us last night, and I went upstairs and made Nina come down to the cellar. She was not at all willing. It is all very well, I have a charming safe cellar, and she sleeps on the ground floor above me, which I consider foolish. The cellar is much nicer when return shells are considered.

We have been trying to make three sets of apparatus out of two, which has not been easy, but I think they are going to work all right. The two assistants at Number 86 hospital were called up at four-thirty for work, and have been kept steadily at it all day, so when Nina and I have done our work this afternoon we are going to take over for a bit there, because they are sure to be wanting rest. The doctors are all nice and very enthusiastic about their work: one had kept a long bit of a man's intestine as a treat, to show us all the holes in it. It had been perforated in four places, and he said, "If it had not been for your X-rays I could not have known where to cut; as it was I went straight to it and the man will now live."

We saw a great deal of company the last week before the attack began. Rudyard Kipling and Percival Landon came to see us, then suddenly I came across Byard, the singer, in the full dress of an Army captain; he was most kind and gave us some bully beef. (Some British guns had arrived the week before.) Then Mr. Arthur Stanley appeared (Chairman of the British Red Cross), with Mr. Pennant, Colonel Stanley, Sir Ernest Clarke, Sir Courtauld Thomson and Lord Monson, and Mr. Stanley has given us all we asked for, i.e. a new Fiat chassis for our third apparatus, and a new runabout for Nina who has been trundling about in her coal van, the Vauxhall, all this time in Gorizia.

13th May.

After all, we were unable to help the others yesterday as we had our own work to do, not only in the town

GORIZIA

here, but had to go off to the English hospital at Villa Trento, some fifteen kilometres away. Met our other pet lambs going out to a job, but they were so unhappy about their machine that we had to go with them to help put it right. Then got a wire from twenty kilometres in the opposite direction, an Italian hospital, piteously begging us to come and put their machine right as it would not go. That we refused, we simply cannot do mechanics for other people as well. We sent Carrara to see about it and he discovered that the coil was burnt out, so they are done for the moment. Sorry for them, just at this critical minute, but it can't be helped. The birds are just yelling, trying to drown the guns.

We got back last night at 11 p.m. after seeing to the Cormons apparatus, which was showing signs of giving up the ghost. It was pitch dark, not a ray of light, except lightning, which was very helpful, and flashing of guns on all sides; me driving. It was most thrilling, and I only once drove into a mule, and we left two mule carts sitting one on top of the other in the darkness of a deep ditch. I could not see what became of them because at that moment I drove into the back of a cart which had chosen to stop under an archway without mentioning it, but nothing happened beyond shouts on both sides.

16th May.

The night before last, after an extra busy day, Nina and I got in about 9 p.m. to dinner and after developing plates had gone to bed, when there came a telephone message from the assistants at 86: " We are so tired we cannot sit up to-night, will you take our night's work? " We were rather unsafe, as it was only their second night there; however, we tumbled out of bed and went, in pouring rain and pitch darkness, with

"A MINOR EVIL"

Stagni, our Corporal Major, clinging to the outside of the car on one side and Sterzi, my special boy, clinging to the other, me driving, they jumping down and running ahead when impossible to see another inch. It was very difficult to get on as troops were massing up to the Front and we had got into the middle of them. We arrived at the hospital at about 11.30 p.m., took over, drove the assistants to bed and stayed till 6 a.m. We had a most interesting night. There is a first-rate abdominal surgeon, by name Solaro, there, and we were working for him. They could only bring the wounded in by night, and all the passages were crammed with them, lying in rows close together. They were not all for our mobile field hospital, which was a branch of Professor Baldo Rossi's section for abdominal operations only, the rest of the hospital being for quick passers through, and only the very urgent cases for immediate operation handed over to our section to deal with.

One case was very interesting. The man had been hit just below the ribs and the piece of shrapnel had travelled across and down, the surgeon found it had touched the aorta, had gone behind the stomach, cut away the attachments behind the peritoneum and gone through all the intestines. He had to ladle out every coil and sew up every hole. It took hours and he said if he missed one hole all his work would be for nothing. He had done twenty laparotomy and abdominal operations that night out of thirty cases. I know less about doctoring than anybody, but having seen so many operations I now feel quite capable of doing them myself. Anyway, he didn't find his bit of metal and finished, saying it did not matter at all, as it was a minor evil, and all the shifting of insides had lost it. He said that it had probably settled into quite a harmless place.

GORIZIA

We were rather worn out yesterday after our two whole nights out, so went to Cormons in the afternoon to see how the others were getting on. It was such a comfort getting away from the noise for a bit that I went and snored for two full hours. When we got back to Gorizia we found that the corner of our house had been hit and the wall of the garden knocked down for the third time; stones and gravel were everywhere, and leaves and branches all over the streets. They *had* made a mess while we had been away! The hottest fire from the Austrians there has been yet, and they say we must expect the same to-day. An aeroplane came yesterday and dropped bombs and immediately afterwards the guns began. Now another one is soaring over our heads, so I expect the bombardment will begin again soon.[1]

After the exciting time mentioned in the last few letters I went back to Cormons and was very busy, as the hospitals were full. Most of our patients were men whom we had already seen in Gorizia and radioscoped . . . now the surgeons wanted plates to operate by. Nina was still quite happy in Gorizia, but I was very glad to be out of that continual noise for a bit. I was privately rather worried at her staying alone there, but she was quite immovable and said it was her duty, and nothing would budge her. Mine, I knew, was in Cormons, hence whence. Miss Gretton was also in Gorizia, but in a hospital some way off. What made me anxious was that Nina was always toiling backwards and forwards from our house to the hospital along a very unhealthy road. It was not of the slightest use fussing, though it was rather agitating hearing the guns going day and night and not being there.

[1] The expected return bombardment never came off—a few shells came over, but nothing to speak of.

THE DENTIST

Meanwhile, the assistants worked like niggers. During those few days they did ninety-seven examinations in one day. Our highest, I think, having been sixty-nine one day, and fifty-seven and fifty-four the following days.

Cormons.

Been having toothache, but even that was cheered by something amusing. I had to go to the military dentist's tent, a huge marquee put up in the corner of a field, and hidden from aeroplanes by trees. On my entering the tent about twenty officers, each draped in a white sheet, rose to their feet, clicked their heels and made low bows. The bows rather lost their effect as each man had his mouth fixed wide open by a gag. I then joined the ranks of the sufferers and was tortured in my turn.

Heavenly hot weather has come at last. One of the dynamos, rather the worse for wear, proceeded to come adrift from its moorings and travel about in the car, so we had to send a message into Gorizia for Nina to come out with her machine to do our work for us, and we felt much abased. Steady hard work now in eight hospitals to-day, and two of the three dynamos out of action.

The General's A.D.C. has just been to report that one of our assistants is sending dangerous letters through the *borghese* (civilian) post! The authorities had made us censors for our section and this woman, annoyed at having to show us her letters, as all the others did, has been posting them privately: result, they have all been stopped and returned to us. We had her up and told her that she would be sent home if it ever occurred again; I am afraid she will have to go, as she is quite undisciplined, and talks against us to the others, also, I will own, to our faces—which is not so bad.

GORIZIA

10th June, 1917, Gorizia.

Three times a day they call up from the Comando Supremo to tell us the time. When there is much shelling everybody's watch plays tricks, so this excellent regulation has been issued in order to keep them right, perfect agreement about the time being absolutely indispensable.

Very peaceful at present. I am in Gorizia, with nothing but birds and flowers and an occasional faraway gun. I am delighted that my car could not go out this morning, otherwise I should at this moment be sweating away at Cormons, with dust and glare and lorries and assistants.

You do not know what a worry it is to be clamoured for at such long distances from our usual haunts. We never fail to please (!) with the result that we are called over and over again, even as far back as to Udine and Cividale. We have had to strike, the distances are too great. It means also that on the days when the assistants and the men might have rested, they are unable to do so, as they are constantly sent for to base hospitals, to which cases, already radiographed by us at the immediate front, have been evacuated.

We have a new head of *sanità* who is most inconsiderate at present and is heaping more and more work on us, very flattering, but it cannot go on.

I am writing at the window and have just had the most delicious whiff; there is a strange, very sweet jasmine in this garden which has a milky fluid when you pick it. What could it be?

The Italian Army has a strange form of punishment for delinquencies amongst the men. Nina and I saw a case the other day. A huge ring of soldiers were in a field and a man in full marching equipment was running round the outside of the ring, with another man after him, both running as hard as they could go,

HUNTING LUST

the man behind beating the one in front with a whip on any part of his person that he could reach, the rest of the soldiers hitting at him with their belts as he passed. I wonder what he had done?

There is a great deal of talk about peace going on, and people are saying this is the last war; I wish I thought so, but I don't see how it can ever be. If you think, hunting and killing have been going on since all time. We consider ourselves civilized and yet are all anxious to kill our fox, and are sorry for hounds when, after a long run, the fox gets away. And out shooting, how annoyed people are when they miss, yet no one will willingly run over a rabbit or a chicken on the road. In war we do all we can to help the wounded on both sides and yet do our best to kill. It is all so illogical. Nina and I have had many experiences of the hunting lust in this war. We were invited into a gun-emplacement the other day and anxiously watched the officer in command of the gun laying it on to a convoy of men and mules on the far side of the valley. He adjusted his alignment and tried again and again to get them. Sometimes the shell burst in the valley below, and with an exclamation of annoyance he elevates his piece. This time the shell goes over the convoy. We leave him in despair, he will never hit them, and the last we see as we look across the valley is the procession of men and beasts calmly continuing their way, by this time probably out of range. We go off down the mountain-side feeling how much better we should have done it, and almost regretting not having asked the officer to let us try.

Again—the day they took Gorizia; the *alpini* running over a single railway-line hanging in the air over the river Isonzo. The brickwork has all been shot away and the line hangs in a long curve unsupported in the air except by the uprights of the viaduct at each end.

GORIZIA

They are attacking the town of Gorizia. With bated breath we watch, man after man loses his footing and falls down into the wicked current below . . . more are coming, plenty to take the place of those that are gone, they have reached the other side and are charging up into the town. Bravo! they have done it. Do we think of those who have fallen and have been washed away? Not a bit of it; all that counts is that the Italians have taken the town of Gorizia.

Another time we are walking down the street in Gorizia. The Austrians are shelling the market-place, and the noise has been going on so long that no one seems to mind it. A figure runs down the street towards us, stumbles and falls, rolling into the gutter, where he lies quite still. We realize quite well that he has been hit by a piece of shell, or perhaps a shrapnel bullet, but it is not our business; men run out from a neighbouring house, pick him up and carry him in, shutting the door behind them, and we proceed peacefully on our way, arguing about a case that we have just been X-raying or discussing the merits of some new radiographic material.

What can have happened to our nervous systems that we take it as all in the day's work and go quietly on with our job, never thinking of it again? . . . Perhaps we had steeled ourselves to see anything and had received so many nervous shocks that our sensitiveness was dulled? I hope this last explanation is the true one, as one can then understand how human flesh and blood was able, day after day and month after month, to stand the horrors of the trenches without going raving mad. . . .

One day when we were just leaving the Zagora tunnel an officer came up and asked if we would give him a lift. We refused, as we had made a rule never to take anyone whom we did not know in our cars; the

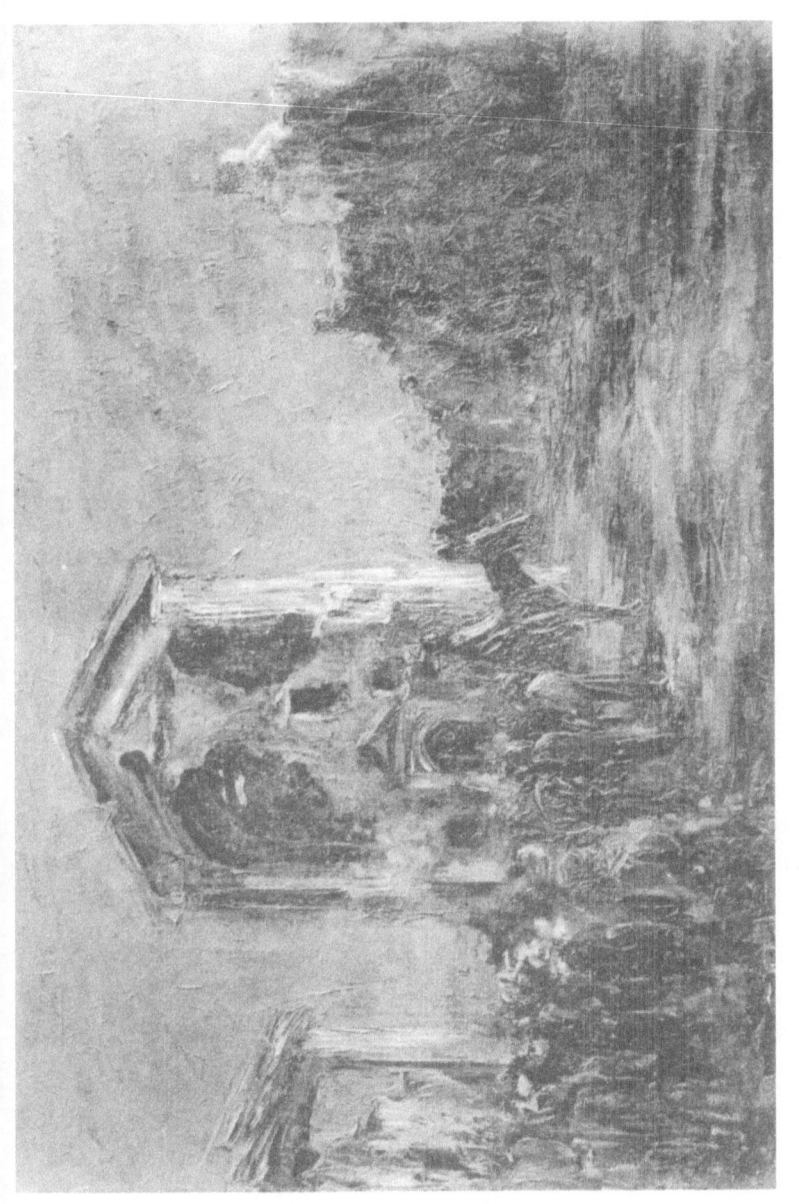

Sant' Andrea. Relief troops taking over the trenches under cover of darkness, near Gorizia

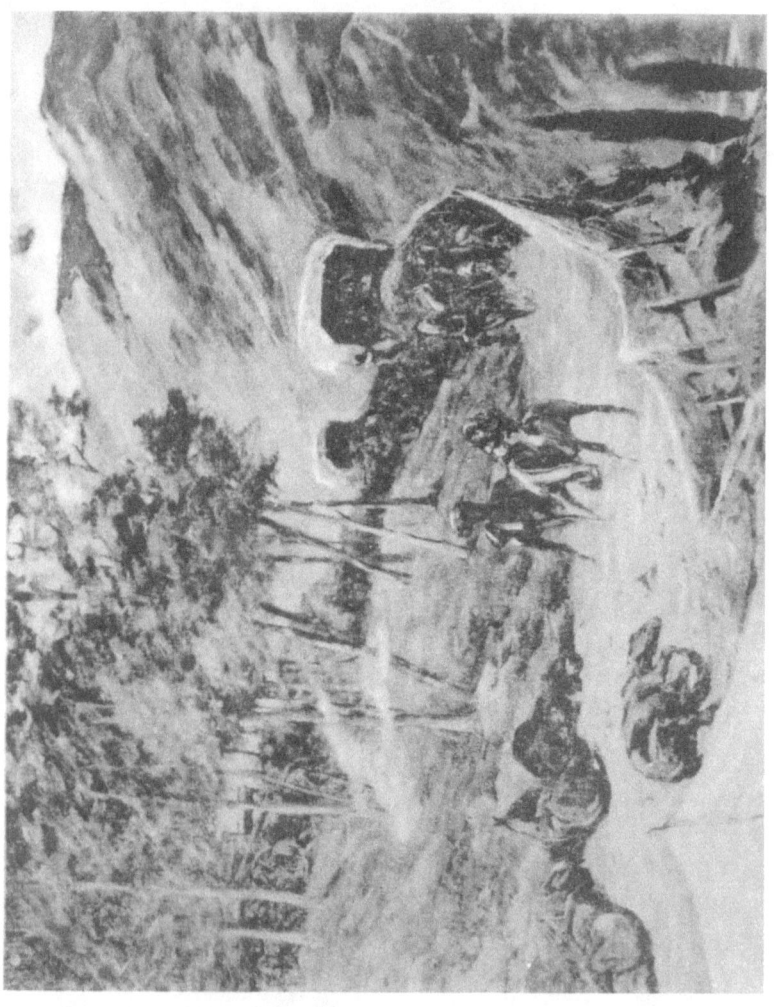

THE CURVE OF DEATH, NEAR ZAGORA, 1917

"THE CURVE OF DEATH"

reason being that our Italian was not good enough for us to be sure of detecting a foreign accent and we might inadvertently carry a spy. However, this man showed us his papers and repeated his request, saying that it was well known that we were under the protection of either Heaven or the Devil, as we so often went up and down the road the men called the Curve of Death without being hit, and that he had some very important despatches that he particularly wanted to arrive safely. Of course we laughed and took him up.

At that same *curva della Morte* another day we found a huge gun (*marina prolongata*) hopelessly stuck. They had been trying to get it up, and after sticking for some time it started to run backwards. Thirty or forty men tried to hold it, but it was far too heavy to manhandle. I was glad that our car, which I was driving, was above and not below this terrifying object which was slowly gathering speed notwithstanding all efforts to stop it. Nina got out of the car and ran down the steep bank to stop troops, lorries, etc., which were coming up to the hairpin bends below, and finally the monster, rapidly increasing pace, rushed over the edge of the cliff and fell down into the valley below. I believe it hit no one. . . . Another time we saw a lorry full of men that was going up the other side of the valley, tip over at the corner of a hairpin bend, all the men jumped for their lives and not one was hurt, but the lorry leapt from hairpin bend to hairpin bend, just missing troops, cattle and *camions* all coming up the road, and finally ended in the river Isonzo where it disappeared.

About this time Tito, our Ritz cook, was taken from us and we were in despair. A posse of carabinieri arrived at the house and arrested him. I demanded to know what he had done, and they said that they did not know, they had only had orders to arrest him and lock him up. Nina and I consulted what to do, we could not submit to losing him without a struggle. So I wrote to the Chief of the Staff making complaint that our cook had been arrested without acquainting us, that we, as his commanding officers, had every right to be notified if he had done anything worthy of punishment, and we demanded to know why he had been removed from our section. It was a very dignified and pompous epistle, which ended by an appeal for his return. That evening he reappeared, smiling, and settled down to work again as if nothing had happened. Several days afterwards we were dining at mess and the General, in shouts of laughter, told us that his mischievous junior staff had apparently for long coveted Tito, as the best cook on the Front excepting his own; so they had made the plan of accusing him of some fault and getting him arrested. They had then meant to let him out of prison and take him for their own mess. "But," he added, "they had bitten off more than they could chew when they tried to take your man from you, and I shall see that it does not happen again."

We were very proud of the smartness of our section, who were always clean and well turned out. The only time the men ever became slack was when there was severe shelling which was always demoralizing. When Nina was in Gorizia she noticed that as the shelling became more violent, so they became more dirty and untidy. She had them all up before her and told them that they were a disgrace to the section and to the Italian Army. She then went on a long round of visits to hospitals and dressing-stations, leaving them to digest what she had said. On her return, about seven o'clock in the evening, she was rather puzzled to see one of the men evidently watching for her return at the corner of the street. As soon as her car came in

THE SECTION

sight he rushed away and she came in, not knowing what mischief they might have been up to while she was out. To her amusement she found the whole of them standing to attention in the courtyard as for a parade. The Sergeant told her that, directly she had left in the morning, they had all set to work and washed, shaved and cleaned themselves and their uniforms, and never would they disgrace the section again—and they never did.

24

A HOLIDAY

July, 1917.

ONE day, when I was passing Villa Trento, on the way back from Udine, I met three staff cars, with a lot of English and Italian officers in them. They waved to me to stop, and lo and behold! the Duke of Connaught was in one of them. He said that he was on his way to see us in Cormons. On hearing that Nina was in Gorizia and that I was on my way there, he said that he would like to come there instead, as he particularly wanted to see her (having known her for many years), but said that he must hurry as he must be back in time to dine with the King of Italy. I assured him that he could quite well do it in the time, and he asked me to go ahead in my car and show the quickest way into the town. I was rather intrigued by a heated confabulation which took place between the Duke and the officers in attendance. It then turned out that their orders were not to take him close up to the Front. However, he was highly amused at the idea of seeing Gorizia and told me to go on, saying where we went he could go, only I must be quick.

I drove as fast as the crowded roads would let me, and was rather horrified when, going through the village of Podgòra, the Austrians started putting a few shells over, and my brain was busy wondering what would happen had I led him to his death. Luckily it was only a mild outburst and by the time we had crossed the Peuma bridge over the Isonzo, all was peace again.

The Duke insisted on going up on to our roof, when he heard that we could see the Austrian trenches from there, but we dared not let him stay there long, as his red collar could so easily be seen. As he was coming down, Nina's sergeant came to report that a civilian of the town had been to our sentry on the gate to ask him if the English General who had just arrived was not the Duca di Connaught, the uncle of the King of England. This made us very anxious as we knew that the town was full of spies, and we hustled him away as soon as possible, I piloting him over a different bridge to the one we came in by.

Just as we got over the bridge a strafe began, and very glad I was that we had not been a few minutes later. I returned immediately to the house and found that it had been hit, and the house the far side of the road had been knocked flat. So the enemy had obviously realized that he was there and had tried to get him. Nina removed a piece of shell which had stuck in our front door, not three minutes after he had left, and sent it to the Duke as a souvenir of his visit to Gorizia.

Nina now has a car lent her by the Comando till her new one comes, so she started this morning at 7 a.m., while I sprawled in my cool cellar till 10 a.m. I must agree with her that there is a blessed peace here (when they are not firing). I have a most darling little smooth-haired Fox terrier, under-jawed, and with a tan head. Nina found her being towed along the Gorizia road by a soldier on a bicycle, very hot and very tired, and bought her for me. I should think about seven years old, and she already has a great culte for me. I can't

A HOLIDAY

take her everywhere and she weeps buckets when I leave her. She doesn't understand Italian but makes very good guesses at English. The soldier says she had been left in some vacated Austrian trenches, so I suppose that she thinks that "Come here" is nearer "Komm her" than "Vieni Quà." Anyway, she is blissful, except when shelling begins at night when she crawls trembling under my pillow, and even if I have to shoot her when I leave she is at least having a nice time now. I have called her Merna, which is the place where she was found.

9th July, 1917.

We have just had our first English luncheon party which consisted of General Hamilton, Colonel Buzzard, Colonel Moberley and Captain Williams, who are all very kind and helpful when we want anything. They brought us a lot of English helmets the other day, asking us all to wear them as they think them thicker than the Italian ones. They are decidedly heavier, but very comfortable.

Now Nina is ill, isn't it a pest! Only we are much comforted by having a very good doctor, the head one with the English troops, who has taken us under his wing; Major Elliott is his name, and he has been a doctor at Como for years, and since the War began has been in service at Malta and here. So he knows all about hot-weather diseases, etc. Nina has been firmly put to bed for a week or ten days and then, if fit, is to go for another ten days to a convalescent home. He says she ought to be all right by then. It is a sort of ptomaine poisoning, and is evidently the *end* of an illness. She has insisted on going on with her work although she has been very seedy for the last two months, with fever every night, and at last, three days ago, I went and fetched the doctor without telling her. Poor lamb, she was so glad to be ordered to bed, she has had no holiday for twenty months, and the doctor says she simply must go away or she will break down altogether.

Last night De Martino, one of the engineers, came in about 11 p.m. to say, "I hear you are going to sit up all night. Please let me sit up instead of you. I will bring my work here, and I can cook Benger quite well, and could call you if Mrs. Hollings wanted anything." (He goes to his own work at three in the morning, miles away from here, and gets back at 9 p.m.) They really are wonderful friends and would do any mortal thing to help us in a difficulty.

20th July, 1917.

Nina and I had a heavenly drive yesterday, a new way back from the tunnel, over all the ground that had been fought over; we got hopelessly blocked by the crowds of prisoners being brought back from the Bainsizza Plateau.

We were standing by the side of the road, waiting for an opportunity to get on when we saw an officer waving to us from a tump overlooking the road. Unlike most people, he had only a cap on and not a helmet, and on getting out of the car to go and join him we found that it was the King, surrounded by a large group of officers. He sent his A.D.C. down to meet us and say that he wanted us to come up and watch the enemy guns go by; they had only been taken that morning. . . . He was rather stranded, as the road beyond was being shelled and his car was not able to get to him. We, of course, offered him ours, but he would not take it, asking us, as we were going that way, to tell his car, if we saw it, to come on at once. We stayed on the tump watching the prisoners and guns for nearly an hour and then went on our way. We found the King's car, sheltering behind a rock, and sent it on post-haste to him.

The King and Queen have asked us to go and stay with them at Sant' Anna di Valdieri, near Cuneo, directly we can get leave. We have applied, and the General says that now at once is the best time, so we are off to-morrow. We purpose to kill two birds with one stone and go to Turin and see what has happened to the new Fiat car promised us by Mr. Arthur Stanley, which has not yet materialized.

24th July, 1917.

At Sant' Anna di Valdieri it is beautifully cool, and I was quite keen to get up and go out by six o'clock this morning. It is a narrow valley with always a nice breeze, and they have built a quantity of tiny houses for their guests; Nina and I have one to ourselves. The river is straight under our windows. The Queen gets up very early to fish, and we shall probably do so soon also, but are not really expected to appear till eleven-thirty, luncheon, and then a siesta till tea; after tea, fish and paint till dinner at eight-thirty. The Duchess of Aosta is here, and the Duke of the Abruzzi.

26th.

I am enjoying myself, paint all morning, sleep all afternoon, fish all evening—a most regular and healthy existence. This afternoon we are going to another river farther up the mountains, taking dinner with us; no walking farther than we want to, as there is always a motor within hail. Everybody kindness itself, and most anxious we should do exactly as we like and not overdo it. The Crown Prince, Beppo as he is called, interests me enormously; he is the most marvellous small boy I have ever met, and I don't see why anyone

FISHING

should ever bother to grow up. He knows everything there is to know already; he is twelve and a half, about five feet eight inches high, and deeply thrilled by "style." We played a game this morning with one of his books, of putting a hand over the writing and guessing the date of old furniture. He was never wrong once, even knowing the transition periods and all. There is no question of history you can stump him with, and his sketches *à la* Bakst are cram full of character and not drawn in the least like a child's drawing. Instead of toys, he showed me, with great pride, a collection that he keeps under his pillow which consists of valuable miniatures, snuff-boxes and all sorts of *bibelots*!

Yesterday's expedition was a great success; the Queen caught twelve trout and Nina, the brute, eight; me, only two, but the biggest of the lot. It rather spoilt my pleasure putting on caddis worms as bait. You decapitate three with sharp scissors and thread them on to the hook, the fourth you put on complete, and they wave their hands at you as you do it, it makes me feel quite sick, much worse than ordinary worms. The Queen was much amused at our squeamishness, and finally put them on for us; she is as active and as graceful as a chamois, jumping from rock to rock in the middle of the rushing torrent with perfect comfort. These mountains are lovely, very *escarpé* and rocky, with chamois and wolves and even ibex. The wild flowers are very exciting too, a saxifrage covered with cobwebs and closely packed with red flowers, a lovely lichnis with grey leaves, a tall pink flower like phlox all coming up amongst wild lavender which is everywhere, and then there are quite big primulas (rather an ugly pink) and pale yellow foxgloves in masses next to orange lilies and a tiny red rhododendron and,

A HOLIDAY

close to the snow, edelweiss, and big things which I believe are mulleins.

We go back on Saturday, just about right, I think. It is a mistake to stay too long if we are being a success, and we must get back to make preparations. We have the new car, too, to drive back to Cormons from Turin. It will be a long and weary drive, but better than boiling in the train as we did coming, at least driving there is always a breeze.

N.B.—We have just got a wire to-night from the General to say "Return Immediately," so we are leaving three days before we meant to.

On receiving the telegram from the General of our Army we left Cuneo for Turin where we had arranged to pick up the new Fiat which Mr. Arthur Stanley had promised us. Mr. Becker, with whom we had stayed on our way to Cuneo, met us and took us to the Fiat works. There we found that although the car was ready no actual order from the Red Cross had been received to give it to us and they would not give it up without a guarantee, so Mr. Becker very nobly guaranteed that the money would be paid and also that we were right and proper people to take delivery of it. We slept at the Beckers' house that night and started in the new car next morning at seven o'clock, meaning to sleep at Padua. On coming to a long, smooth stretch of flat road we thought, here was an opportunity to test the pace of the new purchase and we fairly let her rip. We were going about seventy kilometres an hour when suddenly out from a side lane rushed about ten schoolboys on bicycles, straight across the road. We were taking it in turns to drive and I happened to be driving at that moment; it was no good to jam on brakes as at that pace it would have meant turning the car over, so I did my best to get through them and, to my surprise, managed it, leaving the boys scattered all over the road in various recumbent positions, as one and all had capsized. Why we did not capsize, too, I do not know, as we ran the car right up the bank at the side of the road and off again. As I got full control of the steering and slowed down, we looked back and heard shouts of " Viva l'Inghilterra " from the boys seated in the middle of the road. We waved back, and, seeing that no one was hurt, continued at a more sober pace, congratulating ourselves on having got through without having killed anyone.

Our journey was very hot and very long, so we stopped for a rest about the middle of the day and lay down in the ditch by the side of the endlessly straight high road which goes across the whole width of the North of Italy. I do not know what Nina did, but I know I went sound asleep on the hard ground, with lorries thundering past every moment, covering us with fine white dust, so that we hardly recognized each other when we woke—I personally was awakened by an earwig crawling into my ear.

We had to pass through Mantua, one of the most lovely little cities in the world. But, beautiful as it was, we were very glad to leave it, as we had an adventure there which might have ended very badly for us.

In many of those Northern Italian towns they have Customs officials to prevent people taking in foodstuffs without paying tax. The *Custode* stopped us as a matter of course and asked if we had anything to declare ; Nina leant back and reached for some white bread rolls that we had over from our last meal, offering them to the man as a treat for his children. He at once yelled, " You are German spies, you are talking German," and, turning to various people loafing round the gates, shouted again and again, " Spies, spies." In one

A HOLIDAY

second we were surrounded by a roaring mob, all shouting, " Spie, spie, al fiume."

I do not know what the end would have been, and things looked very ugly, when I luckily caught sight of an officer in uniform in a one-horse carriage just coming into the piazza. Leaving Nina to the tender mercies of the crowd I jumped out of the car and pushed my way through to the officer's carriage. He sprang out to meet me, and saying quickly, " I know who you are, go into the carabinieri's post," pushed me up the steps, and shouting, " Fools, donkeys, imbeciles," jumped into our car and standing on the seat by Nina harangued the mob, saying we were English and allies, that he knew us well and had seen us working on the Front to help the wounded. In a moment the crowd had turned round into abuse of the Customs official. The last we saw of him was being hustled towards the river, where they meant to give him the ducking they had intended for us. I asked if anyone could help him, but the officer said it would do him good and teach him a little sense. By this time (everything had happened so quickly) the carabinieri had appeared on the scene and demanded to see our papers. They, of course, were in order, but we were asked to leave the town immediately as they said that they could not be sure how long it would be before the mob changed its mind again, and they wanted to get us away as quickly as possible.

Our next adventure on that journey was of quite a different sort. We arrived at Padua about 10 p.m., the excellent *padrone* of the hotel at once got us food and suggested that we should have a bottle of an especially fine wine to pick us up. The name of the wine was Goccia d'Oro (drops of gold) and the colour of it was pure gold. It was excellent but very strong, I only had half a glass, Nina had two,

! !

and then we went up to bed. My room was on a different floor to hers and looked out on to a balcony. My head was already whirling with the wine I had drunk, and I crept thankfully and giddily into a large four-poster covered with a mosquito-net, leaving my window open; I took my revolver into bed with me. In the middle of the night I was awakened by a noise at the window; I lay watching it, and presently saw an arm come in, followed by a leg. This was too much and I sat up, saying in my best Italian, "If you come any farther I shall shoot." The leg and arm were hastily withdrawn with a humble "Scusi, Signora," and I heard no more. Next morning as we were starting, the very unwashed boots of the hotel came close up to me and said in a low voice, "I hope you will not say anything about what happened in the night. I regret deeply that I disturbed you, I thought the room was empty and I only meant to come in and sleep on the bed"!!

I was rather sorry to see how embedded in the ordinary Italian mind is the conviction that if you are English you must be a drunkard or at least a strong drinker.

I was coming back from Gorizia alone one day at about 8 a.m. and stopped my car by a small garden just outside Podgòra to go and pick some flowers. The villa was in ruins, but the flowers were lovely. I had a big armful and was on my way back to the car when a little officer suddenly appeared and with a salute, followed by a beautiful bow, invited me to come into their Mess, which was close by, and drink a glass of cognac. He was much distressed when I explained, with many thanks, that I did not drink brandy at all, nor did I want strong drinks at that hour of the morning, and I left him looking sadly after me murmuring to

A HOLIDAY

himself, " But I thought that all English people drank brandy at any time of the day or night."

Of course I can't deny that there have been one or two episodes since our men came out here to justify his supposition. The other day Marchese Rosales, who was Head of the Comando di Tappa in Romans, came to us in a state of mind fit to be tied! He was a pompous soul and full of his own importance (he had been very kind to us when we first came out, helping us to get our house comfortable and our orderlies well turned out, etc.) and was positively spitting with wrath. It appears that two English privates of Gunners had got gloriously drunk on absinthe in the little town of Romans and were dancing in the piazza with a mocking crowd of Italian soldiers round them. Our friend, thinking that this was an unseemly display, advanced magnificently across the piazza to wave them away. The two, who could not have been as drunk as they seemed, looked at each other and, exactly at the same moment charged our Marchese with their heads down, as in a football scrum. They caught him in his middle, doubled him up and sent him flying backwards through his own soldiers! Not young, and swelling with outraged dignity, he ordered their instant arrest by carabinieri. They were seized and put in cells, while he telephoned to British Headquarters to say where they were, telling the story and asking that they should be sent for. No one paid any attention to his demands until next day, when they were fetched without any message or apology. Some days after, he received a message from British Headquarters demanding his presence at a court-martial on the two men, where he was requested to give evidence. Again I must remind you that he thought himself the biggest swell on the Front, and was deeply offended at the peremptory tone of the notice. However, he thought " All English are

LACK OF COURTESY

barbarians. Perhaps they did not mean to be rude or ill-mannered"; so he told one of his clerks to signify to the British General that he would do himself the honour of attending the court-martial. . . . The day came; no car was sent for him, and when he telephoned and asked at what time he was expected and how he was to come, the answer was, "Let him come with the old woman who sold the drink"; they could come together in the mess cart which would be sent for them. Needless to say Rosales did not go with the old woman, but when he did arrive in an Italian military car he was told to wait on a bench outside the courtroom until he was wanted, and there he sat with the old woman and other witnesses for half an hour, when he ramped home and refused to go again.

Even then no official apology reached him, only two or three gay young subalterns came to his office, demanded to see him when he was very busy and then asked where they could buy the best wine for their Mess, and what would he recommend.

This kind of thing has not made the English beloved, particularly as the order has now been promulgated in the Italian Army that their soldiers are not to have any wine, as, if they do, the English soldiers get hold of it and make themselves drunk: such a pity, as the Italians had been so delighted that the English were coming, and this order stopping all wine for everyone alike has made distinctly strained relations. One never sees an Italian soldier the worse for drink, at least we never have in all the time we have been here.

All our present adventures consist of strugglings and battlings with our interrupters and condensers which have been giving us hell. Nina practically lives in Gorizia now and I am *imboscata* here at Cormons struggling with machinery. She says Gorizia is so nice and peaceful (!) compared with the noise and clamour

A HOLIDAY

of passing *camions* and the amount of people coming in here. If she likes living in an underground room with all the windows stopped up by sandbags, it is not for me to argue, but it is not to my taste; so I stay here and cope with the assistants and go in whenever there is extra work to do there. Nina spends all her spare time making up new machines. She has become quite crazy on machinery, which is an excellent thing as we are both now mechanics to the section and do much less radiography since Sir Frederick Treves fussed you by declaring that we were getting dermatitis from the rays.

After working so long ourselves we found it very difficult to let others take it on, but when we began lending apparatus and assistants to the different operating centres, as well as having the two X-ray cars always on the road, we found we had plenty to do to keep the plant in order. We managed altogether to raise by hook or by crook five machines, and had lent many of our spare parts to hospitals whose X-rays would not work.

At first we had scandalized our new electrician by the things we used to do to our machines; but after a time he found that although we knew no theory of electricity and could not discourse on the matter, yet experience on our apparatus for nearly three years had taught us the way to get the best results they were capable of giving; we had learnt how to locate an injury in our plant as quickly as the plant enabled us to locate a foreign body in a man.

So the three of us used to travel the country in different directions, doing our best to mend and put various apparatus in order.

25

BAINSIZZA PLATEAU

A FEW days after the retreat of the Austrians over the Bainsizza Plateau, we received a message from the General asking us to go up to the new ground just taken by the Italians, and see whether the roads were possible for our apparatus. So we took our little touring Fiat up to sample the going for the heavier cars, and packed it full of gauze swabs and thermometers, which we knew were very much needed by the advanced dressing-stations. We crossed the river half-way between Plava and Canale, as the usual bridge was down, and finding ourselves so far already from our objective, we decided to go up by a new road that we heard existed near Canale. Canale must have been beautiful before it was destroyed, as it was situated on the river itself, with a series of bridges connecting both banks. There were still remains of houses to be seen on the bridges, and its position was on a lovely curve of the river, with high wooded mountains on either side.

The road proved not to be finished, so we had to return to Plava and go up by the wonderful road which the Italian engineers had made up Monte Kuk: seven and a half kilometres of road with fourteen hairpin bends, and wide enough to take three lorries abreast, all made in twenty-one days ! It was very crowded, and we stuck hopelessly at one of the bends ; a big naval gun being towed up by two huge tractors had refused to turn the

BAINSIZZA PLATEAU

sharp corner, and had stuck right across the road. The only way to move it was for one of the tractors to climb the steep bank, towing the gun with it, and then to insert jacks under the gun, and once on the balance, to put twenty or thirty men to swing it bodily round to the new direction, with twenty others to steady its nose with a rope for fear it might possibly overbalance. We sat and watched this wonderful performance, which went off without a hitch. It took about an hour and a half, and we remained comfortably in our car and ate our luncheon.

The Bainsizza Plateau is very wild and beautiful, with grey rocks sticking up out of the ground everywhere. There obviously had been plenty of trees, but they were the usual sad sight, all blown to bits and the bark all gone, leaving them standing white against the scorched and furrowed ground. The Austrian dug-outs looked like so many rabbit-burrows up the sides of the ravines, and there were signs of the enemy's rapid flight at every turn—ammunition-dumps, gun-carriages, and large heaps of boxes containing food; in one place we passed they had left two field-guns and all their ammunition, as well as a traction-engine. They had been trying to get their guns up out of the pit where they had been hidden when the Italians had fallen upon them and captured the whole lot, turning the guns round and firing them after them.

There was no shelling going on as we left the mountain to go across the plateau, and it was so lovely that we told our Italian driver to go steady, because we wanted to have time to see the country properly. We were going first to Batè, and to reach this we had to pass a little house where the English Ambulance had established itself. On our way down we saw masses of shell-cases of all sizes and shapes, and the demon of souvenir-hunting took possession of us. We got out and picked up quantities, stowing them into the car. We then proceeded on our road, and stopped at the English Ambulance Section to pass the time of day with them. We found them much worried, as it appeared that a *camion* had been hit not half an hour before our arrival on the very spot on which we had been so happily culling souvenirs. They had been watching us through glasses, and said the road was always being shelled, and that the Austrians could see every car that came along it. The Austrians were obviously in a kind mood at the moment we chose to play by the roadside! They were kind to us all that day, because, having to go to Zbrdo, the Englishmen were good enough to say that they would take us in an ambulance car, as more likely to escape being fired at than our private one, which looked like a staff car, and we started for Zbrdo with Mr. Dickenson in his ambulance, a gigantic Red Cross flag stretching from the bonnet to the back of the car.

They cheered us by telling us that the road was in full view of the Austrian line the whole way, but that so far they had never been personally fired on, though everybody else had! We went very fast and bumped about wildly, as the road was practically non-existent, but got there without any mishap. We found our doctor-major whom we had come to see, and he seemed much pleased at getting the thermometers, which he said were very difficult to obtain and were broken in quantities by the men. We were just getting up to go when a shell came over with a scream and landed plump outside the house, followed immediately by another that spattered stones and other things in through the door. The Major seemed somewhat worried, and said it was impossible for us to start, so we politely sat down again and began to make conversation; but the shells arrived faster and faster, and the Major got up saying the house was not safe and we must come into a cave a little way off. I do not know what the others felt about it, but I know I should have much preferred to stay where I was under a nice strong doorway to running out into the street at that moment; but we had to do it, and I have seldom run so fast. It was lucky that we did run, as a high explosive hit the church tower just as we all bolted down like rabbits. We were followed by a little surgeon who had been in the fields and had been caught in the storm. He was very blown and shouting with laughter at his escape. After a bit the firing died down, and we emerged from our shelter and gained the car, which had not been touched. Nina confided to me in a whisper that she had been hit on the ankle by one of the stones which had been hurled in at the door. We did not mention it, as our companions would have been so distressed, but it made a beautiful bruise. Later on one of the big *sanità* officials heard of it, and came to find out if she had been wounded, but she could not say that she had, having had many a worse bruise playing hockey in her youth. The kind official was much disappointed, having hoped to be able to give her a wound stripe.

We have to thank the surgeons for their unfailing patience and help; given perseverance, goodwill and untiring attention to the minutest details, anyone can learn to be extremely useful to surgeons in finding and locating foreign bodies and fractures. The finding and diagnosis of disease is, of course, a totally different matter, and this no amateur ought to attempt. If we were asked to radiograph or radioscope anyone for suspected disease, we always agreed to turn on the rays for the surgeon and allow him to look, but refused to have anything to do with it ourselves beyond taking plates.

Professor De Cigna, who had done a lot of radio-

RECOMMENDATIONS USELESS

graphy and was one of the first Italian surgeons we worked for, used to show us everything he could, normal and abnormal, explaining and helping in every way. Dr. Sbrozzi, a well-known brain surgeon, was also most helpful, so that before we had been out long we took to doing all the screening ourselves, as we found that quite a lot of the surgeons had no idea of radiography and could not see the simplest fractures even.

September, 1917.

We have been trying to get *Valore* medals, or even mentions for the assistants, who have worked so hard. They deserve them quite as much as we do and have been in quite as dangerous places, but nothing seems to have any effect. The same answer always : " You have been here two years, your assistants, at the outside, six months." Another answer was : " We cannot give them to every person in a regiment ; we can only pick out and give to those we choose." Polite but adamant, so we have now been bombarding St. John of Jerusalem, and got more or less the same answer from them : " Your assistants will have the War Medals, and they can choose whether they will take the English ones or the Italian ones." We were asked by St. John of Jerusalem to mention a few names of people, both English and Italian, who, we considered, had been of real use to the section, so we mentioned, besides our own assistants, an excellent electrician and mechanical engineer, Major Tettamanzi by name, who had given up his own hard-earned rest to keep our plants in working order. No matter how tired, he would always stagger in whenever he had a spare moment to run over our wires, etc., and make sure that all was working right. They sent us a list to fill in, and then paid not the slightest attention to it, although medals are being chucked right and left to people who do not deserve them half as much.

6th August, 1917.

We propose leaving here 15th September, and shall be very sorry to go. Anyway, we shall send our heavy baggage off on that date. People are being very nice to us about our work; Sbrozzi said yesterday, "I cannot tell you how much I shall miss you, although I would not move a finger to prevent you going. It is the highest time you went home, but I should like you and Mrs. Hollings to know that I consider most of the success that I have had as a surgeon during this war to be due to you both."

28th August.

We are busy inspecting and mending all our apparatus so that all shall be ready and in order when we leave, and we are only doing an occasional hospital when it is very urgent and when there is no time to get an assistant into Gorizia, so don't fuss about our being burnt by the rays. I also spend a good deal of time on the top of the house sketching and watching the attacks gradually developing on all sides.

One of the assistants is twittery and whiney, another is frankly cross, and my boots squeak unceasingly. Nina had a touch of sun yesterday and I feel sick. I am so feeble-minded that I cannot see which is right, to trail on with a war job when you know you are tired out and go on till you collapse and become a general nuisance, or to insist on going home.

I have often been asked what was our nearest escape during the War. It is very difficult to say. Once, after a burst of shelling, I dug a shrapnel bullet out of the cover of the car which was just over my head; another time a large shell went to ground under Nina's bed in

A NEAR THING

the cellar in Gorizia. Luckily it did not burst and it remained there for all the rest of the time we stayed in the town.

One day Nina and I were driving up the Corso in Gorizia on our way to our house. There was a good deal of shelling going on at the moment and one of the big plane-trees which lined the road was hit, just in front of our car; the shell twisted it round and tore it off at its thickest part, leaving all the fibres sticking up. It looked as if a giant fist had wrenched it off. The top of the tree was hurled across the road immediately in front of our car and through the shop windows on the opposite side; these had been all planked up, and it blew the planks back into the street as it crashed through them. Our windscreen was smashed to pieces by the draught made by its passing and the back of the car, luckily empty, as we were both sitting in front, was filled with débris, glass and bits of plank and pieces of tree. We fortunately had on helmets which received several good raps, but nothing penetrated.

On getting home we were sitting out in the garden, feeling somewhat exhilarated after our narrow escape, when we heard the sound of another big shell coming. Nina and Corporal Stagni bolted for the house at the first sound but I, idiotically, did not move. Result . . . my hat was blown off by the draught of the passing shell and my hair felt as if it was being pulled out by the roots; I had a very sore head for nearly a week after, and learnt a lesson not to play the fool.

The Austrian shooting was very good. They meant to get the house of a certain general and put one shell into the dining-room, where it went behind a case of empty siphons and did not explode, and another into the General's bedroom, which he had happened to leave half an hour earlier than usual that morning, and a third exploded in the garden in front of the room where he worked. No one was even wounded, but it was not the fault of the shooting!

Our house in Gorizia had a most convenient roof, and when we had time to spare we used to lie flat on the top of it, so as not to show above the parapet, and watch the troops assaulting San Marco and San Gabriele. So near were we that we could hear them shouting as they ran to the attack. San Marco was assaulted again and again while we were there, but the Italians, try as they might, could not get it; they used, with great effort and sometimes terrible losses, to get half-way up, and rumours used to float down to us that they had taken it, but they were always driven back again. The top was practically impregnable, having machine-guns hidden in caves all round; and a little *bersagliere* officer, who had led his men over and over again to the assault, told us that there was a point beyond which his men simply could not go, for they were mown down in rows and nothing could live. San Marco was never taken while we were there, but San Gabriele was several times, and then lost again.

To have two people of equal seniority in a command is usually a risky proceeding, but our partnership was the greatest success, and except for occasional sparring, which cheered us all up, we thought alike about most things and were a very good balance one to the other. My partner had much more dash and go, I had been born with a large bump of caution and had been trained to dogged work, so the combination was a good one and neither of us could have done without the other. But she was twelve stone, and I was nine, so when it came to a physical tug-of-war she had me beat.

We had been working hard at one of the hospitals in Gorizia all the morning, the streets as we walked to our work were quite empty as the enemy were shelling the upper part of the town and the civilians were all in

A GOOD PARTNERSHIP

hiding in the vast cellars and passages which run under the streets there. We had taken several plates and were just going home to develop them when we remembered that we were short of developer.

A discussion between us promptly arose, Nina wishing to go to the nearest chemist, who was in the market-place at the end of the street, to buy the ingredients, I, of a more cautious disposition, wanting to go to a chemist the other side of the town, as the market-place was receiving steady attention at that moment from the Austrian batteries and was by no means a wholesome spot. However, physical strength won the day. Notwithstanding my clinging to her coat-tails, my partner, at a fast run, crossed the empty market-place towards the chemist's shop, the back of which had just been blown out by a shell. The place, when we reached it, was one mass of lime dust and débris, broken glass everywhere, and naturally no one to be seen. But from under the counter, which was still intact, came a voice, the voice of the chemist, "Help yourselves, Signore, I am not coming out," and he directed us where to search. After a minute we found what we wanted and, throwing the money under the counter, we ran for our lives, not a moment too soon, for as we reached the other side of the piazza two shells burst, one in the shop itself and one behind it, to be followed by a third in the market-place. Looking back through the clouds of dust and smoke it did not seem as if anyone could have escaped destruction and we mourned the little chemist as lost; but, strange to say, we were hailed in the street some days after, and there he was. We did not recognize him, never having seen him, but he knew us all right and we made great friends.

Nina and I had arranged that whoever spoke first in a tight place should be obeyed without argument. In the last case perhaps Nina had spoken first, I don't

BAINSIZZA PLATEAU

remember . . . but another day we were motoring back towards Cormons and had reached a village called San Lorenzo di Mossa just when a high explosive burst in the main street, raising great clouds of dust and bringing the buildings clattering down all round. My partner was driving and I shouted, " Left, quick ! " She swung the car left-handed into a side street at top speed as another shell fell just in front of us, and we found ourselves in the middle of the most ghastly mess. A shell had exploded a minute before in the middle of a large ring of mules who had all been tethered head in towards each other, about 200 I should think. They were in pieces everywhere, many with legs missing and huge gaping wounds, struggling all over the road and fields, trying to drag themselves away. The sight was indescribably horrible, and even our orderly, who was in the back of the car, was in tears. There was nothing we could do, we should have only been in the way if we had stopped, and we had our own work to attend to, so we rushed on, leaving the terrible scene behind us; it left a memory never to be forgotten.

We had been strongly recommended to keep away from the rays (our hands and eyes having become somewhat affected by them), so on the 31st September Nina and I handed the command of our section over to Mr. Pinsent, an architect, who had already been working at X-rays for some time in Verona, and after many affectionate farewells to all the friends we had made during our two years' stay in Italy we went home.

Some months later we received a letter from General (now Field-Marshal) Badoglio asking us to come back and continue our work, this time to be attached to the Italian Army, but the Armistice came just as we were ready to start, so we did not go.

A LETTER TO KEEP

Letter to us both from the Hon. Sir Arthur Stanley, Chairman of the British Red Cross

17th May, 1917, Rome.

DEAR COUNTESS HELENA. . . .

I cannot leave Italy without writing one line to tell you both how glad I am that I have been able to pay you a visit and to see something of your wonderful work. Everywhere I have heard nothing but praise and admiration of your courage and your devoted service to the wounded . . . and I can assure you that I as Chairman of the British Red Cross am just as proud as you must be of the wonderful name you have made for yourselves . . . probably prouder! Whenever you are next in London do please come and see me. It will be a very real joy to hear of your new exploits.

yrs. sincerely,
(*signed*) ARTHUR STANLEY.

26

SCRAPS

AND after the War? What then? As with many other people, we were incapable of sitting still, or of resuming a normal existence. So we went to France to work with the Americans in the Terres Dévastées.

What a strange experience that was. The Americans liked to pretend that a state of war still existed and wanted all the hardships they could get. We did not grudge them their adventure, but we had no wish to share their discomforts which they created just for the fun of it.

My partner and I had signed on as chauffeurs, but struck at the amount of unnecessary work expected of us. Our cars had to be clean and ready by 8.30 a.m., often we were not in to luncheon until 4 p.m., only to find the remains left over from the meal the others had had three hours before. We then had to go out again, carrying goods to different villages and often not returning until 10 p.m.

Even Sundays we were supposed to take the rest of the workers out joy-riding all over the country. Nina had been patiently submitting to this treatment, but when I arrived some ten days after her we struck for regular meals and shorter hours, absolutely refusing to work all Sundays as well as all week-days. The head, a very nice woman called Miss Hadley, agreed and

RABBITS

some sort of regular organization of the drivers was arranged.

Miss Hadley came into the common-room one day when we were all together and asked if any of us knew anything about the keeping of rabbits. Only Nina and I put up our hands, and before long we wished heartily that we had not done so. She announced that about 2,000 rabbits were arriving that evening by train, to be distributed for a nominal sum amongst the peasants of the neighbouring villages. Would we take charge of them, if we understood their habits and ways. We had only four hours to make arrangements for their housing and food. The housing was not difficult. The château, which was near Soissons, was built on a terrace with high steps leading up to the entrance on the ground-floor, and under the ground-floor were large, light, dry cellars, the ceiling supported by stone arches. Here, we thought, the rabbits will be dry and safe. We bought hay, corn and bran, and ordered cabbages to be delivered daily by the thousand; then we went off to the station to meet our charges. They had been sent loose in railway trucks and the first trouble began when we found many had been crushed by others sitting on them. Our ambulances were not nearly large enough for the quantity sent, so we had to go into Soissons and collect vans and lorries to carry them. They took hours to unload, but at last we got all of them into their new home.

Before their arrival we had spread all their food out in long lines, but they all wanted to eat the same cabbage and to our horror the same crushing and squashing began which had ended so disastrously in the railway truck. Till midnight and past we struggled with those nightmare rabbits, picking them up and putting them out in rows with their noses pushed into their food, only to look round and find them all heaped up again. At last we gave it up and hoping for the best went to

SCRAPS

bed. Next morning we hurried down before breakfast; many were alive and eating, but many more were dead, crushed and suffocated by the others. We sorted the dead from the living and went to report. A sale was quickly arranged and many found a home, but every morning and every evening the corpses were removed in barrow-loads, till only two remained and those got down a drain and were no more seen. The smell of rabbit has always made me shudder ever since.

Our work in France at that time was not exciting, but we had one episode that might have ended badly had it not been for the pluck of an American chaplain. A great many Chinese were employed in the neighbourhood and were all quartered in a large camp about two miles from the town of Soissons. One night something annoyed them and they broke out, killing the French sentry at the gate. Then, arming themselves with scythes, hammers, picks and anything else that they could find, about 400 started out to loot Soissons. One of the clerks employed in the camp slipped out on his motor-bicycle and dashed into the town to warn the inhabitants. He went to an American padre who could speak Chinese. This man without hesitation jumped on to the back of the motor-bicycle, directing the clerk to take him to meet the mob. Having reached a narrow bridge which the Chinese, on their way to the town, were obliged to cross, this plucky padre and clerk wedged their bicycle across it and waited until the mob appeared, waving their weapons and shouting. The padre then advanced calmly towards them, with his arms held up and calling in Chinese to them to halt. They did so but with angry gestures. He addressed them, asking what was their complaint, and promising to have it looked into if they would return quietly to their camp. The marvel was that the Chinese listened to him. And then a man stepped forward saying they could not return

BRAVO, AMERICAN PADRE

as they had killed their sentry and would themselves inevitably be killed in revenge by the rest of the guard. The padre gave his word that nothing would happen to them, and that he himself would lead them back and see that the French did nothing to them: a rash promise which, however, succeeded. He then placed himself at their head and led them back to the camp. Luckily the French, seeing him in front, did not fire and the town of Soissons was saved. I never heard what their complaint was in this particular case, but know that there was a good deal of trouble with the Chinese labourers that were employed in tidying up after the War in France, because of the lack of sufficient water for their ablutions and ceremonies.

It was an unpleasant thought that they had meant to loot the town of Soissons, and we should undoubtedly have been the first to have been murdered as our château was between their camp and the town.

One day the order came that six of us drivers were to go to Paris to collect some new Ford vans which had just arrived at the depot there. Nina and I and four others were chosen to go. The cars were all said to have been inspected and passed as ready for the road by the head of the depot, and each was supposed to have its full complement of oil and petrol. We proceeded in convoy with Nina bringing up the rear. Unfortunately her car stopped in the middle of Paris and she had to get out to make it go again. Meanwhile, we had all serenely pursued our way and only found that she was missing when we arrived at the gate on the road which left Paris for Soissons. When we discovered her loss, I turned back to look for her, leaving the rest of the convoy to go on home. I toiled round the walls asking at each gate if the officials had seen a lady dressed in khaki and driving a Ford van. At last I reached the one she had gone out by. Apparently she had headed for Compiègne instead of for Soissons.

By repeatedly asking people on the road I traced her nearly as far as Compiègne, but in that town I could hear no news of her. The reason I was so anxious was that we had been repeatedly told that the forest was full of *apâches*, escaped prisoners and Chinamen who had run away from their battalions, and we had all been warned that it was not safe to be there alone, especially at night. I toiled on through the forest, turning my head-lights in every direction, up every side road as I came to it and blowing my horn in hopes that my partner might hear it and answer with hers, if her car were broken down somewhere within hearing. About 2 a.m. I gave it up and went on to Soissons; as I drove in at one gate of the château she walked in through the other. This is the story she told us. It appears that her car had run out of petrol in the Forest of St. Denis, luckily not far from a woodcutter's hut. She made her way to this; the people there were very kind and urged her to stay the night, saying the forest was not safe, that it was, as we had been told, full of *apâches* and, they added, *revenants*. Nina, however, was obdurate, she said that we should all be so anxious if she did not turn up and that she must go on, on foot, if they had no petrol to give her. It was fourteen or fifteen kilometres; she was not very young and it was rather a foolhardy thing to attempt, but she did it in safety and with a very interesting experience. She had been tramping for ages along the cobbled road and was getting very footsore and tired when she suddenly saw in front of her some English soldiers climb out of the ditch on one side and run crouching across to drop into the ditch on the other side of the road. She was close enough to see quite clearly how they were dressed and particularly noticed that they wore Glengarry caps, putties, and carried

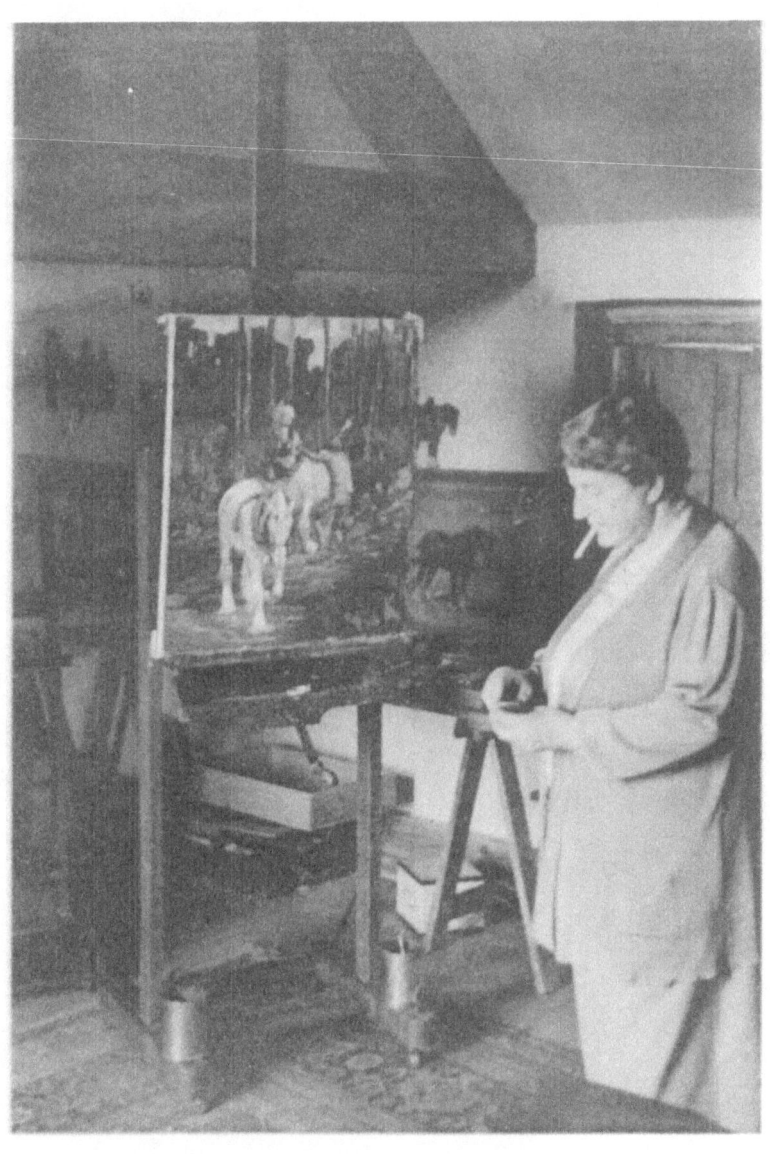

LADY HELENA GLEICHEN AT WORK
IN HER STUDIO

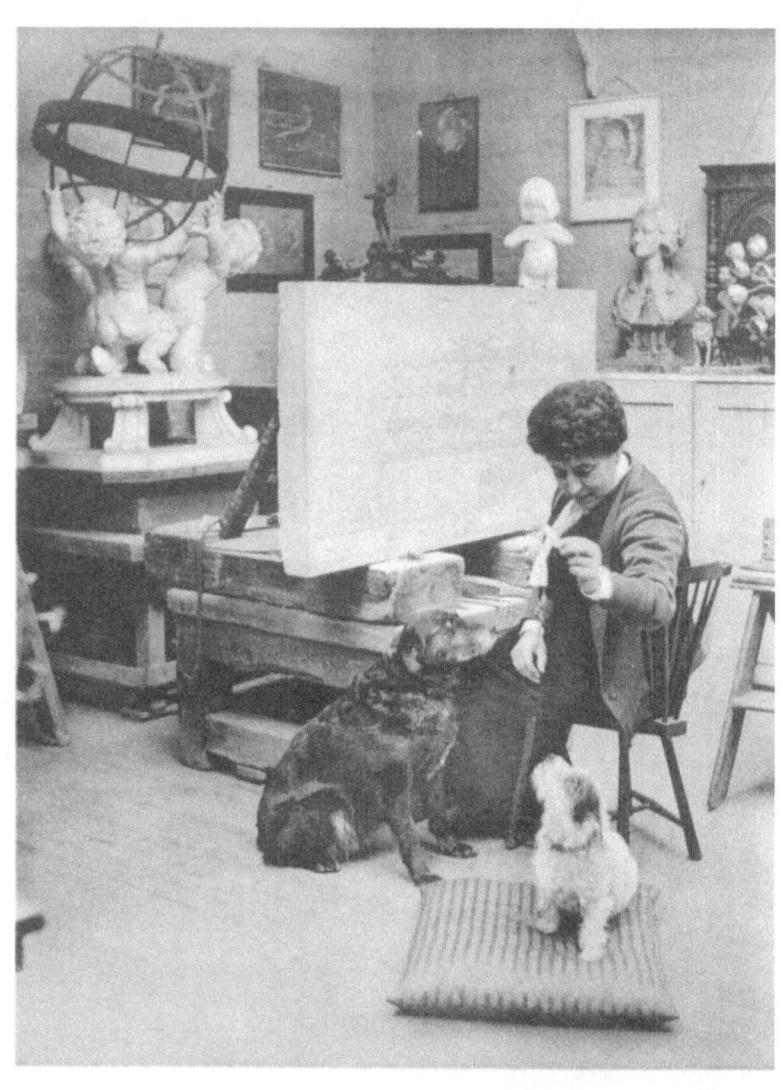

LADY FEODORA GLEICHEN AT WORK

SECOND SIGHT?

cavalry carbines. She estimated them to have been about thirty men.

A couple of days afterwards we were showing to an officer of the British Graves Commission a place in the woods where we had found some English graves, which he had not known of, and I asked her to tell him what she had seen that night. She was rather loth to, but was at last persuaded. He was silent for a moment and then said, " Those were the Ayrshire Yeomanry, who were cut to pieces on that road early in the War. They had not yet been issued with helmets and were wearing Glengarry caps, putties and, of course, carried carbines."

I must add that the gentleman has since denied that he made this statement; but I was present and heard him say it. In any case, whether they were the Ayrshire Yeomanry or not, it is certain that Nina Hollings saw these men. She was a very tired woman and was probably in a more receptive state than if she had been normal. I always feel that the power of seeing ghosts only comes to you when your mind is in a super-sensitive state, either from illness, tiredness or the like, and you are then able to record impressions that are always in the atmosphere round you, though as a rule you cannot receive them.

After returning from France we bought a house in South Wales. My family grumbled rather at the distance from London, but during the last two years of her life my sister Feo became so enthusiastic over the beauty of the country, that she spent every moment she could spare from her studio with us. Nina blew off steam by lecturing all over England on the subject of Italy's part in the War. We had found that very few people here understood how much had been done by the Italians. I, not having the gift of the gab, settled down to paint all I could remember of what we had seen while out there. I had lots of rough sketches to go by, which I had done on the spot, and the atmosphere of dust and murk was thoroughly engrained in my brain and quite unforgettable.

I worked hard, and during the next few years had quite a number of one-man shows—in London, Paris and Hereford, and in the Birmingham Municipal Art Gallery. In Milan also I had an exhibition. There the Italian authorities lent me the big rooms in the Palazzo Sforzesco, known as the best gallery in Italy, and where I was lucky enough to sell several of my war pictures to the Government. People have often asked me why I have nothing to say about my painting life. I suppose because one can no more help doing one's work than one can help breathing, and so one does not talk about it. The principal charm of an artist's life is that there is always the hope and the possibility that one's work may improve, if only one tries hard enough. How often have I left off painting and looked with despair at what I have been doing—it is bad in every way, to-morrow I shall break it all up and start again. And to-morrow comes; I go into the studio and lo! the painting is done; it has finished itself in the night or the pixies have finished it for me. Then there are other days, when you feel on the very crest of the wave, everything has gone well from the beginning (in itself a very bad sign), your composition balances, your tones are true, your colour is good. You put the canvas into a frame and then you see that what you thought so good is utterly wrong. It is a sad fact that what looks well out of a frame never looks well in one, I suppose because a square or oblong frame hanging on a wall in a four-square room is against nature. You cannot take a piece of nature, surrounded by miles and miles of sky and atmosphere, and expect it to look right, crammed into artificial surroundings. So there is a great deal to

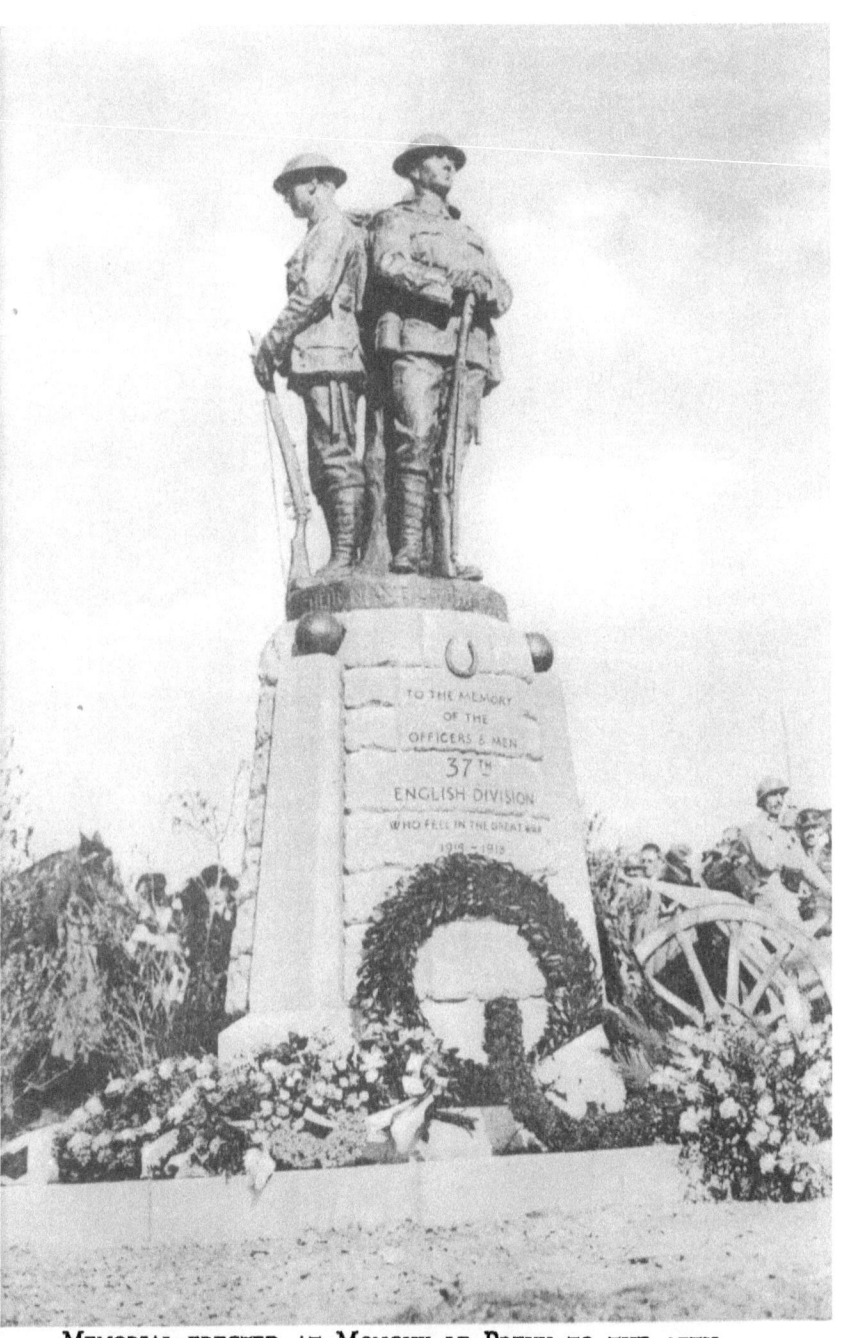

MEMORIAL ERECTED AT MONCHY LE PREUX TO THE 37TH DIVISION, COMMANDED BY THE AUTHOR'S BROTHER, MAJOR-GENERAL LORD EDWARD GLEICHEN
[*Sculpsit F. Gleichen*]

MY SISTER FEO

be said for those moderns who paint things that do not have the faintest resemblance to nature.

My sculptor sister, Feo, died in 1922. She was an irreparable loss to me in every way and her advice in my work had always been the greatest help and encouragement. Her vision was always clear in all matters belonging to others and she seldom made a mistake in giving advice when others came to her in difficulties; she was never offended when her advice was not taken and she had no petty meannesses. She had undying zeal and thoroughness in all she gave her mind to and was the most responsive person that ever existed, equally ready to enjoy anything with you, or, if you were out to fight, always equally ready to oblige. If you wanted an argument she would hurl herself in on the opposite side, without a moment's hesitation and with the clearest reasons for doing so, made up on the spur of the moment. The most charming of companions, too, as she had the widest possible powers of perception and enjoyment. Her generous praise of others and her ability to make them feel that she appreciated them and their work or thought them worth listening to, drew the best out of people, and even the stupidest felt clever when talking to her. In her own work she was intensely prolific in ideas, her difficulty, she often said, was in eliminating, never in creating. I should like to write pages more about her and her work, but do not feel that this is the place to do it.

One morning, some long time after her death, I was brought a letter from Rome addressed to her. I opened it and found it was from someone quite unknown to me, signing herself Isobel MacAllister. In it she appealed to my sister to help Alfred Gilbert, the celebrated sculptor, to return to London. He was very unhappy, she said, feeling himself an outcast from his own country; "and," she added, "think what a loss to England, all his good work is going to foreign countries where his talent is appreciated. What is the matter with the English people that they can let the best sculptor that England has produced since the time of Alfred Stevens live in penury abroad?" This letter interested me very much, as, besides my own enormous admiration for his work, I knew how much my father and sister had both appreciated his genius; I knew also the sad story of how he had gone abroad under a cloud many years before.

King Edward VII had had a personal feeling against him for never having finished the magnificent tomb to the Duke of Clarence in St. George's Chapel at Windsor, and King George V had naturally the same feeling of indignation, so I well realized that it would be hopeless to try and reinstate him without the King's consent. I also realized how difficult this would be to obtain . . . so I at once took the letter over to Sir Frederick Ponsonby, the King's private secretary. He was very doubtful as to whether King George would ever consent to receive him or to encourage the idea of his return to this country, but he was willing to help in every way he could. Gilbert had been accused by his enemies of selling in Bond Street some of the figures which belonged by rights to the Duke of Clarence's tomb, and he told me afterwards how this story had got about. He had employed a relation of his to work in his studio at the time he was making these figures. The young man had secretly copied some of them and then sold them as Gilbert's work, and made quite a lot of money. I asked why, if he knew this, he had not defended himself and told the King what had really happened. His answer was: "How could I, when I knew that if the story had become public the mother's heart would have been broken and she would never have been able to look anyone in the face again? . . . Besides," he said, "no

ALFRED GILBERT, R.A.

one who knew my work could ever have taken those things as mine."

Gilbert had many enemies for the following reason. He was, like many artists, utterly unable to manage money and with no idea of its value. His work was the only thing that counted in his life. A really great artist, such as he was, will never let his work leave his studio until he is satisfied that he can do no more to it, and that it is the best he can produce. Gilbert was seldom satisfied, he could always see something that might improve it and make it more perfect. The consequence was that he frequently came to the end of the money that had been paid him in advance for a commission; other people might be waiting for their orders to be carried out, but Gilbert would go on working at the first commission, and use the money of the second, and even of the third or fourth, to improve the first.

Sculpture is an expensive form of Art, especially Gilbert's, as he loved using precious stones, gold and silver to beautify his work. His casualness thus made enemies of the people who were waiting for the completion of their own orders, and even his own profession began to say that it was too much and amounted to dishonesty. This it never was, dishonesty was not in him, only concentration on his work to the exclusion of all else. He always used to say how he wished that he had lived in the glorious time of the Renaissance, when artists could live and work in monasteries, or under the care of great patrons, without a thought except for their work. Often I heard him sigh for the days of Lorenzo di Medici.

At last people could bear his ways no longer and a violent movement was started against him. All his creditors raised their voices as one man, and Gilbert imagined himself to be completely bankrupt. (That this was not true was proved after he had gone abroad, and he paid up all his creditors.) The matter of his bankruptcy came before the Council of the Royal Academy who called upon him to appear before a special Committee of Enquiry. Here, from all he told me, I gather that he lost his temper completely, indignantly threw up his membership of the Royal Academy and left the country in rage and misery.

Alfred Gilbert was seventy-two when he at last came back to England. At first he would not hear of returning, and I thought that I should have to go over myself to try and persuade him; however, this plan was soon knocked on the head as, when the King heard what I meant to do, he sent me a message saying that I was not to go. I therefore wrote to Gilbert's cousin, Mr. Walter Gilbert—the well-known metal-worker (who made the beautiful gates for Buckingham Palace)—and asked him to come and see me at St. James's Palace. He came and promptly offered to go himself to Bruges, promising not to come back without him.

We received a telegram in a few days saying that they were arriving, would we take a room for Gilbert somewhere in a quiet place. Miss MacAllister busied herself about this and Gilbert was brought to see us on his way from the station. He was painfully agitated, with shaking hands and a way of snapping at his shoulder every minute and rolling his eyes up to the sky. After a few weeks' peace in my studio he lost all these tricks and became quite normal.

King George had agreed to his return on condition that he finished the Duke of Clarence's tomb before accepting any other work, but Gilbert had no means whatever. He could not buy himself clothes or a ticket to come to England nor even his daily food; much less could he hire a studio, buy tools and materials nor pay to have his work cast in bronze when finished. So

I LEND GILBERT MY STUDIO

the King most generously agreed to find the money again for the figures which had never been completed years ago, while Gilbert's friends supplied all else. Violet, Duchess of Rutland and the Duke of Portland, always good friends to him, gave some clothes and my brother gave him a coat besides other things; my share was the loan of my studio in St. James's Palace, with the tools, modelling stands, etc., which had belonged to my father and sister. So in July, 1926, he found himself established with clay, wax and plaster, besides some beer to refresh himself with.

This reminds me that his charming enemies, not content with accusing him of dishonesty, also accused him of drinking. Needless to say, I did not know him in his youth, but I do know that this was not the case in his old age, as I used to go down to the studio at any hour during the two years he worked there and never did I have the slightest cause for suspecting anything of the kind.

During the time that Gilbert had my studio I became ill and had to retire to bed on a diet of milk for six weeks. Every day he used to come up and pay me a visit, and much of interest did he tell me. Stories of how, when starving in Belgium during the War, he used to go out into the fields to eat raw turnips, the only food he could get. The Germans, he said, tried to persuade him to go to Germany and work for them, but he said that nothing would induce him to work for the enemies of England, rather would he continue to eat raw turnips in Belgium! In order to gain a pittance he taught small children to draw. A story is told of him that after the War he was given a commission to model a heroic statue of Victory for a certain town. He hired a large barn which he turned into a studio, where he set to work. When nearly finished the council of the town which had given him the order came to view it. The ten or twelve stout gentlemen in frock coats with their hats in their hands stood in awe before the beauty of the huge winged figure. It was perfect, exactly what they wanted. They congratulated him and filed out. He called to his workmen, "A ladder, quick, also a hammer—no—nothing else, only the biggest hammer you can find." He hastened up the ladder and began smashing everything he could reach: head, wings, drapery, his men on the ground below begging and imploring him to desist. "Are you mad?" they cried. When at last, worn out and exhausted with his fury, he descended the ladder, he explained: "If people like that admire my work, how bad it must be! I shall begin all over again tomorrow," and he walked off to his lodgings. Many people might think that this was a lunatic thing to do, but it is a good example of Alfred Gilbert's point of view: never to allow a piece of work to leave your studio before you are satisfied with it.

Soon after his return the Royal Society of British Sculptors voted him the gold medal of their society, the highest honour they could give to any sculptor. Gilbert, instead of being pleased, was infuriated. "All these years have my brother-sculptors neglected and ignored me, they did not care if I was alive or dead and now they come offering me their beastly medals . . . let them keep their medals for themselves."

He was walking up and down the room, raging with indignation and hurt feelings. For a whole hour did this continue, while I exhorted him not to be such a fool. Could not he see that everyone was trying to make up for all he had suffered in the past; this was their way of apologizing and showing their appreciation of his genius. No, he could not see it. Suddenly he swung round. "Would you like me to accept? If you would I will do anything to please you, even to humbling myself in the dust," and he hurled himself on

THE MEMORIAL TO QUEEN ALEXANDRA

his knees beside my bed, seizing my hands and bursting into tears. I think I had tears too as I congratulated him and we wept together. Hastily, before he could change his mind, I wrote to Sir William Reynolds-Stephens, the President of the Royal Society of British Sculptors, saying that Gilbert would accept the medal with much pleasure and considered himself much honoured by the Society. Sir William answered that he would come and present the medal himself.

Soon after this the President of the Royal Academy, Sir Frank Dicksee, came to pay me a visit to talk about reinstating Gilbert as a Royal Academician. There again I had a struggle with him, but I won. It is not generally known that the Royal Academy, Burlington House, is directly under the King, so nothing could have been done about this without the King's consent. Not only had this been obtained but His Majesty had graciously signified his willingness to give Alfred Gilbert the order to carry out the Memorial to Queen Alexandra. This really made the poor old man happy. He had adored Queen Alexandra for all her kindness to him when he was in trouble and he felt that now truly he had been received back into the fold. All trouble was not, however, over, as the committee who were arranging the details of the memorial had some strange idea that Gilbert would model the figures and that an architect should design and model the base, etc. When Sir Lionel Earle and Sir Cecil Harcourt Smith told me this I knew that there would be a rumpus. Gilbert, who was as great a designer and architect as existed, would never allow this. In fact, very few sculptors would consent to such an idea. He was fit to be tied. Never would he permit anyone to dictate to him about his work or have anything to do with it. Have an architect to do his work when he was designer, sculptor and architect himself. Never—rather would he throw it all up!

SCRAPS

Finally, however, when he had won all round, he became pacified and started work on the Memorial in a studio which had been arranged for him in the old stables of Kensington Palace. Here he spent the last years of his life, happy at last. The money for his work was handed over to Sir Philip Freeman, a well-known solicitor, who generously gave his services so that Gilbert should not be bothered with money affairs, and at last he had his wish—that he should live only for his work, untroubled by worldly cares.

I met him crossing the courtyard of St. James's Palace after the unveiling of the beautiful centre group of the Queen Alexandra Memorial and asked him if he were not disappointed that his design had not been carried out in its entirety. (He had planned some very fine, decorative bronze railings to take the place of the wall which at present faces St. James's Palace.) "Not a bit," he said, " all the drawings and designs are finished to scale and some day, long after I am dead, the whole thing will be erected and they will realize what a beautiful work of Art they possess."

Alfred Gilbert knew and realized well his own genius, and I remember his saying to me one day, when I was carelessly throwing some of my paintings into a cupboard and one missed and fell on to the floor, "How can you treat your work like that, it is your creation and the work of your imagination and even the least of sketches is worthy of being treated as you would treat your child; you would not knock your child about, so why knock your work about?"

To return to Wales.

The people were charming to us, but we felt that we were foreigners in the land for at least eight years. Then just four years before we left (owing to one of our usual monetary crises) they took us on as friends and neighbours and we were very sorry at having to go. While in Wales I determined to learn how to shoot so that my nephew, Valda Machell's boy, should have someone to go out with when he came down to stay with us for his holidays. So I made friends with a very nice publican who had previously been a game-keeper, and I used to revel in the long days spent wandering over the mountains looking for game, of which there was plenty: grouse, hares, rabbits, woodcock (these latter nearly always to be found in the holly bushes which abounded on the hillsides). Wild pheasants, too, and occasionally partridges, but of these latter very few. There was a wonderfully wild bit of upland country above Llangattock which stretched away to Brynmawr, where herds of Welsh ponies could be seen grazing and where the crowing of grouse could be heard. When this moorland reached the valley of the river Usk, it broke into huge rock cliffs which were inhabited by ravens, buzzards and kestrels; merlins, too, there were. Foxes lived in the rocks and hundreds of little blue rock pigeons roosted there. I am always rather ashamed when I think how one day's shooting of these little pigeons drove them away from their home and I never saw them there again. The keeper had suggested our going to the rocks one evening and he got forty and I twenty-nine—they made good sporting shots as they flew very high, and we, no doubt, gave much pleasure to the old people in the workhouse to whom we gave them for their dinners; but I have always regretted the massacre.

There were deep caves in these cliffs which had never been fully explored, and it was said that a man had crawled through them and come out at Brynmawr, seven miles away. The cliffs were very steep and slippery and I hated it when the keeper used to walk firmly along the sheep-tracks on the face of the rock and I crawled shaking after him, not liking to own how giddy

SCRAPS

I was and how afraid of slipping. As one gets older one loses the eyes in one's feet and must watch them or they will put themselves into foolish places.

Besides wandering over the hills in search of game we did a good deal of fereting, which was good practice and which gave me the chance to see quite a lot of interesting natural history.

Once I was standing waiting with my feet each side of a small round hole, too small, I thought, for a rabbit to squeeze through, when to my vast surprise a full-grown fox very stiffly pulled himself out through it and walked quietly off without paying the slightest attention to me. Another time, when rabbiting, I was walking up a fence and happening to look through it, saw a fine, fat rabbit sitting very still with its back towards me, apparently watching a weasel rolling about in the grass in front of it. I had often heard of the hypnotic effect a weasel or stoat has on its victim, but had never seen the process before. The weasel was playing in the most delicious way, just like a kitten, and as I watched got closer and closer to the rabbit until it was actually jumping over it, back and forth. By this time I thought it best to interfere and at my first movement the weasel fled. As the rabbit still remained immovable I climbed the fence and picked the poor little brute up. It was quite unconscious, and seeing that the weasel must have been biting it before, as it had a nasty wound on its neck, I gave it to the keeper to kill. It was better dead.

Baby weasels are such nice things to watch; I once saw a whole family, father, mother and children, romping on the stump of an old tree; rolling over each other, chasing up and down and over, into holes and out of holes in the bark. One stir on my part and they were all gone, in the flick of an eye, never to appear again, though I waited for half an hour.

Before leaving the subject of ferreting, a day at this

A HEREFORD BULL

game comes very clearly into my mind. The keeper's old father, who had been a keeper before him, had come with me to help with the ferrets, and we were spending a dreary time waiting for one which had laid up, he one side of the hedge and I the other. There was a gate on my right which led into the field where the old man was. Suddenly I heard a snort and looking up found that a big Hereford bull had come silently across the field behind me and was standing only a few yards off, looking over the gate. Oddly enough he had not seen me, and rather foolishly I drew his attention to myself by asking old Griffiths what I had better do. "There is a bull here," I said. The old man only answered, "Mind the ferret, my lady." As can be imagined the ferret was the last thing I cared about at that minute, and I looked wildly round for some cover. The bull had suddenly become aware of my presence close to him and swung round towards me, bucking as he did so. I could not help admiring his grace and perfect balance; great heavy brute as he was, fully six years old, and moving as lightly as a thoroughbred. The hedge was far too thick and high to scramble through or over, and besides, I had broken my leg not long before and was only just off crutches; the field behind me was a forty-acre field and there was not even a bush in sight, so the only thing to do was to stand still. The bull got between me and the hedge and there, after a good buck, he proceeded to tear up the ground with his horns. This was too much, and I fired one cartridge between his horns and just above his back, keeping another cartridge ready for a second shot should it be required, but to my amazement he dropped his head almost to the ground and walked away across the field as if the weight of the world were on his shoulders. The only explanation of his surprising behaviour is that the flash and noise together so near to his head must have scared him stiff, and I have since been told that if you can only make sufficient noise to frighten a bull that he is the most cowardly of animals. It was very lucky for me as I could not have run or dodged him in any way with my lame leg. I heard afterwards that he was very bad-tempered and was usually kept locked up, but that he had managed that day to break down the door of his loose-box and had got out without anyone knowing.

I took a different piece of rough shooting most years while I was in Wales, some quite good, others very chancy.

My bag for the season of 1928 was ten rabbits and one cock pheasant! But the one cock pheasant made up for all.

One afternoon I called the gardener, Bufton by name, and said, " There is a cock pheasant on my shoot and I have got to get him, come and help." We walked for an hour, seeing and hearing nothing of the bird, when suddenly I spied him in the corner of a field nearly half a mile away. We hastily held a whispered consultation and settled that Bufton should make a big détour and try and head him towards me, and that when he saw him he should stand on a gate and wave his hat; I was then to go direct to where we had first sighted him and put Hebe (my labrador) on his trail.

There ensued a most exciting hunt: Hebe followed his scent well, and now and again I caught sight of him speeding ahead, but nothing would induce him to get up. Bufton's hat, a white one luckily, showed again and again, farther and farther away. I had to put Hebe on to a strap as she was too fast for me. We kept this up for the best part of two hours, till we were all, except the pheasant, worn out. Then Bufton's hat began to come nearer and Hebe and I thought it time to take cover. Still nearer came the white hat, when with a

A SUCCESSFUL STALK

sudden rush Bufton pounced at some reeds the far side of a stream and out ran the cock at full speed across the field and away. And the whole business had to be done again. Never have I seen a bird run so fast, Bufton, scarlet in the face and perspiring at every pore, running hard to head him off, Hebe and I breathless behind. Another half-hour passed with occasional views to keep up our enthusiasm, then he disappeared. There seemed to be no scent now as Hebe could do nothing. The beastly bird was lost, he had us beat. Suddenly, from a bush, almost at our feet, up he got with a whirr and a clatter and away across the stream, the first time he had taken to his wings, a hasty shot and I got him, Hebe bringing him back with pride across the water. It was just dark, and we returned in triumph at five-thirty after one of the most exciting hunts I have ever had, with a fine large cock pheasant for the pot. I wonder how old he was. He had to be boiled for hours and even then was barely eatable. He knew a great deal.

I have often been interested to find how neither birds nor animals seem to notice red. I have a terra-cotta coloured coat which enables me to see a great deal which is usually hidden from people who wear other coloured garments. A fox has walked right up to me when I have been standing in his path and only when he actually touched me did he start away, and was off like lightning. One evening I was waiting for pigeons in a larch covert when a hen pheasant flew in, meaning to settle on the nice piece of red earth, when she suddenly discovered that it was not earth but a human being that she had meant to settle on. She threw herself nearly over backwards in her effort to stop, tail feathers spread fanwise, claws stuck straight out in front of her; she emitted a squawk of terror as she fled off into the darkness of the woods. Another time, again wearing the

SCRAPS

same coat, two little quarrelling finches bumped into my chest, to their horror and my amusement.

One more animal story: I was hunting on Exmoor with the Devon and Somerset. It was very hot and I was tired, so I stopped on one of the hill-tops and got off my horse to let him feed while I lay down in the heather and watched hounds working over the other side of the valley. They disappeared soon and I got very sleepy. Suddenly my horse looked up from where he was feeding. I raised my head to see what he was looking at and found that a hind and calf were standing on the track close beside me. They were listening to the hounds which were still far away. Presently the hind turned to the calf and gave a grunt, upon which it gathered its legs together and jumped a big jump, which landed it right beyond a great clump of heather. There it lay down so that I could just see the twitching of its ears, and the mother trotted on down the track, twice stopping to look back; then she went on at a steady, long, swinging trot. I remained where I was for about half an hour hoping the hind would return; the calf's ears were still twitching now and again behind the clump. Then hounds appeared on the track of the hind and when the huntsman came up I told him about the calf and he sent the whip on to stop them. John Fortescue, the author of *The Red Deer*, told me that I was extremely fortunate, for he and many people living on the moor had never seen such a thing, though it was known to happen.

When we had to leave Wales we searched long and far for another house and could find nothing that suited us. One house I went to see was very old and lovely, but most inconvenient as the hall was divided into cubicles so that you had to go from one into the other, through several doors, whenever you wanted to cross to the other side of the house. I supposed that it had

THE HOUSE WITH CUBICLES

originally been a refectory for monks and each one had dined alone. Some years after seeing this house, I met the owner and told her that I had been to see it and the reason that we had not considered taking it. She asked me when I had been there. I told her and she looked at me astounded. "But," she said, "it is impossible, I took all that panelling out of the hall over sixteen years ago when I first inherited the house, and I had it all put upstairs, you can see it there now." I assured her that it was only two years before that I had visited the house, when we had been leaving Wales, but I saw that she did not believe me and only thought me mad.

It is rather curious that I have several times seen houses as they were in other days. I was having luncheon with my cousin Violet Farquhar at Shaw, a beautiful old Elizabethan house, near Newbury, and happened to ask her when they changed the front door, as I remembered that the last time I had been there, a year or so before, I had come through a colonnade of white pillars on the opposite side of the house. Violet looked up at the butler and said, "You had better ask Bailey, I am ashamed to say that I know very little about the architecture of this house, but he has been here a long time and knows all about it."

I turned to the man and he said, "The front door has never been altered to my knowledge but, about a hundred years ago, they enclosed the old colonnade which used to be the other side of the house so as to make a passage to the kitchen, and if you wish I will show you the white pillars which are still visible inside the passage." We went with him and saw the wall which had been built, shutting in the colonnade, which had looked so beautiful when I saw it in another life. Another time I had the same kind of experience. We went over to Hampton Court in Herefordshire, and while talking to our host I happened to mention that the last time I had been in the house was when a Mrs. Burrell was living there, and that we had come in by an entrance with stone pillars on each side, much farther down the road and through what is now the garden. I added that I liked the present entrance much better. Lord Hereford burst out laughing and said, "You must have been here in the time of Charles the Second then, because this entrance was made in the seventeenth century when the old one was done away with. If you like I will take you after luncheon to see the remains of the old stone pillars which were on each side of the gate in those days and which you seem to have seen in a former life."

How I wish I could turn this gift of sometimes seeing the past to some advantage; at Glastonbury, for instance; but unfortunately I cannot produce it at will.

A ghost story.

Nina and I were motoring through Worcestershire and ran through a very heavy rainstorm. It was some time ago and we were in an open touring car so got exceedingly wet. We suddenly discovered that we were near the village of Bredon and I bethought myself that as I was an honorary member of a country club near there it would be a good plan to go in and get a good meal and a comfortable bed. Also, it made a good excuse to sample it, as I had never been there before.

We drove up to the door of a beautiful old manor-house and asked if we might see the secretary. The secretary being out, the housekeeper appeared and agreed to put us up, if we were not very particular as to what rooms we had, as she said the club was very full. This statement struck us as rather surprising, as we had only seen one old man reading in the corner of the very dark hall that we had passed through, and the servant who had answered our ring at the front door had said he was sure they could take us in, as they had no guests.

A GHOST

The dinner, I can remember nothing of, the house seemed dreary and dark and we were glad enough to go to bed, after our long drive. We were given two fairly good rooms opposite each other on either side of the main passage, on the first floor. My room was a longish room with one window only and a powder-closet in the corner opposite to the door by which you entered the room from the passage. My bed was in the other corner against the wall and opposite to the window. Thus the door into the passage and the entrance to the powder-closet were right at the other end of the room from my bed. I had with me a rough-haired terrier, called Puck, and I was sitting up in bed reading and brushing my hair with Puck asleep on my feet, when he suddenly rose slowly, with every hackle up and growling beneath his breath.

I looked up and saw a little figure come through my door, which was shut, trot across the room and disappear into the powder-closet. Puck's fear communicated itself to me, when I grasped that the figure was only clothes. No face, no hands, no legs or feet ... just a smart, full-skirted coat (blue-grey in colour, I think, but of this I am not sure) with sword stuck at the correct angle, a white bob-wig tied with black ribbon, buff knee breeches and buckle shoes. He trotted across quite fast so that I only realized these details afterwards. Puck by this time had crawled shaking on to my pillow, and I did not wait for the little gentleman to come out again, but seized my pillow and a blanket and fled for my friend's room, across the passage, where she luckily had a good sofa where Puck and I spent the remainder of the night. I should add that the figure that I saw was not more than three feet high.

Next morning we asked for our bill and the housekeeper brought it up herself, so we asked the history of my room, telling her what I had seen. She apologized deeply, saying it was quite true that the room was haunted by the figure of a little man. "We know nothing of who he is," she said, and then she added, "I only tell you this because I am leaving here to-day, we servants are forbidden ever to mention the ghosts. But, oh, mam, the place is full of ghosts and our lives are unendurable here, so I am leaving and hope never to see the place again."

I believe the old manor-house is no longer a club, probably the ghosts became too much even for the club guests.

"I HAVE HEARD" IS NOT SO GOOD AS "I HAVE SEEN."
—Chinese proverb.

It took us some time to find the house of our dreams, but we found it at last. We were coming back late one evening from a fruitless search in Worcestershire and on our way home we stopped at a garage on the Ledbury-Ross road to fill up with petrol. I casually asked the boy at the garage if he knew of any empty house near by, as we liked the look of the country so much. "Yes," he said, "there is an old house just across those fields which is empty, and I know that the owner wants to let it or sell it. You go through a white gate up what is called the Monk's Walk, but you won't be able to get into the house as there is no one there to let you in at this time of night."

It was about 9 p.m., and we knew it would take us nearly two hours to get home, but it might be worth while to be a bit late. We turned up the lane indicated by the boy, and as we drove through the gates leading down to the house were overcome by the beauty of it. The whole country was flooded in brilliant moonlight and not a detail of the old red-brick house was lost. It

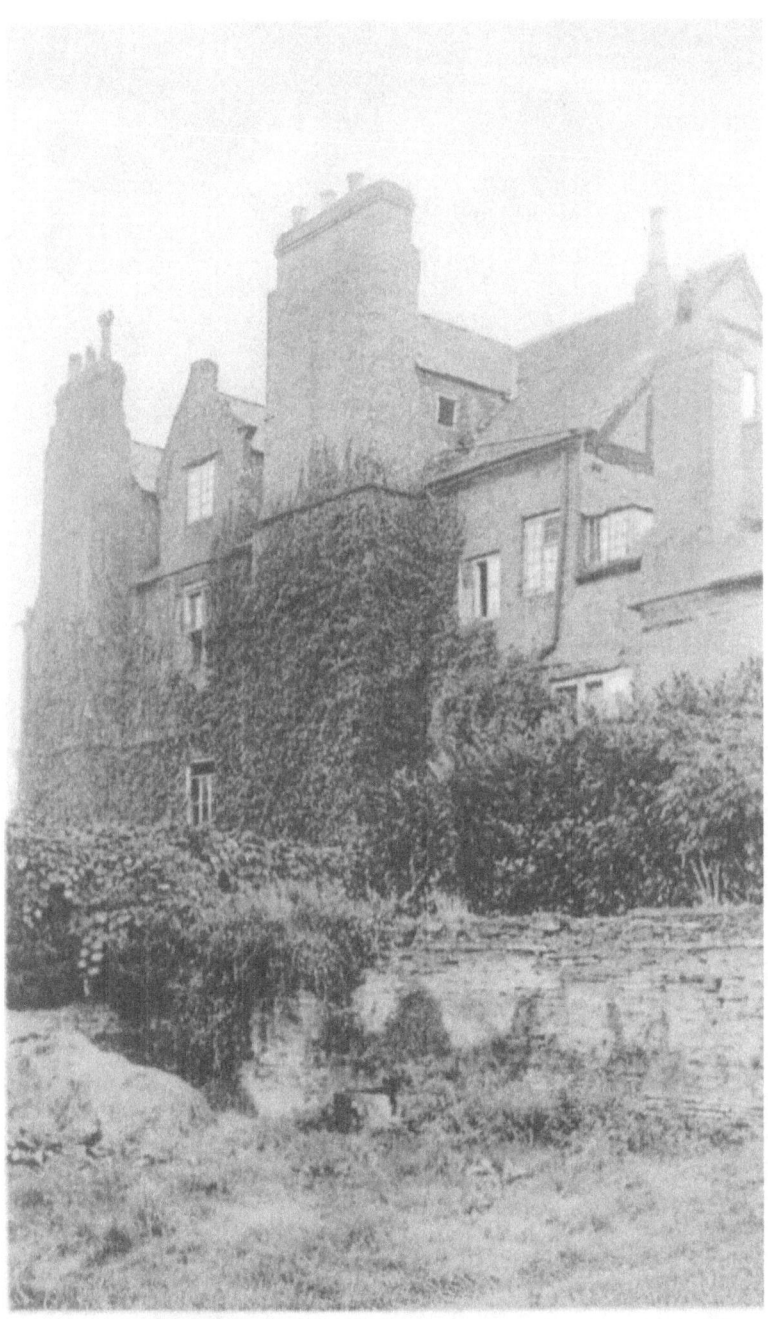

HELLENS . . . . .

HELLENS
[*Statue of Pan in foreground by F. Gleichen*]

was partly Tudor, partly Stuart period, and on one side stood a lovely dove-cot with the letters "F. and M. W. 1641." When we prowled round we found a defence tower at the back of the house, evidently of much later date.

What a house, and what a situation, looking across fields to the distant Malvern hills which were quite visible, so bright was the moon.

Now, how to get in. The windows were most of them mullioned and barred, but one was Georgian or early Victorian, and we inserted a knife under the bolt and climbed in, followed by the dogs. The room we had invaded in this lawless fashion was panelled with Queen Anne panelling, painted white, the next was a square hall with an old staircase reaching to the top of the house. Passing through this we went into a large, high room which we found afterwards was called the Great Hall, a finely proportioned room with a plaster frieze, date Charles II, and a huge open fireplace. The moonlight pouring through the old leaded windows added to the beauty of the rooms and our breath was taken away by the thought that the house might, with some manipulation, perhaps become ours.

We rushed from room to room, becoming more and more enthusiastic and fully aware that we should never be able to buy it but hoping that we might at least hire it for a period.

We got home to Wales by midnight still talking hopefully of what we would do if it ever became ours. I skip all the writing and arguing that from then on took place, but after endless discussion—rather to our terror and against the advice of all our friends, who feared bankruptcy for us—Hellens became ours. We bought it and for nine blissful years have lived in it.

The exact history of the house has been difficult to ascertain. According to old documents in the Hereford

SCRAPS

Museum, it seems to have belonged to one Joan Helyon in about 1100 and then was called Helyons, not Hellens. Joan married into the Walwyn family and from then on to the eighteenth century it belonged to Walwyns. Part of the house was burnt down and was rebuilt by Fulke and Margaret Walwyn in 1641, when they also built the dove-cot and put their initials on it. In the eighteenth century the property went to relations of the Walwyns, i.e. Nobles and Radcliffe Cooks. We seem to have had the doubtful distinction of being the first people ever to buy it, every other owner having inherited it.

One room had the name of being haunted, but we soon stopped that by the simple expedient of taking down the panelling. Behind it we found walnut shells galore and skeletons of rats and mice, quite sufficient to account for all the strange noises heard in the room and which had given it the name of being haunted. The panelling cost the large sum of £6 to take down and we expected it would cost about the same to put up in the Great Hall, but to our horror we could find no one to put it up under the vast sum of £100, a quite unobtainable sum for us after buying the house and moving all our furniture, etc. Then a marvellous thing happened. A friend of my mother's came to see what our new home was like. She said she would like to give us a "hansel," a Scotch word for a present to people settling into a new home. We were very grateful and suggested a new lamp, as we wanted one badly. "No," she said, "I shall find something presently," and she wandered away round the place by herself. When she came in to luncheon she asked us what all the oak panelling was doing stacked in the mill-house. We explained, saying that we meant to put it up eventually but must wait a little. "Oh," she said, "there is my hansel, have the work done as pleases you best and

TOO GOOD TO LAST

send me the bill." So that is how the Great Hall at Hellens was panelled.

Rooks came to build in the copse the first spring we were there, a sign of good luck which delighted us both. Then I had to find a studio. The first thought was to turn the larder into one; it faced north, but I did not like to spoil the old window, and without widening it it was not possible to get enough light, so as we knew we could never keep hunters again, I turned the hay-loft into a lovely studio and the architect, Maurice Chesterton, put me in a good high window looking towards the north. Result, the best studio I have ever had and a perfect light for painting.

One of our first visitors remarked with commiseration, "You two poor imbeciles, you have bought the biggest house in Herefordshire." But it was not true, the house looks big and its rooms are big and high, but there are very few of them and we have only room for two guests besides our two selves.

Our furniture luckily is all of the right date and looks as if it had grown with the house, and as my sister Valda was leaving her old place up in the north just at the time that we bought Hellens, she lent us what extra we needed. We walked into the place having no alterations whatever to make. Electric light, hot-water pipes, everything ready for occupation. What a bit of luck.

Now in 1939 comes a new war, when only young people can be of use and old experience counts for nothing. Everything has to go into the melting-pot and Hellens must join the rest.

FINIS

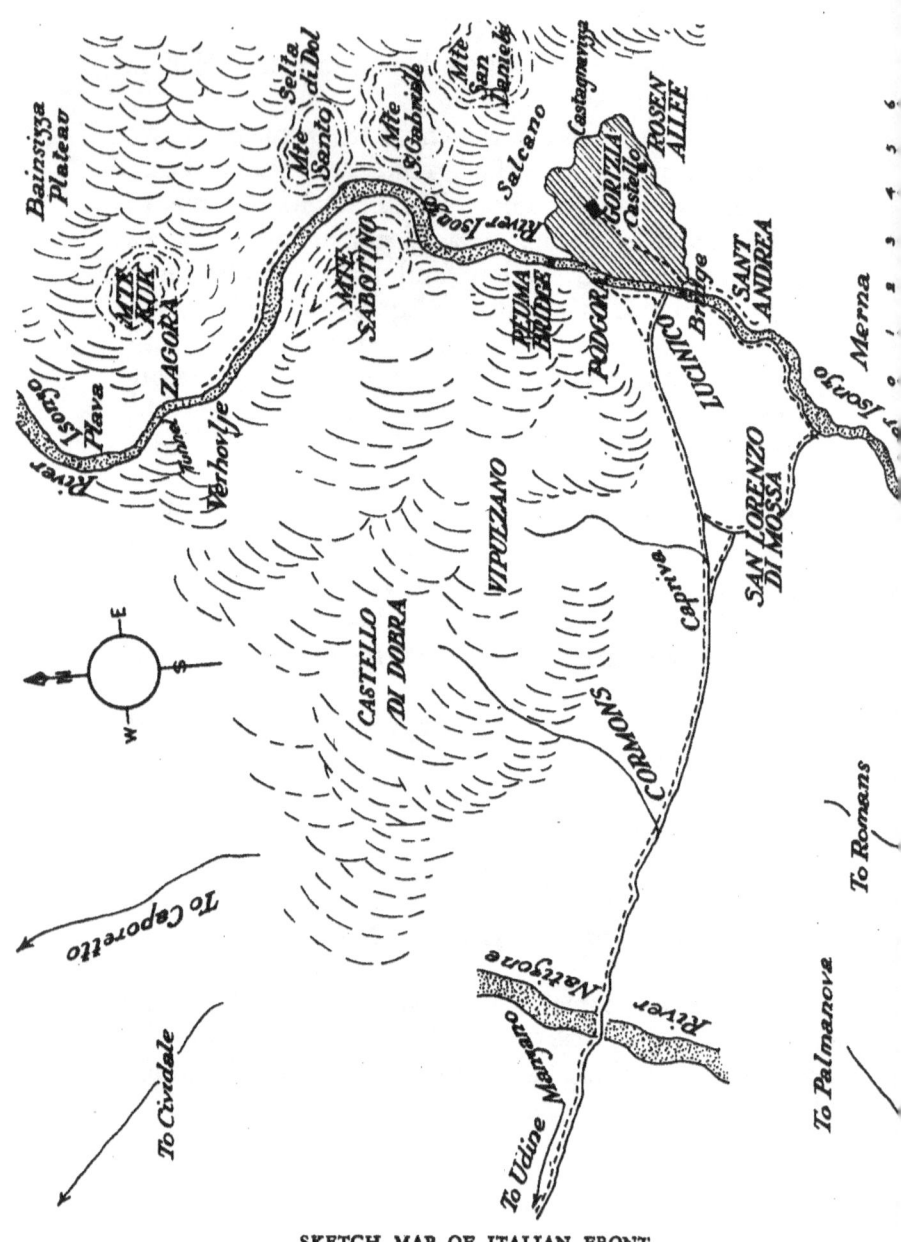

SKETCH MAP OF ITALIAN FRONT

Appendix

And now of Unit IV I must speak. Unit IV consists of two intrepid ladies, a motor-car or so, a soldier servant or so, and a movable X-ray apparatus. For nearly a year, when I met them – and now for more than a year, for they began in December 1913, these ladies, the Countess Helena Gleichen and Mrs Nina Hollings, have been passing quickly from field-hospital to field-hospital with their merciful van-load of magic, and thus making possible swift and accurate operations which, but for them, would in many cases either never have been performed at all, or have been dangerously, if not fatally, delayed.

I don't know to whom the credit is due for first seeing the possibilities of a mobile installation of this kind, but few thoughts for the amelioration of the soldier's lot can have been happier. Certainly no two practitioners of the mystery can ever have worked with industry more untiring or with greater zeal than these two ladies.

To see Unit IV at work is the very remarkable experience which we had on our second evening. Outside the hospital in the inevitable darkness, was the motor-carriage containing the dynamo. From this an India-rubber pipe wound its way along a passage and so into a little room where people moved like silhouettes against faint fluorescence, and where there was no sound but the buzzing of the sparks. By degrees one could make out the dramatis personae of this shadowy play. Sitting by the wall, with her hands controlling the current, was Mrs Hollings. In a corner was one of the orderlies watching the machinery. On a stretcher in the centre was a powerful Italian soldier stripped to the waist, above whose body the other necromancer was passing a luminous square of glass. Beside her stood the two medical officers of the hospital, the captain and the lieutenant. It was Rembrandt again: "The School of Radioscopy".

Leaning by the side of the operator, over the wounded man, I was able to share her field of vision. For some time the bullet, or piece of shrapnel, or whatever object it was, eluded us; and then suddenly with a little shout of exultation she announced its discovery. The next thing was to adjust a movable plummet immediately over the spot on the square of glass, turn on the ordinary light, slide the glass away, and – for the surgeon's guidance on the morrow – immediately beneath the plummet, now swinging no more, to mark the man's skin with an indelible pencil. The mark would tell the surgeon that somewhere below it a foreign substance was lodged. But it would tell him only that. Necessary also to inform him how deeply he must cut, and for this purpose the man was moved on his side, and again the search was begun: this being a more prolonged task, since he was a big man and the rays had therefore the greater distance to penetrate. With the marking of the second spot the proceeding was finished, and case No.3423 on Unit IV's books (not bad for two ladies in a foreign war zone in a little under a year!) was carried back to his bed and case No.3424 was brought in. Since the poor fellow was, however, in great pain and the splinter very small, it was decided that he must be photographed – a less interesting proceeding for the spectator.

That night we were the guests of Unit IV, and I looked through the album in which some of their most remarkable photographs are preserved, and heard the story of a recent adventure, told with the utmost simplicity as though quite a matter of course. A shell had fallen among some soldiers beside the road, and the ladies had arrived just in time to comfort one or two who were dying, and carry the others to a hospital. This and similar deeds won for them the Medal for Valour.

From *Outposts of Mercy*, by E.V. Lucas, London, 1917, pp 28–31.

INDEX

Abdul Hamid, Sultan of Turkey, 13-14
Abruzzi, Duke of the, 290
Adam, Paul, 126
Alexandra, Queen, 11, 322-3
Alma-Tadema, Sir L., 9
Annaly, Lord, 59
Anspach, Margravine of, 19
Aosta, Duchess of, 290
Aosta, Duke of, 192
Ashby, Professor Thomas, 135-6

Badoglio, General, now Marshal, 187, 207, 308
Baird, Captain, 169
Baring, Maurice, 35
Baring, Tom, 35-6
Baruzzi, Lieutenant, 227
Beaumont, Count Étienne de, 126-30
Beaumont, Hubert, 182
Becker, Mr., 292
Belfield, Mrs., 172-4
Bellegarde, Rhodina, Contessa, 227
Berry, Major, 73
Biggar, Mr., 73
Bismarck, Prince, 72-3
Borsari, Captain, 217
Böttiger, M., 68
Bouhy, M., 21
Boulongne, Paul de, 126
Burgh, Tommy de, 55

Burrell, Mrs., 331
Buxton, Mr. Gerald, 78
Buzzard, Colonel, 288
Byard, Captain T., 275

Cadorna, General, 183, 195 *n.*
Calabrini, Marchese Carlo, 226-227
Calderon, Mr., 22, 24
Capello, General, 136, 151, 207, 216, 218, 250, 252
Carrara, 273, 276
Cattaneo, General, 241, 267, 269
Chapman, Miss, 262, 267, 273-4
Charles II, King, 7, 331
Cigna, Professor De, 183, 185, 302
Clarke, Sir Ernest, 275
Clary, Count, 73
Connaught, Duke of, 286-7
Corkran, Sir Victor, 20
Cowans, General Sir John, 132
Craven, Countess, 62

Dale, Will, 89
Dickenson, Mr., 301
Dicksee, Sir Frank, 322
Dunkley, 80-1
Dunmore, Earl of, 10

Earle, Sir Lionel, 322
Edward VII, King, 21, 317
Elia, Marchese, 226

INDEX

Elisabeth, Empress of Austria, 11
Elizabeth, St., of Hungary, 19
Elliott, Major, 288
Eugén, Prince, 68
Eugénie, Empress, 20, 63–5, 67–73

Fadda, Surgeon Major, 214
Farquhar, Violet, Lady, 330
Feisal, King, 21
Ferdinand, King of Bulgaria, 14–15
Fortescue, Hon. Sir John, 35, 329
Freeman, Sir Philip, 323

Gabriel, Major, afterwards Sir E. V., 141
George V, King, 83, 317, 319–320, 322
Gilbert, R.A., Sir Alfred, 317–23
Gilbert, Walter, 319
Gladstone, Mr., 11
Gleichen, Count, xi
Gleichen, Countess, afterwards Lady, Feo, 9, 20–1, 34, 36, 57–8, 81–3, 95, 97–100, 104, 314, 316
Gleichen, Countess, afterwards Lady Valda, *see* Machell, Lady Valda
Gleichen, General Count, afterwards Lord Edward, 9, 37, 40–1, 58, 73–5, 192, 220
Gloucester, Duke of, 7
Gonzaga, Prince, 227–8
Goodall, Will, 79
Gotland, Signor (ambulance driver), 243
Grant, Miss, 262
Greece, King George of, 11–12

Gregory, Lady, 73
Gretton, Miss, 253, 262, 274, 278
Gustavus Adolphus, King of Sweden, 68

Hadley, Miss, 310, 314
Hagenbeck, Herr, 70
Hamilton, Duke of, 72
Hamilton, General, 288
Hanbury-Williams, Miss, 262, 267
Harcourt-Smith, Sir Cecil, 322
Hass, Signor, 162
Hereford, Viscount, 331
Hewitt, 145–6, 207, 217
Hohenlohe Langenburg, Prince Hermann, 15, 65–7
Hohenlohe Langenburg, reigning Prince of, xi
Hohenlohe Langenburg, Prince Victor, *see* Victor, Prince
Hohenlohe Schillingsfürst, Gustav, Cardinal, 25–7
Hollings, Hilda, afterwards Mrs. Lindsay Venn, 63, 95, 97, 100–1
Hollings, Jack, Lieut. 21st Lancers, 127
Hollings, R.N., Lieutenant-Commander R. E., 182
Hollings, Mrs. (Nina), 13 *n*., 41–54, 55–6, 58–61, 63, 72, 74, 83–6, 89–94, 97–9, 102, 109, 125 *et seq.*, 132 *et seq.*, 138 *et seq.*, 145 *et seq.*, 160 *et seq.*, 170–2, 176–80, 182–183, 185 *et seq.*, 196 *et seq.*, 211 *et seq.*, 226–7, 231–7, 239–42, 243 *et seq.*, 257 *et seq.*, 274 *et seq.*, 286–94, 297–8, 299–315, 331

INDEX

Holstein, Feo (Princess Feodora of Schleswig Holstein), 40-1
Hoyos, Count, 16-17
Hoyos, Count Alec, 17
Hoyos, Count Eddy, 17
Hoyos, Countess, 16

Italy, Crown Prince of, 290-1
Italy, King of, 178, 197, 221, 226, 255, 289-90
Italy, Queen of, 221, 226, 290-291
Johnstone, Hon. Lady, 216-17

Kelly-Kenny, General Sir T., 63, 70-1
Kent, Duke of, xi
Kerr, Captain Richard, 88, 94
Kipling, Rudyard, 275
Kitchener, Lord, 21
Knapp, Dr., 162, 205-6, 212

Laking, Sir Guy, 20
Lambert, Captain Rowley, 5-7
Landon, Percival, 275
Landreani, Captain, 206-7
Lawley, Sir Arthur, afterwards Lord Wenlock, 133
Legros, Professor, 9
Leiningen, Princess Feodora of, xi
Leiningen, Prince, xi
Lemon, Arthur, 9, 28-30, 32-4
Lemon, Mrs., 31
Lilliefors, Swedish painter, 68
Lombardi, General, 215, 218-219
Longhurst, Colonel, 59

MacAllister, Miss Isobel, 317, 319

Machell, Lady Valda, 9-10, 21, 81, 87, 115-19
Machell, Colonel Percy, 21
Machell, Roger, 193, 324
Mackenzie Davidson, Sir James, 126, 168, 175-6
Martino, Signor De, 289
Mencières, M., 125
Mensdorff, Count Albert, 35
Moberley, Colonel, 288
Monson, Lord, 134, 136, 160, 182, 188, 216, 275
Monvel, Boutet de, 20
Moodie, Major Pigot, 102
Mount Stephen, Lord and Lady, 35-6
Munthe, Dr. Axel, 69 n.

Nansen, Fridtjof, 70
Nicholas II, Tsar of Russia, 68-9
Nightingale, Florence, 21
Northcliffe, Lord, 201-2, 218

O'Neale, Mrs., 172

Paget, Mr. Harry, 9
Peñeranda, Duke of, 95
Pennant, Mr., 275
Piacentini, General, 248, 253
Pietri, M. Francesco, 63
Pinsent, Mr., 308
Ponsonby, Sir F., afterwards Lord Sysonby, 39, 317
Ponsonby, Sir Henry, 18
Ponsonby Fane, Sir Spencer, 39
Ponzio, General, 182
Porter, Mr. John, 78
Portland, Duke of, 320

Radcliffe, General Delmé, 168-9, 182, 218, 257

INDEX

Raimondo, Tito, 253-4, 283-4
Rennell, Lord, 11 *n*.
Reynolds-Stephens, Sir William, 322
Ribblesdale, Lord, 82
Rosales, Marchese, 296-7
Rossi, Professor Baldo, 277
Roversi (orderly), 180, 183, 253, 260-1
Rutland, Violet, Duchess of, 320

Saggini, Medical Inspector, 234
Santucci, Colonel, 215
Sargent, John, R.A., 29
Sartorio, Sig., 181
Sauteiron, de St. Clement, Colonel, 134
Sbrozzi, Professor, 228, 263, 303-4
Sbrozzi, Signora, 228
Seymour, General Lord William, 31
Seymour, Admiral of the Fleet Sir George, xi
Shaw, Captain, 5
Smith, M.F.H., Dudley, 62
Smyth, Dame Ethel, 219, 236, 239
Solaro, Signor, 277
Spencer, Earl, 99
Stagni, Corporal, 277, 305
Stanley, Colonel, 275
Stanley, Sir Arthur, 131, 275, 290, 292, 309
Sterzi, 277
Sullivan, Sir Arthur, 20
Sweden, King Oscar of, 67-8

Tettamanzi, Major, 303
Theed, sculptor, 7
Thomson, Sir Courtauld, 275
Tordella, 270
Toscanini, Cavaliere, 207
Trevelyan, George, O.M., 136
Treves, Sir Frederick, 298

Victor, Prince, of Hohenlohe Langenburg, xi, 3-10, 13-14, 18-19, 21, 25
Victor, Princess, of Hohenlohe Langenburg, 15, 19-21, 25, 27, 34
Victoria, Queen, xi, 7, 18-19, 36

Wales, Prince of (Duke of Windsor), 178
Wantage, Lady, 55, 57
Wemyss, Lady Eva, 125
Westminster, Duke of, 76-8
White, Sir William, 12
Whitehead, 145-6, 152, 154-6, 159, 170-4, 189, 201, 205, 207, 211, 227, 231-2, 253, 261
Whitnell, Miss, 237-9
Williams, Captain, 113, 288
Wilson, General Sir Henry, afterwards Field Marshal, 128
Woodroffe, Miss, 253, 262

Young, Mr. Geoffrey, 237

Zorn, Anders, Swedish painter, 68
Zucco, Count, 135

www.ingramcontent.com/pod-product-compliance
Lightning Source LLC
Chambersburg PA
CBHW031605210526
45464CB00004B/1437